Bruce Lee
The Evolution of a Martial Artist

by Tommy Gong

Bruce Lee Foundation

Bruce Lee
The Evolution of a Martial Artist
by Tommy Gong

Special Projects Editor: Vicki Baker
Copy Editor: Gretchen Haas
Graphic Design: John Bodine

Library of Congress Control Number: 2014932112
ISBN: 978-0-89750-208-5

Printed in the United States of America

Third Edition 2017

Disclaimer: The adoption and application of the material offered in this book is at the reader's discretion and sole responsibility. The author, Black Belt Communications and Bruce Lee Enterprises are not responsible in any manner whatsoever for any injury that may result directly or indirectly from practicing the techniques and/or following the instruction given within this book. Since the physical activities described herein may be too strenuous in nature for some readers to engage in safely, please consult a physician prior to training. The specific self-defense practices illustrated in this book may not be justified in every particular situation or under applicable federal, state or local law. The author, Black Belt Communications and Bruce Lee Enterprises make no warranty or representation regarding the legality or appropriateness of any technique mentioned in this book.

Dedication

This book is dedicated to Bruce Lee, the founder of *jeet kune do.* Bruce, although we never met, you have been a hero to me since childhood and throughout my adulthood. Your inspiration continues to guide us toward our personal liberation.

This book also is dedicated to the memory of Ted Wong, who passed away in late 2010. Ted Wong dedicated his life to the practice, preservation and perpetuation of jeet kune do around the world and was an integral part of the leadership of the Bruce Lee Foundation. He was my *sifu,* and in Chinese culture, one's sifu is much more than just a teacher or instructor, but more like a father figure and/or mentor. I expected to have numerous conversations with Sifu Ted regarding the information contained in this book, but he passed away before the primary writing began. In the same way Ted had to carry on the teachings of jeet kune do without his sifu, Bruce Lee, I had to pick up the pieces and finish the journey of completing this book on my own. However, since I spent ample time with Sifu Ted over many years, he prepared me and I gained the confidence to complete it. Thank you, Sifu Ted, for all that you shared with me. I will treasure it for the rest of my life.

—Tommy Gong

Ted Wong and Bruce Lee

Tommy Gong and Ted Wong

Table of Contents

Acknowledgments

There are many individuals I'd like to acknowledge for their parts in creating this book.

First and foremost, I want to acknowledge those who shared their memories of Bruce Lee and the development of his personal expression, jeet kune do, including Bruce's wife, Linda Lee Cadwell; Taky Kimura; Allen Joe; and the late Ted Wong. Credit is also due to two additional students of Bruce's: Peter Chin and the late Jesse Glover. Much appreciation to Bruce Lee associate and karate champion Mike Stone. Without their insights into Bruce, this book would have never taken shape. I am especially indebted to Linda, who provided editorial assistance and guidance in completing this project.

Many thanks to Bruce's daughter, Shannon Lee, and attorney Kris Storti for providing the photos of Bruce Lee from the Bruce Lee Enterprises archive, which gave this book life. Over the years, Perry Lee (no relation to Bruce) has collected many rare and unique items related to Bruce Lee, and I am grateful that he provided some of his collection for this project. I am also indebted to Allen Joe and Mark Chow, the youngest son of the late Ruby and Ping Chow, for providing photos from their personal family albums. Also, appreciation goes to Andy Kimura for posing with his father to illustrate the earlier Seattle techniques. Thanks to Professor Dan Lee (one of Bruce Lee's first-generation students of jeet kune do) for his Chinese terminology suggestions as well as his Chinese calligraphy of the jeet kune do characters.

Much gratitude goes to the research team who assisted in framing the interviews, including Greg Rhodes (who provided access to his lifelong Bruce Lee Chronology project), Jeff Pisciotta, and my jeet kune do students Benton Chan, Vincent Dequito, Evandro Lee, Helder Lee, Dennis Pierre, Dini Wong and Ron Wong. For their work on the first edition of this book, I am also grateful to Tyler Tichelaar, who served as editor; to Vera Wallen, Louis Awerbuck, Jeff Pisciotta and Eric Punsalan for providing editorial assistance; to Will Johnston for providing photo research; to Mat Ptacek for cover design and image processing; and to Adelina "Eileen" Dequito for book layout.

I also want to acknowledge the efforts of biomechanists Martyn Shorten, Eric Pisciotta and Jeff Pisciotta for providing a biomechanical analysis of the evolution of some core techniques of *Jun Fan jeet kune do.* They graciously wrote the appendix analyzing the earlier and later techniques from a scientific standpoint. Much gratitude to the individuals who served as test subjects during the data capture sessions (Taky and Andy Kimura, Allen Joe, Tommy Carruthers and Jeff Pisciotta). Last, I want to express great appreciation to my lovely wife, Sherry, who provided the Chinese terminology in Appendix E, as well as her continued support.

This book would not have been created without the generous financial assistance of Gregory Smith Sr., who provided the videography and photography services, and Jerry Lee, who graciously facilitated the printing of the first-run edition of this publication.

Foreword by Linda Lee Cadwell

Over all the years since Bruce passed away, I have often mused about how he managed to get so much done in such a short time. As I have gotten older, I am more aware of how young Bruce was when he died at 32 years old and yet he was so wise beyond his years. I think to myself, How did he pack so much into just a few years? How was he able to get from there to here in a relatively brief span of time?

In this book, Tommy Gong has laid out the paths Bruce chose in his lifetime to develop his martial art of jeet kune do and his philosophy of self-actualization. He traces every aspect of Bruce's growth including the physicality of fighting, the science of biomechanics, the psychology of human nature and the philosophy of living a fulfilled life. Tommy Gong has drawn a road map for you to travel from Hong Kong to Seattle, Oakland,

Los Angeles and back to Hong Kong to witness key incidents in Bruce's life that led to his fast-paced evolution from student of *wing chun* to founder of the most refined martial art in the world, jeet kune do.

Tommy Gong brings a gold-plated background to the study of Bruce's personal journey. Tommy's sifu, Ted Wong, was a close friend and personal student who probably spent more one-on-one time training with Bruce than anyone else. Bruce considered Ted to be a pure student because previous martial art training did not clutter his mind. In the many decades since Bruce passed away, Ted continued to study and teach only jeet kune do and to refine his understanding of Bruce's art both physically and philosophically. As Ted's student, Tommy was able to glean an insightful perspective on how Bruce's mind worked.

Tommy's research on this project has been impeccable. In an effort to understand Bruce's progression toward artistry in the martial arts, Tommy interviewed numerous former students. He spent time with Bruce's assistant instructor, Taky Kimura, in Seattle, and with Bruce's Oakland student and good family friend Allen Joe. Tommy learned about the sciences of kinesiology and physiology with experts like Jeff Pisciotta to further his understanding of the efficiency of Bruce's movements. He researched former childhood classmates of Bruce's to delve for the answers to how a skinny kid from Hong Kong became the most prominent martial artist and philosopher of the 20th century.

Tommy's innate curiosity drove him to search deeply into Bruce's motivation toward excellence. His powers of observation combined with a keen intelligence have provided the reader with an interpretation of Bruce's odyssey that resonates with depth. In this book, Tommy makes available to every man and woman the story of a remarkable man, but in so doing he lays out a blueprint that will inspire the reader to create his or her own path to success.

At a very young age, Bruce felt he had within him a great creative and spiritual force that would allow him to overcome obstacles and realize his dreams. Tommy took this inspiration to heart by searching for the source of Bruce's genius and, in so doing, realized one of his own dreams of chronicling the evolution of his sifu's teacher, Bruce Lee.

In writing this book, Tommy has exhibited a spirit of generosity that goes beyond everyday acts of kindness. He has literally put years into the research of this material and taken time away from his family in order to complete it. In addition, the royalties arising from the sale of the book will go to the Bruce Lee Foundation in an effort to realize its goals of preserving and perpetuating Bruce Lee's art. On behalf of our family and all the supporters of the Foundation, we are grateful to Tommy; his wife, Sherry; their two sons, Derek and Darin; and all his helpers who assisted in the publication of this book.

If Bruce were here today, he would be proud of this book because it goes beyond just mere glimpses into his life and seeks to explore how he translated thoughts into action. Tommy's sifu, Ted Wong, would be equally proud that his student had drawn from his teaching the essence of jeet kune do. I believe both Bruce and Ted would say to Tommy, "Job well done!"
—Linda Lee Cadwell

Foreword by Shannon Lee

This book is tremendous for a variety of reasons. It is the first book that the Bruce Lee Foundation has undertaken to write and publish. It is most clearly a labor of love for the organization but in particular for author Tommy Gong, who is also a board member. He spent countless hours of his time crafting this work solely for the benefit of the BLF and my father's legacy. The others of us on the board are eternally grateful.

Second, this volume is also a very interesting look into my father's journey as a martial artist. His evolutionary process is captured in a very intriguing way in these pages. It is placed in time, in history and in context, and it is organized in such a way as to create a path for the reader to follow that is clear and filled with lots of interesting scenery and landscapes. It paints a picture of a man in a process, which is what my father most certainly was. Always the eternal student, my father never considered himself as having peaked or finalized anything. He was constantly becoming and this book tells that story in a captivating way.

Evolution, though it has quotes and thoughts in it that have been revealed before to the public, speaks in a way that is unique and refreshing. If you are a martial artist, you will appreciate not only the journey but the combinations of movement and philosophy, humanity and genius, technique and experimentation that Bruce Lee demonstrated in his lifetime. This book definitely reveals something unique about the nature of jeet kune do and Bruce Lee that should not be missed.

Finally, I would encourage the reader not to skip the book's appendixes, in particular the appendix on biomechanics as it reveals for the first time the scientific efficacy of my father's evolutionary process. That section also provides an interesting point of view and discussion of a fascinating scientific area for anyone curious about the science of movement.

The BLF is proud to be able to add this book to the continuing legacy of Bruce Lee. It is a must-have for anyone interested in my father's martial process and jeet kune do. Thank you for supporting the BLF and helping to further the reach of my father's legacy for generations to come. May you enjoy all this book has to offer!

In the spirit of JKD,
—Shannon Lee

Preface by the Author

"More wing chun-oriented" was the way the late sifu Ted Wong described the Seattle curriculum Bruce Lee taught in the late 1950s to early 1960s. In 1967, Ted began training at the Los Angeles branch of the Jun Fan Gung Fu Institute in Chinatown, and he later became Bruce Lee's private student and training partner. I began my studies under Ted during the mid-1980s, and I learned everything I could about Bruce Lee and jeet kune do, but there weren't nearly as many resources available then as there are today.

A few years later, I traveled to Seattle on a road trip with some JKD students from Japan who studied jeet kune do under Dan Inosanto. One of them, who had moved to Los Angeles from Seattle, had previously trained under Taky Kimura, whom Bruce put in charge of his Seattle Jun Fan Gung Fu Institute branch when he moved to Oakland. This student took us to visit Taky, who was very kind to us, inviting us to join his class in the basement of his Seattle grocery store where he continued to teach a small group of students. During the class, I recall being instructed to keep the rear heel down and put more weight on the rear leg when learning the stance; then we lined up together, facing our training partners to practice trapping techniques.

Before training under Ted Wong, I had received my initial training in jeet kune do in Oakland/Berkeley from Greglon Lee, the son of James Lee. James was put in charge of the Oakland Jun Fan Gung Fu Institute branch when Bruce left Oakland to do *The Green Hornet* television series in Los Angeles. While I recognized some similarity between the training in Oakland and Seattle, I saw differences between what I was learning from Ted and the Los Angeles era. Not only were the stance and technique different, but also the timing and rhythm. By experiencing the training from the different eras of Bruce Lee's development as a martial artist, I realized he was going through an evolutionary process during his dozen or so years living in the United States and moving between Seattle, Oakland and Los Angeles.

In reviewing Bruce Lee's evolution in martial arts, one should be able to witness his transformation from the earlier *wing chun gung fu* he learned in Hong Kong to what would later become jeet kune do in Los Angeles. The contrast is stark! I recall reading about it in Dan Inosanto's earlier book, *Jeet Kune Do: The Art and Philosophy of Bruce Lee*, but to experience it was much more eye-opening. During the late '80s, when helping Ted create the manuscript for his book with William Cheung, *Wing Chun Kung Fu/Jeet Kune Do: A Comparison*, we wrote that when comparing Bruce's earlier and later students, the casual observer might find it difficult to believe they were taught by the same instructor, even those students who primarily practiced only what Bruce taught them. What a fascinating journey Bruce Lee took in developing his very personal expression in the martial arts.

In the late '90s, Bruce's widow, Linda Lee Cadwell, called together many of Lee's students to join the Jun Fan jeet kune do Nucleus/Bruce Lee Educational Foundation, the non-profit organization whose goal was to preserve and perpetuate his teachings. The uniqueness of each era of Bruce's development and his evolution were further exemplified when students directly taught by Bruce passed on to the attendees what he taught them during the organization's five annual seminars. As a result of their sharing what they learned from Bruce, many differences in Bruce's methods became apparent. However, I believe they discovered they had a lot more in common with each other, especially when it came to Bruce's fighting principles and philosophical underpinnings. At the same time, the world was getting a bigger glimpse into Bruce's personal writings through the group's newsletters, the *Bruce Lee Magazine*, and full-length books covering all things Bruce.

The Nucleus

For me, personally, it was a very rich period of exploration into Jun Fan jeet kune do and Bruce Lee's life. I became the unofficial videographer for the Nucleus when we received a generous donation of some high-end video equipment to document the organization's events and conduct personal interviews with first-generation students. While the Nucleus did not last, I think some very important work was accomplished during those years. Typically, when people are interested in studying jeet kune do, the main reason is that they are inspired and motivated by Bruce in some fashion. Consequently, they desire to learn and experience his way of martial arts and training methodology in order to understand him better. The Nucleus provided an unprecedented opportunity to study Bruce and jeet kune do by giving public access to many of his personal notes and to meet with the many people who personally knew him.

Those years reinforced my view that by chronicling Bruce's life in the United States through his students from Seattle, Oakland and Los Angeles, a history of the evolution of Bruce's development as a martial artist and the creation of jeet kune do could be written. The combination of his writings and his students' oral testimonies serves as the definitive case study of Jun Fan jeet kune do from which a beginner can pursue his or her journey of jeet kune do.

When Bruce Lee's daughter, Shannon, asked me to serve on the new Bruce Lee Foundation's board of directors, I wanted to continue the work that was started in chronicling jeet kune do's development. I asked Taky Kimura, Allen Joe and Ted Wong, who became the Board of Directors for the Bruce Lee Foundation, to provide their firsthand accounts of Bruce during his martial arts development. They were all profoundly affected by their relationship with Bruce, and I feel extremely fortunate that they agreed to be involved with this book. I was equally excited that Linda Lee Cadwell, Bruce Lee's widow, agreed to be involved as well. She was the only person who could have convinced so many of Bruce's students to work together while serving as Nucleus board members, and she was present during all three eras of Bruce's development in Seattle, Oakland and Los Angeles. I was glad they agreed to the proposal that royalties generated by this book's sales would solely benefit the Bruce Lee Foundation to further its mission to preserve and perpetuate Bruce Lee's legacy.

This book endeavors to shed light on the development of jeet kune do, looking into what moved Bruce to evolve as a martial artist. It asks, "What drove him to modify his techniques and training methods, influencing his direction and development as a martial artist?" We are especially fortunate to illustrate his martial arts development through the demonstration of techniques by Taky Kimura, Allen Joe and Ted Wong. In an attempt to connect the dots between what may be seen as completely different arts, I hope to inspire the reader to continue his or her studies of jeet kune do and the case study of Bruce Lee's life, while at the same time finding the best within his or her individual self.

Although this book chronicles the development of jeet kune do during Bruce's lifetime, it is by no means the final word. The destination for each individual will take a different path, so the final chapter is for you to write by discovering what works best for you, and to be on your own personal quest for excellence on your martial arts journey.

Notes on Sources

Primary interviews were conducted with Linda Lee Cadwell, Allen Joe and Ted Wong in April 2009 and with Taky Kimura in October 2009. Supplemental information from short conversations took place with Jesse Glover and Peter Chin. Jesse was Bruce's first student in Seattle, and Peter was one of Bruce's last students in Los Angeles.

I am also indebted to Linda and Shannon Lee, who provided access to the Bruce Lee Enterprises Archives, including his many personal writings and letters that were accumulated over the years. All quotes without sources noted are from the Bruce Lee Enterprises Archives.

All images of Bruce Lee appearing in this book, unless otherwise noted, are courtesy of the Bruce Lee Enterprises Archives.

—Tommy Gong

Introduction

What Is Jeet Kune Do?

On July 9, 1967, Bruce Lee named his personal expression and approach to martial arts *jeet kune do,* which translates as "the way of the intercepting fist." He especially liked the stop-hit technique from the sport of fencing and wanted to come up with a term describing the very nature of the technique. But on so many different levels, jeet kune do meant so much more to Bruce than simply intercepting an opponent's attack. He truly desired to free his followers from the confines of martial arts styles and traditions, claiming JKD to be the only nonclassical form of Chinese *gung fu.* Having no bias in combat, being neither "for" nor "against," one begins to take on the true nature of *yin* and *yang* when embracing this philosophy. With its structure being described as "a circle with no circumference," so there are no boundaries, making it a "formless form," one cannot fathom or truly understand and grasp JKD; as soon as you think you have grasped it, you have lost it. (That is, "As soon as you have a way, therein lies the limitation.")

Lee liked to describe his truth in martial arts philosophically. He encouraged followers to blaze their own paths in their personal development and excellence in martial arts, to have faith and trust in themselves when taking directions that might even stray off the Bruce Lee path. But with this open-ended, sometimes circular approach to martial arts, what is the starting point for the layman or beginner? Although it is easy to understand the endgame for followers potentially doing their own thing based on their personal journeys, what are the beginning steps?

A Common Beginning

One element all of Lee's first-generation students share is having received firsthand training experience in *Jun Fan gung fu*/*jeet kune do* from him, whether it was early on in Seattle or Oakland, or later in Los Angeles. Although all the students started from various martial arts experiences and backgrounds before studying with Bruce, and they have taken their training and personal development in different directions since then, they had this common starting point.

But what exactly is the common message or theme these students acquired from Lee? What is his legacy? Is it only his philosophical messages of "being like water" and "discovering your own truth"? Is it the compilation or distillation of all the martial arts that he delved into, or just the ones he utilized? Over the years, diverse viewpoints even among the first generation students exemplified the very fluid and personal nature of jeet kune do. Some desired to refer to the system comprised of techniques and training methodology as Jun Fan gung fu, then relating jeet kune do as the liberation from rigid traditions and classical styles in researching and developing onward, while others desired to refer to Lee's complete journey of martial arts as jeet kune do, since it was occurring throughout his lifetime. Some feared that within a very short period of time, what was taught as JKD would bear little resemblance to what Lee taught and practiced, while others argued that in order to progress the art, it must continue to adapt and change.

At the same time, because of Lee's iconic status around the world, his persona has become a commodity, and associating oneself with his martial arts has been a means to financial gain. Worse is when individuals who have little if any training in JKD take his writings or sayings (often misinterpreting them), and develop "their own style" yet continue to call it JKD since they are "doing their own thing." In this way, and as a result of over-commercialization, the essence of jeet kune do can be lost.

Why Jeet Kune Do's History Must Be Preserved

The term *Jun Fan jeet kune do* was adopted in January 1996, during a landmark summit meeting in Seattle with Linda and Shannon Lee, along with many of Bruce's first-generation students. This meeting served as the precursor to the formation of the JFJKD Nucleus/Bruce Lee Educational Foundation. Actually, it was Shannon's suggestion to merge the two terms (Jun Fan gung fu and jeet kune do) to describe her father's complete journey in martial arts, and everyone in attendance unanimously agreed.

Jun Fan jeet kune do serves as the definitive case study for Jun Fan gung fu and jeet kune do because it endeavors to give a clear and accurate picture of Bruce Lee's legacy to martial arts—physically, scientifically and philosophically. I remember Linda paraphrasing a statement made by Pete Jacobs (a student of Lee's in Los Angeles) during the Inaugural JFJKD Seminar held in 1997 in San Francisco: "We can't possibly predict in what direction he may have gone, most certainly we can predict that he would have continued to grow, evolve, change, but we can't say what that was" [or would have been]. In this way, JFJKD serves as both the historical reference for what Lee practiced, trained and taught during his lifetime, and also the inspiration or catalyst encouraging followers not to follow blindly their *sifu* (teacher) and/or style, and to discover the truth for themselves.

Although Lee's message prescribed having no boundaries when looking to improve one's martial arts, it becomes increasingly important to document what he taught and practiced so future generations will have a chance to experience what the first-generation students did during their time with him. As a result, the art of Jun Fan jeet kune do showcases the common ground that first-generation students share so the historical reference and context of his evolution in the martial arts during his lifetime could be preserved. When examining Lee's personal notes and letters, and hearing the recollections from his students, one can discover the building blocks of jeet kune do. In this way, Lee's body of work is basic source material, providing the beginning student some initial steps to study and explore, and a path to understanding JKD.

An interesting viewpoint is that—while some differences may exist between Lee's martial arts when it comes to his time in Seattle, Oakland and Los Angeles—little delineation occurred in his evolutionary development toward jeet kune do. Lee developed JKD throughout his time in America. It was, by no means, a smooth, gradual process, but for him, change happened out of necessity. His process was akin to the modern evolution theory of "punctuated equilibrium," which proposes over thousands or millions of years that species maintain a relatively stable existence, but when evolutionary changes occur, they are rapid and abrupt, not smooth and gradual. Punctuated equilibrium appears to describe perfectly Lee's methods because he was known to be inspired by something early on, only to drop it or even criticize it later. As he became enlightened through investigating various topics such as kinesiology, or the science of movement, he came to fully understand how to use a certain fighting principle and then modified his methods accordingly. Furthermore, events such as an altercation in Oakland, wherein Lee was challenged by a Chinese martial artist, resulted in an abrupt change in Lee's approach to the martial arts. Although he bested his opponent, Lee concluded the match lasted entirely too long due to his strict adherence to his previous training, and he immediately sought out more efficient combat methods.

In many ways, the exact timing of these inspirations is difficult to pin down, because much of what was happening to Lee was occurring simultaneously. For instance, he was already influenced by Western boxing and fencing in his early years in Hong Kong. The question is: When did certain elements come to full fruition in his development as a martial artist? Similar techniques were taught in all three schools, yet certain discoveries he found useful during his evolution were reflected in his private practice and training. Although it is convenient to chronicle Lee's development by dividing it between his Seattle, Oakland and Los Angeles periods, much overlap exists between "eras" since he continued to have contact with students from all three. In fact, each era could be equally served by referencing the many students he had. Nevertheless, the three eras provide the reader points of reference for placing dates, events and Lee's development into context so that each school provides a glimpse along the evolutionary path.

One must realize that Lee studied physics, biomechanics, nutrition and training theory, and he used scientific methodology to validate what he was doing. He researched what he did not know, developed hypotheses, tested his theories using himself as the test subject and then concluded whether or not they worked. One could say that Lee used the science of combat when formulating his style of "no style." It was not simply choosing what he liked or preferred, but rather what was proven to be the most effective. In this way, not only the "what" and "how" were learned, but also the "why." Perhaps the need to understand "why" is the most important lesson he left us.

Taky Kimura and Bruce Lee

James Yimm Lee and Bruce Lee

Dan Inosanto and Bruce Lee

We can use JFJKD as an invaluable tool because it provides a point of reference when discussing Lee's evolution and various interpretations of it presented through the years since his passing, whether we're talking about *wing chun,* Jun Fan gung fu, jeet kune do, JKD concepts, original JKD, etc. During the mid-80s, there was dissension within the JKD family over the purity of the art versus the infusion of different martial arts based on one's personal journey. Today the focus has shifted to how much wing chun was done in Seattle, Oakland or Los Angeles, but the same negative criticism still continues, despite its pointlessness.

This book places the various elements of Lee's earlier and later training in context on the JFJKD timeline. Although trapping techniques had less to do with JKD later on, it was a central theme in Lee's martial art during the earlier and even middle period of his development, serving as a valuable foundation for Lee, and it deserves respect as a valid part of JKD history. Placing techniques such as the *pak sao* (block), the straight lead, and the side kick with its accompanying footwork along the JFJKD timeline should help the reader see things in better context.

Since Lee's passing in 1973, we have been fortunate that so many of his students—those he taught early on as well as those he taught later—shared Lee's teachings with students around the world. During the past few years, their teachings have become even more precious because many of them have passed on. In just the past couple of years since work on this book began, some of Lee's closest students have left us, including Jesse Glover, Lee's very first student in Seattle, and Ted Wong, one of Lee's last students in Los Angeles. These students have left us with a rich history that allows us to understand better Lee and jeet kune do. The first-generation students of Bruce Lee shared a lot in common, so where there were differences, maybe they were more like two halves of one whole that is the formless form.

Jesse Glover and Lee

Ted Wong and Lee

Although Lee did not like to refer to jeet kune do as a style or system, his martial arts movements had a distinct character or flavor. Hence, the balancing act is not to forget his message of liberation and freedom, while being sure to recognize his many other contributions, large and small, so the complete picture of his life can be fully appreciated. In the spirit of being neither "for" nor "against" what JKD is, Jun Fan jeet kune do serves as the two halves of one whole, just like yin and yang, in joining together Lee's legacies in martial arts, from the physical, technical and scientific to the philosophical principles eliminating the notion of self and ego, being like water, and adapting to "what is."

CHAPTER 2

Hong Kong: Research Your Own Experience

When Bruce Lee immigrated to the United States in spring 1959, his first stop was San Francisco. Ironically, he was actually born in San Francisco at the Chinese Hospital on Jackson Street in Chinatown on November 27, 1940, while his parents, father Lee Hoi Chuen and mother Ho Oi Yee (aka Grace Ho), were on tour in the United States with a Chinese Opera group. According to the Chinese lunar calendar, not only was it the year of the dragon but also the hour of the dragon when Bruce Lee was born. At three months old and having already been in his first film in San Francisco, Bruce and family returned to Hong Kong; he would not return to America until he was 18 years old. Since he was born in the United States, he chose to claim his U.S. citizenship and live in America. Through his family's connections in the Cantonese Opera, he initially landed in San Francisco for the summer, staying with Kwan Ging Hong, who had an apartment only a few blocks away from the Jackson Street hospital where Lee was born.

San Francisco Chinese Hospital

Most fans of Bruce Lee in Hong Kong and China know him by the stage name of Lee Siu Loong or "The Little Dragon." It was an appropriate name for such an energetic individual with such a magnetic personality. However, his given name was Lee Jun Fan.

Bruce Lee in San Francisco

Lee Jun Fan: The Name

When Lee was born at the Chinese Hospital in San Francisco's Chinatown in 1940, a nurse in the ward suggested the name "Bruce" as his English name (although he did not know that his English name was Bruce until he was almost a teenager). His mother, Grace, gave her newborn son the name Lee Jun Fan. From its literal translation, "Jun" means "to arouse to an active state" or "to make prosperous." It was a common name for young Chinese boys in Hong Kong, since the Chinese wanted the sleeping lion of the East to awaken. Jun's pronunciation, rhyming with "fun" or "gun," can also mean "to protect" or "to help." Fan (pronounced "fawn," as in "lawn" or "dawn") refers to San Francisco in Chinese.

However, a more personal reason exists for the name Jun Fan. When Bruce was born in San Francisco, his mother was by herself in the Chinese Hospital since her husband, Lee Hoi Chuen, was in New York with the Chinese Opera group. She chose the name Jun Fan since baby Bruce would be her protector while in San Francisco. So Jun Fan means "Protector of San Francisco." Perhaps it was an omen when he first returned to the United States that he landed in the city of his birthplace. Jun Fan gung fu is the term identified with Lee's early development in the martial arts from around 1959 to 1967. It is part of the foundation that formed the basis for jeet kune do.

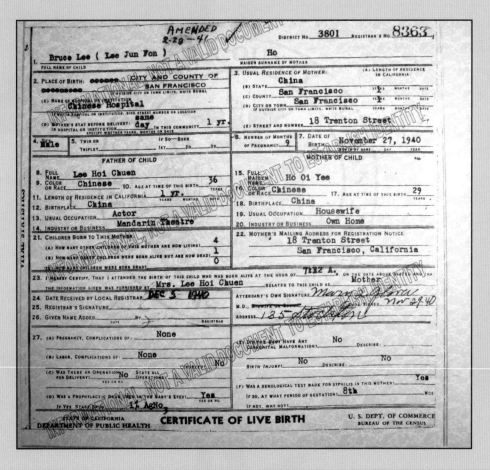

Lee left Hong Kong at a crossroads in his life, just beginning to enter adulthood, with no definite idea of what he would do with his life. In Hong Kong, he had been a child actor, appearing in 20 films by the time he was 18, due in part to his father's involvement with the Chinese Opera and being an actor himself. As a result, Lee was already a celebrity of sorts, throughout his life being recognized from films he performed in as a child. As a young adult, though, it did not appear that he would make a career out of acting.

Bruce was the fourth child in a family of five siblings. The eldest was sister Phoebe, followed by sister Agnes, brother Peter who was a year older than Bruce, and the youngest, Robert. According to his wife, Linda, Bruce was the "ham" among the siblings, a practical joker and natural actor. Bruce had many nicknames, but his family called him Sai Fong or "Little Peacock," a girl's name. This was to fool the Chinese gods into

thinking Bruce was a girl because they might be jealous that the family had a second boy and take him away. Linda recalls that his family always called him Sai Fong.

Bruce was also nicknamed Mo Si Tung or "Never Sit Still" to describe his characteristic perpetual motion and restlessness as a rambunctious child and teenager. Although he had some initial exposure to *tai chi* through his father, Bruce discovered his passion for martial arts when he began studying wing chun, a relatively new style of gung fu (around 200 years old compared to styles that were thousands of years old), under Yip Man in 1953, at age 13. Yip Man fled China in 1949 when the Communist takeover occurred, and he was the first to popularize wing chun in Hong Kong. It is said that when *wing chun gung fu* was formulated, it was purportedly founded by a woman, and as a result, skill was emphasized over strength. It was simplified and streamlined from existing systems so that one could learn the complete system in less time than conventional martial arts in China. During the mid-1950s, rooftop matches pitting practitioners of the various styles against each other were popular in Hong Kong. Wing chun gung fu's straightforward and aggressive approach, in addition to the quality of its stable of fighters, helped build its great reputation as an effective fighting style and allowed a rapid rise for the wing chun school in Hong Kong. While not as graceful or visually appealing as other systems, wing chun found its forté in simplicity and efficiency.

Yip Man and Lee

Although he did not learn the complete system, Lee made much progress in the art during the four years of training in wing chun. Lee was introduced to wing chun gung fu through his schoolmate William Cheung. Lee once told Joe Hyams, a Los Angeles student, that he chose wing chun because of its emphasis on close-range fighting, which Lee thought complemented his nearsightedness. Since he could only see things well up close, the emphasis on close-range fighting might prove beneficial.[1] As it turned out, Lee relied less on his visual acuity and more on his sense of touch when learning wing chun. According to Dan Inosanto, Lee's assistant during the Los Angeles years, the three things Lee especially liked about wing chun were its economical structure, its directness and its emphasis on energy or sensitivity through sticky hands or sticking hands (*chi sao*) training.[2]

Wong Shun Leung was another role model for Lee. Wong's many successful rooftop matches helped build the wing chun reputation. Wong's practical approach to fighting and his Western boxing experience

---

[1] Hyams, Joe. *Zen in the Martial Arts*. New York, NY: Bantam, 1982. p. 27.

[2] Inosanto, Dan. *Jeet Kune Do: The Art and Philosophy of Bruce Lee*. Los Angeles, CA: Know Now Publishing Co., 1994. p. 23.

greatly influenced Lee as a teenager. In many ways, the seeds of JKD were planted in Lee by his foundational training in wing chun gung fu and the guidance of his experienced senior brothers.

Lee was not an exemplary student in school, but once he found a passion for something, he completely devoted himself to learning about it and perfecting his technique through incessant practice. For instance, Lee was sure to practice his wing chun with his friends during recess and lunch breaks at school. Also, to improve his practice of chi sao, he recalled developing a constant energy flow in his arms by applying constant pressure to his arm against his school desk in the classroom. When his arm slipped past the desk and automatically flew up, he realized a key aspect of the way to practice chi sao. This method was not necessarily the way to practice chi sao classically, but Lee discovered an aspect that could make his practice more effective.

Lee's first five years of childhood were marked by the Japanese occupation of Hong Kong, where the Chinese were allowed to live in their homes but were essentially prisoners of war. Linda recalls that Bruce remembered vividly leaning over his balcony, with his mother pulling him back while he shook his fist at the Japanese airplanes going overhead. Following the Japanese occupation, Britain continued to hold Hong Kong as a colony, and many of the British living in Hong Kong continued to treat the Chinese as second-class citizens. Linda believes Bruce's martial arts training helped him deal with the inequities of life: "When that period was finally over, the British colonization could have led Bruce down a different path where he would be filled with hatred and anger, but his martial arts training really steered him down a different path to show people the beauty of the Chinese culture." Through the exercising of his body and mind, Lee gained the confidence to overcome challenges in his life positively. Instead of allowing these challenges to bog him down, he began to turn them into opportunities. Martial arts had a profound effect on him and steered him in a positive direction, helping him to channel his energy.

Lee's affinity for martial arts' philosophy was clear evidence of its positive influence on him. He may have first desired to learn martial arts simply to become a better fighter, but his passion for learning everything he could about gung fu led him to begin studying its philosophy, which serves as the art's foundation. During these formative years in his practice of gung fu, Lee became aware of Taoism and *Ch'an* (Zen). In this way, the young teenager who simply wanted to learn how to fight was transformed into a young adult whose thirst for mastery led to deeper self-examination and gave life meaning.

One must realize that martial arts and its many famous practitioners of the past contributed to the rich tradition of Chinese culture in Hong Kong, especially among male teenagers. Similar to legendary sports figures in the United States such as Babe Ruth, Jack Dempsey or Muhammad Ali, famous martial arts masters were the legend and folklore of Chinese pride and its heroes, including famous masters such as Wong Fei-Hung, Hung Hei-Gun, Fong Sai-Yuk, Huo Yuanjia (Lee later portrayed Huo's student at the Ching Wu school in the film *Fist of Fury,* aka *The Chinese Connection*), not to mention the Shaolin Temple and its Five Elders. Many of Hong Kong's early films dramatized famous martial artists such as Wong Fei-Hung, played by famous actor Kwan Tak Hing, and his archenemy, played by Shih Kien, who would later play Han in *Enter the Dragon.*

As a result, Lee was intrigued with the many different masters and the unique skills they possessed. Although he was loyal to the wing chun system, he was interested in being exposed to many different forms of gung fu. His thirst for martial arts knowledge could simply not be contained within one system. But it was his training in the rich tradition of the Chinese martial arts that provided his introduction to the classical martial arts.

A Valuable and Enduring Lesson in Tao

It was probably during the practice of chi sao at the wing chun school in Hong Kong that Lee discovered a powerful lesson in "being like water":

After four years of hard training in the art of gung fu, I began to understand and felt the principle of gentleness—the art of neutralizing the effect of the opponent's effort and minimizing the expenditure of one's energy. All these must be done in calmness and without striving. It sounded simple, but in actual application it was difficult. The moment I engaged in combat with an opponent, my mind was completely perturbed and unstable. And after a series of exchanging blows and kicks, all my theory of gentleness was gone. My only thought at this point was "somehow or other I must beat him and win!"

My instructor at the time, Professor Yip Man, head of the Wing Chun school of gung fu, would come up to me and say "Loong [Dragon], relax and calm your mind. Forget about yourself and follow the opponent's movement. Let your mind, the basic reality, do the counter-movement without any interfering deliberation. Above all, learn the art of detachment."

"That was it!" I thought. "I must relax!" However, right then I had just done something contradictory against my will. That occurred at the precise moment I said "I" <+> "must" <-> "relax." The demand for effort in "must" was already inconsistent with the effortlessness in "relax." When my acute self-consciousness grew to what the psychologists refer to as the "double-blind" type, my instructor would again approach me and say "Loong, preserve yourself by following the natural bend of things and don't interfere. Remember never to assert yourself against nature; never be in frontal opposition to any problems, but to control it by swinging with it. Don't practice this week. Go home and think about it."

The following week I stayed home. After spending many hours of meditation and practice, I gave up and went sailing alone in a junk. On the sea I thought of all my past training and got mad at myself and punched the water! Right then—at that moment—a thought suddenly struck me; was not this water the very essence of gung fu? Hadn't this water just now illustrated to me the principle of gung fu? I struck it but it did not suffer hurt. Again I struck it with all of my might—yet it was not wounded! I then tried to grasp a handful of it but this proved impossible. This water, the softest substance in the world and what could be contained in the smallest jar, only seemed weak. In reality, it could penetrate the hardest substance in the world. That was it! I wanted to be like the nature of water.

Suddenly a bird flew by and cast its reflection on the water. Right then as I was absorbing myself with the lesson of water, another mystic sense of hidden meaning revealed itself to me; should not the thoughts and emotions I had when in front of an opponent pass like the reflection of that bird flying over the water? This was exactly what Professor Yip meant by being detached—not being without emotion or feeling but being one in whom feeling was not sticky or blocked. Therefore in order to control myself I must first accept myself by going with and not against my nature.

I lay on the boat and felt that I had united with Tao; I had become one with nature. I just laid there and let the boat drift freely according to its own will. For at that moment I had achieved a state of inner feeling in which opposition had become mutually cooperative instead of mutually exclusive, in which there was no longer any conflict in my mind. The whole world to me was as one.

While Lee wrote this essay at the University of Washington after a thorough study of Chinese philosophy and many years of reflection of that key lesson in his training, it showed the deep level of understanding he had achieved during his formative years in Hong Kong. It illustrates how some important lessons early on had a huge influence and set his path in certain directions.

Many other seeds were planted in Lee while he was still in Hong Kong. His brother Peter was a successful fencing champion who provided Bruce with some initial exposure to the art of sword fighting. Through that introduction, Bruce developed an ability to take what he learned from one subject and relate it to another. In this case, Bruce later applied the extreme speed and reflexes required in fencing to his gung fu practice.

In high school, Lee also found himself competing in a boxing tournament. Although he knew little about Western boxing, he won the match due to his aggressive straight punching and efficient simultaneous attack and defense, which he learned from wing chun. Linda Lee states, "Winning that bout was a feather in Bruce's cap, since he proved to himself that he could fight without using leg techniques." In the championship match, Lee bested his opponent who had been champion for the last three years! Again,

Lee adapted his gung fu knowledge to the situation at hand, namely the boxing ring with its rules and regulations and boxing gloves, to come out on top.

Photo courtesy of Allen Joe

James Yimm Lee

In the same year (1958), Lee won the Crown Colony Cha-Cha Championship with his prowess on the dance floor. He was so taken by dancing that he had a card in his wallet listing his 108 favorite dance moves! The dancing helped him develop his footwork and sense of timing and rhythm. Cha-cha dancing also came in handy for him when he returned to America in 1959. While on the ship to San Francisco, Lee was in the steerage class, but he found himself in first class teaching people to dance. And during his brief stay in San Francisco, he performed his cha-cha dancing for some of the Chinese social clubs at ballroom dance parties, occasionally giving gung fu demonstrations during intermission. George Lee (later a student of the Oakland school and Bruce's close friend) met Bruce for the first time on just such an occasion. George was impressed with Bruce's gung fu and he encouraged him to teach, but by that time, Bruce was already making plans to move to Seattle. Bruce also became acquainted with fellow dancer Bob Lee (and Bob's wife, Harriet), whose brother was a well-respected gung fu practitioner in Oakland by the name of James Yimm Lee; James would eventually become a key person in Bruce's life.

Bruce Lee's combined film experience, martial arts training and cha-cha dancing, enhanced by his energy, drive, philosophical outlook and upbringing in Hong Kong, laid the foundation for his coming years in the United States.

In San Francisco

SEATTLE ERA

CHAPTER 3

Seattle: Absorb What Is Useful (Laying the Foundation)

By the end of the summer of 1959, Lee had moved to Seattle, Washington, to begin his academic studies. Fook Young, a gung fu practitioner and former Chinese Opera performer living in Seattle, drove down to San Francisco to pick up Lee for the trip to Seattle.

Bruce Lee, Ping Chow and Lee Hoi Chuen

Bruce's father, Lee Hoi Chuen, had connections in Seattle via Ping Chow, a close family friend and fellow Cantonese Opera performer. Ping and his wife, Ruby, arranged to have Bruce stay at their home while he worked at their restaurant. In 1948, despite racial discrimination, the Chows had been the first to open a Chinese restaurant outside of Seattle's Chinatown. Years later, Ruby was a progressive community activist in the Seattle area, where she was the first Asian-American elected to the King County Council, serving three terms between 1973 and 1985. In the same way, Ruby was equally strong-willed at her restaurant where she insisted everyone earn his keep. Working in a restaurant was challenging for Bruce, who was used to having servants at his family home in Hong Kong.

Lee first attended Edison Technical School for about a year-and-a-half to earn his high school diploma before attending university. During that time, he met his first student, Jesse Glover, a judo practitioner and fellow student at Edison. Glover first saw Lee at a demonstration where he was performing his cha-cha dancing and gung fu skill at a community festival

Images courtesy of Mark Chow

with the Chinese Youth Club. Glover approached Lee about his desire to learn gung fu and Lee accepted, albeit in private training. Shortly after, Lee also took on Glover's roommate, Ed Hart, as a student. Soon things began to take shape and a small group of individuals were training with Lee, including Skip Ellsworth, Howard Hall, Leroy Porter, Pat Hooks, Charlie Woo, James DeMile, Leroy Garcia, John Jackson and Taky Kimura. According to Kimura, this informal group included some ex-GIs—Glover did some

Jesse Glover and Lee

judo and boxing while in the Air Force, and DeMile was a heavyweight boxing champ during his stint in the Air Force. With students of various ethnicities, the group was "like the United Nations," according to Glover. They trained anywhere they could: backyards, parking lots, city parks, baseball dugouts. Glover was the senior student, serving as Lee's assistant to the group.

As Lee was completing his studies at Edison Tech, he was pestered by a karate man who wanted to test his skills. Lee was outspoken when he talked about gung fu, sometimes at the expense of other martial arts. To promote what he was doing, Lee often stated that Chinese martial arts were the predecessor of other martial arts such as those from Japan, or that while karate was a hard style, Chinese gung fu was more of a soft style. One Japanese martial artist in the audience took exception to this statement. Glover recalled that Lee exercised a lot of restraint when the karate man continued to goad him over a period of time, until he had had enough and accepted the challenge.

Glover, Lee, Ed Hart and Pat Hooks

They arranged to have a match at the downtown Seattle YMCA in a handball court. Glover was Lee's second and the referee, while Ed Hart was the timekeeper. When the two men engaged, Lee deflected his opponent's first kick and started to blast him across the court. When the karate man went down on his knee, Lee kicked him in the face and he fell to the floor, lying motionless. Glover thought the karate man might be dead, but he slowly regained consciousness and came to his senses. When he asked Hart how long the fight lasted, he told the karate man twenty-two seconds. He didn't have the heart to tell him it really only lasted eleven seconds.

By the end of 1960, Lee had graduated from Edison Tech. He entered the University

of Washington the following spring. He attended a course in judo at the UW and also spent some time researching it with Glover and Fred Sato, a close friend and a local judo club coach. (Lee gained an appreciation for judo, and in fact, he told Linda later, when their son, Brandon, was four or five years old, that the best thing for their son was to study judo because it involved "using your whole body, bigger movements than say punching and kicking, and the whole body awareness one develops" as a result of its practice.)

Lee took on various odd jobs to earn a little money, such as a newspaper stuffer for the *Seattle Times*. But as his group of students began to increase in numbers, they urged Lee to get a school of his own. Linda says, "Those students convinced him that he could earn a little money by charging his students a nominal fee and then he wouldn't have to work at Ruby Chow's folding wontons anymore."

The first location was in Chinatown (now known as the International District), later moving to a basement location in the same neighborhood. It was during this time that Lee and Kimura really bonded, and Lee eventually relied on Kimura as his assistant. While the earlier training with the initial group was informal, later classes became more formalized. Lee called the school the Jun Fan Gung Fu Institute, since what he was teaching was already deviating from his wing chun training and he wanted to be respectful of the art he originally learned. It also made sense in that "Jun Fan" was his Chinese name.

Taky Kimura: Bruce Lee's Best Man

Taky Kimura's father came to the United States from Japan in the early 1900s to work on the railroads in the Pacific Northwest. He traveled back to Japan for the purpose of marriage and then returned to the U.S. Their family eventually grew to eight children. Taky was number six, born in the city of Olympia, Washington, in 1924. Later on, the family settled in Clallam Bay, a logging community where Taky's father was hired as a foreman for a group of Japanese workers who maintained the railroads.

Growing up in America was fairly rough for young Taky since he and his family faced a lot of discrimination. Eventually, they were accepted into the community when his entrepreneurial father started selling homemade Japanese rice wine during Prohibition. As Taky stated, "We were finally accepted into the community as second-class citizens."

All of that changed when the Japanese attacked Pearl Harbor on December 7, 1941. The Kimura family was sent to an internment camp established by the United States to imprison Japanese-Americans for fear that sympathetic Japanese-Americans might spy for their ancestral homeland. On the day of his high school graduation in June 1942, instead of receiving his diploma, Taky and his family were put on a train and shipped to California.

The first camp was at Tule Lake in California, just south of the Oregon border. The government set up a 72-city-block camp to house almost 20,000 people. Later on, to further avoid the threat of the Japanese-Americans possibly collaborating with the Japanese, camps were set up farther inland away from the Pacific coast, and the Kimuras found themselves in Idaho. They were in the camps for a total of four years.

When the family was released, Taky's father decided to move them to Seattle, but nobody would rent a home to the Kimuras. Taky's older brother scouted out the area before the family arrived, and after being persistent by sleeping on the man's doorstep for a week, he convinced an elderly German gentleman to rent his small one-bedroom house to the family of nine. It took Taky months to obtain a job assisting a Japanese landscaper. Eventually, the family ended up running a small mom-and-pop corner grocery store, and Taky continued the family business until 2001.

The camps had a profound effect on Kimura. In his words, "I had no self-esteem. I ceased to be a human being. When a Caucasian came up behind me, I had to step aside and let him pass, since I was not worthy." Even his parents did not know about the severe depression he was experiencing. However, one redeeming thing that came out of the internment camps was that he was able to learn some judo there, and he continued his judo practice when his family settled in Seattle. The judo community was small, and some fellow students who attended Edison Technical School told Kimura about a young Chinese person who was an expert in gung fu. Kimura was able to meet Bruce Lee and become his student.

Lee could sense Kimura's low self-esteem, so he took him under his wing, despite being young enough to be Kimura's son. Lee was able to help Kimura get over his inferiority complex and accept himself as a person equal to anyone else. As Kimura said, "Bruce was an inspiration, and he was finally able to get through where I felt I needed to get a hold of myself and try to restore some of that normalcy within myself." One of the core tenets of JKD is you must believe in yourself and your capabilities, thereby becoming self-sufficient. In many ways, that is what Lee provided to Kimura.

When the Lees were married in 1964, Kimura was Bruce's best man. Their friendship deepened, and they maintained contact during Lee's continuing journey that took him to Oakland, Los Angeles and eventually back to Hong Kong. Kimura became one of the very few friends whom Lee trusted completely.

In 2009, almost 67 years after missing his high school graduation to be taken to the internment camps, Kimura's martial arts students petitioned the superintendent of schools, and he graduated with the high school senior class, receiving his diploma in the Olympic Peninsula where he grew up.

Taky Kimura's membership card—front and back

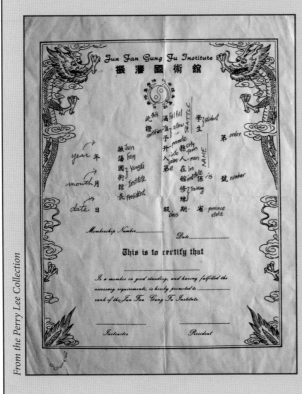 

From the Perry Lee Collection

Doug Palmer was another of Lee's students during this period. He would actually visit Hong Kong, staying with Lee and his family during the summer of 1963. In many ways, Lee's time in Hong Kong was likened to the prodigal son returning. Linda comments about Bruce's first trip home to Hong Kong, "When he left Hong Kong, he had been given $100 by his parents, and he was on his own, so he had to figure out how to make a living and how to get an education. It was a great homecoming at the time." In Hong Kong, Lee actually took Palmer to the wing chun gung fu school to meet Yip Man and witness Lee practicing one-on-one with his former teacher. Out of respect for Yip Man's traditional view of not teaching non-Chinese students and to avoid causing any friction, Lee asked Palmer not to mention learning gung fu from him.

Bruce Lee and Doug Palmer

Yip Man and Bruce Lee

Peter Lee, Ruby Chow and Bruce Lee

By the time Lee returned to Seattle during the fall of 1963, he had decided to move out of the Chows' residence and find a place of his own. As a junior at the University of Washington, he found a big, empty space on University Way that could serve as his studio. It included a bedroom and showers in the back, so Lee actually lived there.

Lee was an excellent martial arts instructor and spent a lot of one-on-one time with his students. According to Linda, "He would explain the movements in such a way that you knew what the purpose was; you weren't just repeating what he was doing or saying. In that way, you had to think, not just copy." Kimura found Lee always positive, never putting anyone

From the Perry Lee Collection

down, and "he had this uncanny ability to look at something and immediately find revelations that we could never fathom. That was the intelligence he had." Lee was also unopposed to accelerating his students' progress. Instead of the slow, drawn-out approach of practicing horse stances and such from a more traditional teacher (which tends to test one's patience more than anything else), he immersed his students in the more practical aspects of what he taught. During Jesse Glover's very first lesson, Lee covered a third of the first wing chun form—centerline punching—and arm positions for single-arm chi sao.

Lee teaching class

On one occasion, Lee took a group of students to a demonstration in the Chinese community in Vancouver, Canada. In some ways, this demonstration was a rite of passage for Lee because he was recognized as a legitimate gung fu practitioner when he performed in front of the crowd. During the visit, he met Tony Hum, a member of the local lion dance team in Vancouver, with whom Lee would become reacquainted when he later moved to Los Angeles. While still based in Seattle, Lee, from time-to-time, made the short drive to Vancouver to buy Chinese books on various gung fu styles.

Jesse Glover and Lee

Martial Art: Jun Fan Gung Fu (Foundation in Wing Chun)

By all accounts, what Lee taught his students during this time period was steeped in the wing chun gung fu he had learned earlier in Hong Kong, although he somewhat simplified its techniques. He adapted some kicks from a few northern gung fu styles to serve as long-range tools supplementing the close-range hand techniques from wing chun, although the kicks were more for speed and distraction than for damaging power. Although he performed higher kicks for demonstration purposes, Lee preferred low kicking for self-defense during this time in his development. Footwork was always emphasized, as it would be in all his schools. The following are principles that display the emphasis on close-range fighting heavily influenced by his training in wing chun gung fu.

Note: *The English terms listed here are followed by the Cantonese pronunciation. Some of the English names are not literal translations, but rather more explanatory to assist the student in learning; for instance, describing the position of a hand technique.*

Principles

Centerline Theory (Joan Sien)

The centerline theory (*joan sien*) is one of the most fundamental principles in wing chun gung fu. The centerline is the imaginary line that runs from between your legs through the top of your head, dividing your body in half. It serves as the rudimentary base from which all defenses and attacks come. You protect the centerline by constantly "covering" or guarding it with one hand, especially since many of the weakest points of the body are located along the centerline.

Despite not completing his training in wing chun gung fu, it is plausible that Lee became aware of many of the theories from the later forms. In the second form in wing chun, *chum kil* or "searching for the bridge," you are taught how to use waist-turning for generating power in strikes. Lee displays his understanding of some of these theories in his writings: "Additionally, the centerline theory allows you to generate more power in your techniques as it serves to coordinate both arm and body, enabling a gung fu man to employ his entire body weight with each strike."

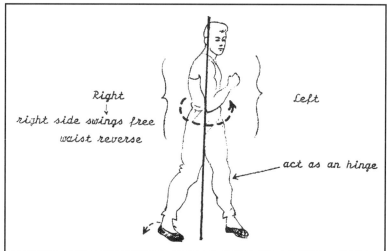

Immovable Elbow Theory (But Doan Jiang)

In conjunction with the centerline, Lee writes: "It has been determined that the ideal distance your lead elbow should be from the centerline is three inches. This allows you to employ the immovable elbow theory [*but doan jiang*], which is fundamental for attack and defense in many styles of gung fu."

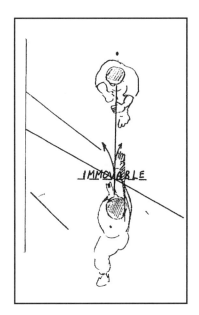

He continues: "It is important when assuming the *by-jong* [ready position] that the elbow of your lead arm remains immovable. With your elbow in a fixed position approximately three inches in front of your body, you'll note that your hand and forearm are free to move in any direction." If the elbows are too close to the body, there is less defensive capability; if they are extended too far from the body, balance is compromised. Lee liked to describe the elbows as the relatively calm eye of the hurricane, while the arms are constantly in turbulent motion with tremendous force.

Four Gates/Corners (Say Gok)

Utilizing the centerline and immovable elbow theories, four areas are created defining the four corners (*say gok*). Within the boundaries created by the immovable elbow theory in conjunction with the centerline theory splitting the body in half, four quadrants or gates are created: the upper outside, upper inside, lower outside and lower inside gates.

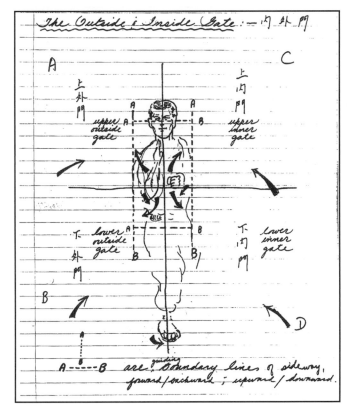

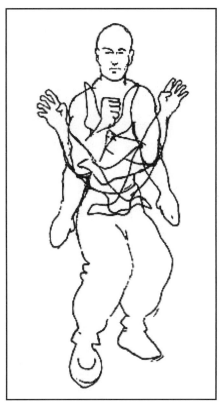

In *Wing Chun Kung-Fu*, written by James Lee with Bruce as its technical editor, the boundaries of the four corners are defined: "In the immovable elbow theory, boundary lines limit the sideward and up-and-down movement of the hand and forearm. The height of the boundary is the eyebrows, and the lowest boundary line is the groin area, although the elbow must never dip below the navel. The width of the boundary extends just past the shoulders." [3]

Since the front or rear hand may defend an attack into any of the four corners, eight blocking positions are created. The four corners dictate the appropriate technique to use when defending against an attack into a particular gate.

Three Fronts (Saam Moon)

The three fronts or channels (*saam moon*) of attack are the upper gate in front of the eyes, the middle gate in front of the hands and the lower gate in front of the legs.

Theory of Facing (Jiue Ying)

The by-jong stance protects the centerline and the three fronts, so that as long as the practitioner is properly positioned and oriented nose-to-nose or "facing" the opponent, it makes it difficult for the opponent to mount an effective attack against the practitioner.

Facing (*jiue ying*) is the critical methodology in making the centerline, the immovable elbow and the three fronts work, since proper positioning in relation to the opponent is vital when engaging: "Since it is crucially important to guard your centerline with the immovable elbow position, it is imperative to know how to face your opponent. When you face your opponent, you are able to preserve your centerline and make it impermeable. If you do not keep facing your opponent (nose-to-nose), you are susceptible to your opponent's attack."

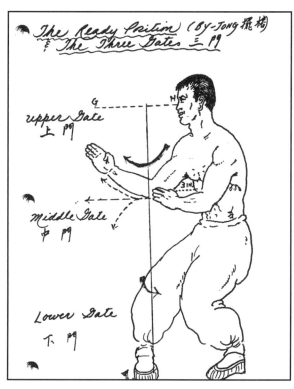

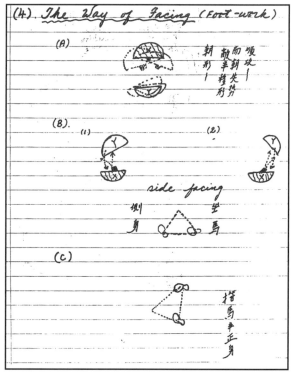

---

[3] Lee, J.Y. *Wing Chun Kung-Fu*. Burbank, CA: Ohara Publishing, 1972. p. 23.

Economy of Movement (Jian Jie De Dong Zuo)

Since the shortest distance between two points is a straight line, direct lines of attack are primarily utilized to minimize the amount of distance to cover and thereby maximize the economy of motion (*jian jie de dong zuo*). No matter how fast you are physically, you can be faster if your movements are structurally fast. In this way, straight-line movements are simply faster structurally than circular motions. Although some advantage may lie in circular motions, whether they be offensive strikes or defensive hand maneuvers, straight-line movement is shorter, and therefore, more efficient. In addition, the condensed boundaries using the centerline, the immovable elbow and the four corners further aid economy of motion: "Practicing economy of movements in both defense and offense and keeping within the boundaries of the four corners is the heart of *sil lum tao* [a little idea]." [4] The sil lum tao is the first form in wing chun, which emphasizes many of the foundational principles described.

Simultaneous Defense and Attack (Lin Sil Die Dar)

Similarly, defending and attacking at the same time is the most structurally efficient method and the epitome of economical movement. A system that typically blocks or defends against an attack before mounting a counterattack gives an opponent more time and, therefore, more opportunity to defend against the counter. But if you attack at the same time he defends, your opponent has little if any time to defend against a counterattack: "Any style which blocks and attacks simultaneously will be structurally faster than a style which incorporates a block and then an attack." [5]

The principle of simultaneous defense and attack (*lin sil die dar*), along with the stop-hit technique from fencing, was a big influence on Lee in eventually developing jeet kune do.

Kimura and Lee

---

[4] Ibid. p. 30.

[5] Ibid. p. 30.

Training Methodology

During his time in Seattle, Lee faithfully practiced wing chun gung fu, and he continued using many of its training methods such as the wooden dummy and training sandbags. Although he had modified some of the trapping techniques from wing chun, the training continued to help Lee hone his skill. He was also fascinated with Chinese martial arts and its many diverse styles, so he experimented with many of the training routines from these systems. Likewise, as he became aware of judo and boxing, he adopted some of their training methods as well. Linda recalls when training with Bruce during the early days in Seattle that she thought he was in terrific shape. His extreme hand speed and ability to control his opponents at close range made him appear invincible. She saw him spending most of his time training, practicing gung fu, honing his technical skills and devoting a lot of time to practicing chi sao with his students. He also supplemented his practicing with some light weight training. His day-planner entries from 1963 illustrate his training program, which consisted of air punching, punching the "sand plate" (wall-mounted sandbags), hanging bag, stretching, forms training such as sil lum tao and a kicking form, the wooden dummy, chi sao and freestyle practice. The following are training methods Lee employed during this time.

Forms Training

Lee became very good at performing many of the gung fu forms he learned while living in Hong Kong and Seattle, some from fellow Seattle-based gung fu practitioner Fook Young. These forms included praying mantis, *choy li fut,* southern mantis, white crane and his original style of wing chun. During demonstrations, Bruce often performed the flashier, flowery routines since they were the most impressive to the crowds, and he taught some of these forms to his early students so they could also perform them. Later on, Lee began to move away from practicing forms because he didn't really believe they had a lot to do with scientific street fighting, which most interested him.

The first form (sil lum tao) from wing chun gung fu was taught in Seattle to learn the basic hand techniques and positioning for chi sao. It was a foundational form for Lee, as was expressed in James Lee's book: "Sil lum tao,

the first form of wing chun, teaches correct elbow position, protection of the centerline, and economy of movements in attack and defense. Since sil lum tao is a stationary form, you will practice all your defensive blocks and offensive attacking tools without taking a single step. The hand movements will later be put to good use in the practice of chi sao (sticking hands)." [6]

Wooden Dummy (Mook Jong)

The wooden dummy comes from wing chun gung fu and is used to develop proper execution of techniques in solo training as well as arm conditioning. The unique position of its three arms and leg attachments allows the practitioner to practice proper positioning of wing chun techniques against an opponent. It provides the practitioner hours of training without a partner and the ability to practice at full power without the worry of physically hurting a training partner.

From the Perry Lee Collection

Top and Bottom Bag

Lee had an interesting blend of modern and traditional training methods. When he stayed at the Chow family residence, he not only had a wooden dummy installed, but also a top and bottom bag from boxing, according to Jesse Glover. The use of the top and bottom bag develops accuracy, proper timing and correct distance.

Lee preferred the top and bottom bag to the speed bag, as he wrote in his notes:

> ### *Platform Speed Bag*
> *Many people think of it as a training apparatus for timing—it's actually for developing rhythm. You don't hit like that.*
>
> ### *The Top and Bottom Bag*
> *The top and bottom bag teaches one to hit straight and fair and square—if hit on the side or top it will be erratic in its movements, and will tell the practitioner that he is not hitting straight.*
> *The almost instantaneous return of the bag to the face will soon teach you how, after having delivered the blow, to recover yourself quickly and get out of danger.*
> *It requires more footwork than the platform speed bag; more variety—and one can also hit upward.*

---

[6] Ibid. p. 43.

Wall-Mounted Sandbags (Sand Plates)

Lee practiced hitting a canvas bag filled with material such as sand or mung beans to develop impact and penetration in his punches as well as develop wrist strength.

Punching Air

To develop speed in his punches, Lee practiced punching without hitting anything, essentially punching air. However, students must be careful not to practice too rigorously or for too long, since damage to the joints can result.

Television Reaction Training

A unique training method Lee used was to practice in front of a television set and watch a program with quick cutaways between scenes, such as a cartoon. When the television show cut to another scene or camera viewpoint, Bruce instantly executed a technique like a punch or kick. This constant awareness and concentration developed quick reactions and reflexes.

Strength Training: Upper-Body Development

During Lee's early years in America, while he was in good physical shape, he was rather slim. He did, however, already have wide lat muscles, which was a trademark of his body when he flexed his lats in the movies. In Seattle, he concentrated on developing his shoulders, forearms and wrists to bolster the power in his punches. He developed these bodyparts through pushups, rope climbing, wrist curls, weight pulley machines and training more like a gymnast, according to Glover, who also saw Lee do some unconventional weight training such as punching exercises with dumbbells, rolling a barbell up and down his forearms, and holding a barbell out with his arms fully extended in front of him at shoulder height. These exercises aided Lee's punches and practice of chi sao by strengthening the tendons and connective tissue in his arms and shoulders.

Limited Cardiovascular Endurance

Lee did not spend a lot of time developing his cardiovascular fitness or endurance, perhaps due to his overwhelming physical speed and reactive abilities, requiring only seconds to end a confrontation. Due to this speed, as with the fight with the karate man in Seattle, endurance was not a factor. Glover recalls that although Lee's speed was lightning fast, his endurance was limited. Similarly, sprinters will have extreme foot speed in the 100-yard dash, but their speed rapidly diminishes as the distance is increased. Glover mentioned that Lee had world-class sprinter speed during the first 40 to 50 yards of a 100-yard dash, but he could not maintain the extreme speed beyond that distance.

Linda Lee: Two Halves of One Whole

Linda Claire Emery was born in Everett, Washington, but when her father passed away of a sudden heart attack when she was only five years old, her mother moved her and her older sister to Seattle. Although Linda was raised with a Christian upbringing, the Seattle environment was progressive due to interaction between people of different races. Seattle has always been a Pan-Asian city, but it also draws people from all over the world, making it a multicultural population.

When Linda attended Garfield High School, the student body consisted of 40 percent black, 40 percent white and 20 percent Asian in the early 1960s, even before the Civil Rights Movement in America. For Linda, it provided wonderful exposure and education for students, not only being multi-cultural and multi-ethnic, but also multi-economic, in that it drew from wealthy and poor areas of Seattle. As a result, Seattle was ready to embrace Bruce Lee.

Linda recalls seeing Bruce for the first time at Garfield High when the school's philosophy teacher invited him to give lectures on Chinese philosophy to the students. She wasn't in the class, but "everyone knew when Bruce was on campus" since he would also demonstrate some gung fu when visiting. Her first impression of him was "no doubt that this was a very vibrant human being, full of energy, and so darn good-looking! So everyone was attracted to him; he was magnetic."

After Linda graduated from high school in 1963, her good friend Sue Ann Kay invited her to the school where she was learning gung fu from Bruce. Linda went to the Chinatown basement location with the "concrete walls and single swinging lightbulb" where he was teaching, and she ended up signing up for lessons.

As Linda was entering the University of Washington as a freshman, she found herself spending time with

Sue Ann Kay, Kimura and Charlie Woo

31

the gung fu students on campus; they would hang out with Bruce, a junior, in the student union building, known as the Hub. "He was always surrounded by students and friends. He was so exciting, so much fun, and so funny, very humorous, always had a slew of jokes," Linda said. When training with the students, Bruce would make a day out of it, with students going out together for lunch or seeing a movie. It was an introduction to Chinese culture and not just martial arts. He introduced them to Chinese dim sum, and Linda put sugar in her tea, to Bruce's disdain. One time, Linda recalls going to an Asian theater to see *The Orphan*, Bruce's last film before he left Hong Kong.

The group also trained on the UW campus on a grassy field surrounded by tall white columns. While Linda was attracted to Bruce, she didn't think she had any chance with him, but while training near "the columns," Bruce asked her, "Would you like to go to the Space Needle?" She replied, "You mean the whole group?" He whispered, "No, just you." On their first date, Bruce presented Linda with a tiny troll doll with long pink hair tied back into a ponytail. He said, "This reminds me of you when you come to the Student Union building after swimming." From that first date on October 25, 1963, they began to date steadily.

During their courtship, Linda spent a lot of time at Bruce's studio on University Way working out, doing homework and going to a Chinese restaurant almost every day for oyster sauce beef and shrimp with black bean sauce. Bruce even enrolled Linda in a Chinese cooking class in the university district and started teaching her Chinese, giving her books to learn some basic Cantonese. During this time, Linda had two "dinners" every day; her time with Bruce was spent clandestinely because Linda's mother did not approve of her dating Chinese men.

By May or June 1964, Bruce decided to leave for Oakland to open the second branch of his Jun Fan Gung Fu Institute, and he was going to move with or without Linda, with whom he was now in love. Although many members of Linda's family did not approve of them getting married, Linda believed in Bruce and insisted on following him to Oakland. Bruce and Linda were married on August 17, 1964. Kimura recalled, "One time, he was already in the movies, he visited Seattle and asked me, 'What do you think about Linda?' I didn't lose a beat; I told him while she may not be the most glamorous person out there, like in Hollywood, she is more Chinese than the Chinese,

you'll never find anyone like that. I closed my eyes, because I thought he was going to pop me, but he said, 'You're right, Taky; I am a very lucky guy.' Linda was part of the yin and yang to him."

When Bruce and Linda started a family, Linda's mother ended up loving Bruce and found him to be a worthy husband to her daughter and father to her grandchildren.

Philosophy: Research in Zen and Taoism

At the University of Washington, Lee ultimately decided to major in philosophy. This decision was the result of his inquisitiveness about things such as why people place a high value on victory as he said during an interview in Hong Kong during the early '70s. And while he saw a strong relationship between martial arts and philosophy early on in Hong Kong, Lee found they had not been presented as thoroughly connected. While he was exposed to both Eastern and Western philosophies in college, he excelled in his Eastern studies, and his most eloquent papers centered on Chinese philosophy and its connection to gung fu, according to Linda. His college papers reflect the huge interest he took in Taoism and Zen and the notions of yin and yang, being like water, and yielding to force rather than opposing it. Having a keen interest in martial arts, Lee was able to conduct a serious study of Eastern philosophies, and as a result, continue to gain a deeper understanding of the martial arts. In this way, for Lee, martial arts transformed from merely a method of exercise or self-defense into a way of life. He wrote that gung fu is practiced not only for health and self-protection, but also for the mind's cultivation. He was very expressive in his writings about Chinese philosophy, whether in college term papers, manuscripts or personal notes. The following are some of the philosophical principles from Chinese culture that Lee found pertinent.

The Truth (Tao)

In a 1962 term paper at the University of Washington, Lee wrote:

The core of this principle of gung fu is "Tao"—the spontaneity of the universe.... Although no one word can substitute its meaning, I have used the word "Truth" for it—the "Truth" behind gung fu; the "Truth" that every gung fu practitioner should follow.... Tao operates in yin and yang, a pair of mutually complementary forces that are at work in and behind all phenomena.

Dark and Light (Yin and Yang)

Lee based his martial arts on the symbol of yin and yang, as he described: "a pair of mutually complementary and interdependent forces that act continuously, without cessation, in this universe. In the above symbol, the yin and yang are two interlocking parts of one whole, each containing within its confines the qualities of its complementaries." The following is a compilation of passages Lee wrote about yin and yang:

Etymologically, the characters of yin and yang mean darkness and light. The ancient character of yin, the dark part of the circle, is a drawing of clouds and hills. Yin can represent anything in the universe as negativeness, passiveness, gentleness, internal, insubstantiality, femaleness, moon, darkness, night, etc. The other complementary half of the circle is yang, which in its ancient form is written with the lower part of the character signifying slanting sunrays, while the upper part represents the sun. Yang can represent anything as positiveness, activeness, firmness, external, substantiality, maleness, sun, brightness, day, etc.

The common mistake of most martial artists is to identify these two forces, Yin and Yang, as dualistic (thus the so-called soft styles and the firm styles). Yin/Yang is one inseparable force of one unceasing interplay of movement. They are conceived as essentially one, or as two co-existing forces of one indivisible whole. They are neither cause nor effect, but should be looked at as sound and echo, or light and shadow. If this "oneness" is viewed as two separate entities, realization of the ultimate reality won't be achieved. In reality, things are "whole" and cannot be separated into two parts. When I say the heat makes me perspire, the heat and perspiring are just one process as they are co-existent and the one could not exist but for the other. If a person riding a bicycle wishes to go somewhere, he cannot pump on both pedals at the same time, or not pump them at all. In order to go forward, he has to pump on one pedal and release the other. So the movement of going forward required this "oneness" of pumping and releasing. Pumping then is the result of releasing and vice versa, each being the cause and result of the other. Things do have their complementaries, and complementaries co-exist.

Instead of mutually exclusive, they are mutually dependent and are a function each of the other. In the yin/yang symbol there is a white spot on the black part and a black spot on the white one. This is to illustrate the balance in life, for nothing can survive long by going to either extreme, be it pure yin (gentleness) or pure yang (firmness). Notice that the stiffest tree is most easily cracked, while the bamboo or willow survives by bending with the wind. In gung fu, yang (firmness) should be concealed in yin (gentleness) and yin in yang. Thus a gung fu man should be soft yet not yielding, firm, yet not hard.... This principle of moderation provides a best means of preserving oneself, for since we accept this existence of the one-ness (yin/yang) in everything, and do not treat it dualistically, we thus secure a state of tranquility by remaining detached and not inclining to either extreme.

Lee continued in the 1962 term paper to state: "This principle of yin-yang (also known as tai chi in Mandarin or *tai gik* in Cantonese) is also the basic structure of gung fu…. The basic theory in tai chi is that nothing is so permanent as never to change."

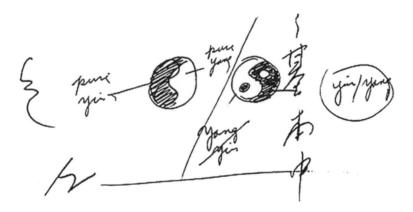

Lee found so much meaning in the yin and yang that he selected it as the base symbol to represent his approach in the martial arts. According to Dan Lee, a student from the Los Angeles era and a longtime practitioner of tai chi, "Bruce added two arrows around the tai chi symbol to further emphasize that the fighting techniques must contain the harmonious interplay of yin (pliable, yielding) and yang (firm, assertive) energies." It emphasized the continuous, unceasing interplay between the two forces of the universe: yin and yang.

However, Lee did not decide to follow the physical movements of tai chi, such as the *Yang, Chen* or *Wu* styles. Although Lee was exposed to tai chi through his father, who practiced its form, it was through his deep research into Chinese philosophy while in Seattle that Lee was convinced of the universal truths of yin and yang that could be applied to all martial arts.

From the concept of yin and yang, Lee observed some vital principles and presented them in his writings:

The Law of Harmony

The application of the theory of yin/yang in gung fu is known as the Law of Harmony, in which one should be in harmony with, and not against the force of the opponent…. As the butcher preserves his knife by cutting along the bone and not against it, a gung fu man preserves himself by following the movement of his opponent without opposition or even striving. [7]

This means that one should do nothing that is not natural or spontaneous. The important thing is not to strain in any way.

A true gung fu man never opposes force or gives way completely.

Be pliable as a spring. Be the complement not the opposition to the opponent's strength. Make his technique your technique.

---

[7] Lee, Bruce. *Chinese Gung Fu: The Philosophical Art of Self-Defense*. Burbank, CA: Ohara Publications, 1987. p. 82.

The Law of Non-Interference

The above idea gives rise to a closely related law, the law of non-interference with nature, which teaches a gung fu man to forget about himself and follow his opponent instead of himself; that he does not move ahead but responds to the fitting influence. The basic idea is to defeat the opponent by yielding to him and using his own strength. That is why a gung fu man never asserts himself against his opponent, and is never in frontal opposition to the direction of force. When being attacked, he will not resist, but controls the attack by swinging with it. This law illustrates the principles of non-resistance and non-violence which was founded on the idea that the branches of a fir tree snapped under the weight of the snow, while the simple reeds, weaker but more supple, can overcome it.

No-Mindedness (Wu-Hsin)

To perform the right technique in gung fu, physical loosening must be continued in a mental and spiritual loosening, so as to make the mind not only agile but free. In order to accomplish this, a gung fu man has to remain quiet and calm, and to master the principle of "no-mindedness" (wu-hsin). "No-mindedness" is not a blank mind which excludes all emotion; nor is it simply calmness and quietness of mind. Although quietude and calmness is important, it is the "non-graspingness" of the mind that mainly constitutes the principle of "no-mindedness." A gung fu man employs his mind as a mirror—it grasps nothing, and it refuses nothing; it receives, but does not keep…. There is nothing to try to do, for whatever comes up moment by moment is accepted, including not-accepted.

A gung fu man's mind is present everywhere because it is nowhere attached to any particular object. And it can remain present because, even when related to this or that object, it does not cling to it.

You should respond to any circumstances without prearrangement, your action should be like the immediacy of a shadow adapting to a moving object against the sun.

Your task is simply to complete the other half of the "oneness" spontaneously. There is nothing to "try" to do, in the final stage of gung fu, opponents, self, techniques are all forgotten. Everything simply "flows."

Non-Action (Wu Wei)

A gung fu man promotes the spontaneous development of his opponent and does not venture to interfere by his own action. He loses himself by giving up all subjective feelings and individuality, and to become one with his opponent. Inside his mind, oppositions have become mutually cooperative instead of mutually exclusive. When his private egos and conscious efforts yield to a power not his own, he then achieves the supreme action, non-action (wu wei).

Wu means "not" or "non-" and wei means "action," "doing," "striving," or "busyness." It doesn't really mean doing nothing, but to let one's mind alone, trusting it to work by itself. Wu wei, in gung fu, means spontaneous action or spirit-action, in the sense that the governing force being the mind and not that of the senses. During sparring, a gung fu man learns to forget about himself and follows the movement of his opponent, leaving his mind free to make its own counter-movement without any interfering deliberation. He frees himself from all mental suggestions of resistance, and adopts a simple attitude. His actions are all performed without self-assertion; he lets his mind remain spontaneous and ungrasped. As soon as he stops to think, his flow of movement will be disturbed, and he is immediately struck by his opponent. Every action, therefore, had to be done "unintentionally" without ever "trying."

Lee communicates this principle in *Enter the Dragon* in a scene that appears in a restored version of the film. He is talking with the Shaolin priest about the level of achievement he had reached in martial arts: "When the opponent expands, I contract, and when he contracts, I expand, and I do not hit, it hits all by itself." In this dialogue, Lee exemplified the notions of yin and yang and unconscious thought and non-action.

Be Like Water

The natural phenomenon which the gung fu man sees as being the closest resemblance to wu wei is water.

In order to survive in combat, the harmonious interfusion of gentleness and firmness as a whole is necessary, sometimes one dominating and sometimes the other, in a wave-length succession. The movement will then truly flow; for the true fluidity of movement is in its changeability.

Instead of opposing force by force, a gung fu man completes his opponent's movement by accepting his flow of energy as he aims it, and defeats him by borrowing his own force. This, in gung fu, is known as the law of adaptation. In order to reconcile oneself to the changing movements of the opponent, a gung fu man should first of all understand the true meaning of gentleness and firmness.... Remember, gentleness versus firmness is not the situation, but gentleness/firmness as oneness is the Tao.

Chi Sao: Philosophy in Motion

Sticking Hands (Chi Sao): The Epitome of Yin and Yang

Lee found tremendous value in practicing chi sao for a few different reasons. The first was developing sensitivity in the arms and proper arm positioning, cultivating a constant energy flow that serves as an automatic reflex for striking when the opportunity arises, thereby giving the practitioner confidence when in close proximity to an opponent. Second, he discovered that the proper practice of chi sao cultivated the mind and exemplified many of the Chinese philosophical ideals when performing martial arts.

Chi Sao: The Culmination of Wing Chun Training

Chi sao is a unique training method from wing chun to develop sensitivity in one's arms. The wrist and/or forearms are attached or connected, "sticking" with those of the training partner in a prescribed manner using wing chun arm positions, and when rolling or rotating the arms, the opportunity to strike the opponent presents itself. Sensitivity is cultivated when the practitioner feels the opponent's attack through the arms and applies the correct countermovement. Lee emphasized that chi sao was not a method of fighting; rather, he found it to be a valuable training method since it is a "flowing energy exercise" requiring continuous movement when harmoniously rolling the arms: "With the flowing energy, the defender 'floats' and 'dissolves' the opponent's force...so as to borrow the attacker's force to complete his counter."

The principles of wing chun are evident in the practice of chi sao, not only in the proper positioning of its hand and arm positions, but also in its key fighting principles: "The practitioner of the wing chun style keeps to the nucleus, letting his opponent move around the circumference. He also learns to move straight from the center out, or 'just enough' from the outside in, with his centerline well guarded by the elbow."

Yip Man and Lee

When Lee taught his students chi sao, he simplified its practice using fewer techniques that were more economical to make it more efficient. As he discovered in Hong Kong, Lee taught that chi sao should be practiced with a constant flow of energy (constant forward pressure) toward the opponent when rotating the arms, so should the opponent's defenses break down or an opening occur, the arm automatically strikes out. When there is emptiness, strike! Jesse Glover also mentioned that Lee began to modify the chi sao positions, attempting to make them more effective, like using the palm instead of the wrist as the point of contact in the *fook sao* position. By honing the physical skills, the techniques in chi sao become instinctive, so the body and mind can be free to make the right movement instinctively.

Mental/Spiritual Benefits of Chi Sao

It was with this instinctive body-mind connection that Lee found most beneficial from chi sao training. Like the flowing movements of the arms when rolling in chi sao, so the mind must also constantly flow from moment to moment with the situation at hand:

> *Movement in chi sao is like a flowing stream—never still. It avoids the "clinging stage" (the mind stopping to abide) and the attaching of one's self to a particular object rather than flowing from one object to another. If you set yourself against an opponent, your mind will be carried away by him. Don't think of victory or of yourself.* [8]

When practicing chi sao, you must forget about success or failure, or devising a strategy to defeat an opponent, leaving the "mind free to make its own countermovement without deliberation." In this way, you listen through your arms and become one with the opponent:

---

[8] *Wing Chun Kung-Fu.* p. 143.

When the opponent expands, we contract; when he contracts, we expand—to fit our movements harmoniously into his attack without anticipating or rushing the action, but simply continuing the flow...our defense should follow his attack without a moment's interruption, so that there will be no two separate movements to be known as "attack" and "defense." The important thing is not to attempt to control the attack by resisting it with force (either physical or mental), but rather to control it by going with it, thus not asserting oneself against nature.

Many of Lee's writings about chi sao express the ideals of Tao and its many philosophical principles:

In view of this, the two practitioners are actually two halves of one whole.

The hands in chi sao should be soft but not yielding; forceful and firm, but not hard or rigid.

When the ultimate perfection is attained in chi sao, the body and limbs perform by themselves what is assigned to them to do with no interference from the mind. The technical skill is so automated it is completely divorced from conscious effort.

As soon as your mind stops with an object of whatever nature—be it the opponent's technique or your own, the mode or the measure of the move—you cease to be master of yourself and are sure to fall victim to your opponent.

Not to localize or partialize the mind is the end of spiritual training. When it is nowhere it is everywhere. When it occupies one tenth, it is absent in the other nine tenths. Let the gung fu man discipline himself to go on its own way, instead of trying deliberately to confine it somewhere. Therefore, during chi sao, you should have nothing purposely designed, nothing consciously calculated, no anticipation, no expectation.

The empty-mindedness of chi sao applies to all activities we may perform, such as dancing. If the dancer has any idea at all of displaying his art well, he ceases to be a good dancer, for his mind stops with every movement he goes through. In all things, it is important to forget your mind and become one with the work at hand…. In chi sao the mind is devoid of all fear, inferiority complexes, viscous feelings, etc., and is free from all forms of attachment, and it is a master of itself, it knows no hindrances, no inhibitions, no stoppages, no clogging, no stickiness. It then follows its own course like water.

Lee and Kimura at the 1964 International Karate Championships

In another passage, Lee states:

Chi sao, or sticking hands in gung fu, is the closest to Taoism and Zen. This art aims at harmony with the practitioner and his opponent. Its principle follows the Taoist principle of wu wei.

All these are simply based on the harmonious interchanging of the theory of yin/yang. As long as we plan our actions, we are still using strength and will not be able to feel our opponent's movements, thus failing to comprehend the true application of yin and yang.

Sticking hands is just like the nature of water: Water is so fine that it is impossible to grasp a handful of it; strike it yet it does not suffer hurt; stab it and it is not wounded. Like water, a gung fu man has no shape or technique of his own, but molds or fits his movement into that of his opponent. It is true that water is the weakest substance in the world, yet when it attacks it can go through the hardest. It can be calm like a still pond and turbulent like the Niagara Falls.

Kimura believed that chi sao was representative of being like water, "since it never ceases to stop, there is no beginning. With everything coming at you, you must be able to neutralize it…The value of chi sao is that it puts you in a yin and yang status when you get into close range."

The Journey Begins

Coming to America was a blessing in disguise for Lee's development as a martial artist because not only was the U.S. the melting pot of people of different nationalities and cultures, but also of the many different martial arts of the world. In Seattle, Lee was exposed to judo, *jujitsu* and karate, arts he had little knowledge of until coming to America. Glover recalls Lee seeing how kicking could be effective as more than a distraction while watching a karate demonstration by Hidetaka Nishiyama in Tacoma during his stay in Washington. The demonstration of power and precision impressed Lee, and his approach in using kicks began to change. Lee would also become a fan of the American sports traditions of boxing and wrestling. Later on, as he moved south to Oakland and Los Angeles, he became acquainted with even more martial arts from around the world such as *savate*, Thai kickboxing, *taekwondo* and *aikido*. He extracted some theories and principles from these arts to test, but instead of examining various disciplines simply to adopt what they had to offer, Lee used them during public demonstrations to illustrate how he and his approach to martial arts were different.

When in Hong Kong, Lee began his formal training in the classical martial arts, but while in the United States, he had to depend largely on himself to mature as a martial artist. This self-reliance largely included self-education by reading profusely and doing research in subjects such as philosophy or science that gave him a better understanding and technical explanation. As a result, he began to realize the need for self-sufficiency, finding answers to his questions from deep within, and discovering a faith and confidence in himself and his abilities:

> As we know that gung fu is aiming at self-cultivation, and therefore, the inner self is one's true self, so in order to realize his true self, a gung fu man lives without being dependent upon the opinion of others. Since he is completely self-sufficient he can have no fear of not being esteemed. A gung fu man devotes himself to being self-sufficient, and never depends upon the external rating by others for his happiness.

Although Lee took a great interest in the classical styles and forms of martial arts in China while living in Seattle, his own personal approach to martial arts was very much "non-classical." He had no qualms about changing a technique or training method for the sake of efficiency or effectiveness. Lee was definitely on a path of personal freedom, but the journey was just beginning.

Note: Taky Kimura provided the following to represent the Seattle-era training presented during the Jun Fan Jeet Kune Do Nucleus' First Annual Seminar in 1997. This curriculum is not intended to be definitive, but rather to illustrate the essence of what Lee practiced during that period.

Seattle Branch Curriculum

Gin-lai or salutation
By-jong (ready stance)
(Incorporating the centerline theory)

Immovable elbow theory
Four-corners theory

Footwork:
   a) Forward
   b) Backward
   c) Shifting right
   d) Shifting left

Sil lum tao (basic form taught in Seattle)

Straight punches, elbow punches and various body punches

Biu jee (finger jab)

Kicks:
   a) Forward straight kick
   b) Forward shovel kick
   c) Side kick
     1) Low side kick
   d) Low toe kick
   e) Groin toe kick
   f) Hook kick (medium and high)
   g) Spinning back hook kick

Chi sao (sticking hands)

Blocks:
    a) Tan sao
    b) Bong sao
    c) Gong sao
    d) Vertical fist punch
    e) Fook sao or elbow-contained bent-wrist block
    f) Palm strikes (vertical, side and palm up)

Techniques:
    a) Pak sao
    b) Lop sao
    c) Chop chuie/gwa chuie

Technique combinations:
    a) Pak sao/lop sao/gwa chuie
    b) Lop sao/chung chuie/lop sao/chung chuie
    c) Chop chuie/gwa chuie/lop sao/chung chuie

BRUCE LEE'S
TAO OF
CHINESE GUNG FU

振藩拳道

以無限爲有限

以無法爲有法

一九六

學生李

CHAPTER 4

Oakland: Reject What Is Useless (The Birthplace of Jeet Kune Do)

What was to become the Oakland period actually began while Bruce Lee was still in Seattle. When Allen Joe was planning to visit Seattle with his family for the World's Fair during the summer of 1962, his good friend James Yimm Lee asked him to "check out this cat." Allen and James had been friends since growing up together in the Oakland area. After returning from World War II, they reunited and discovered they both practiced gung fu—Allen was taking *saam seen kune* (three line fist) and James was traveling to San Francisco for *sil lum gung fu* (Shaolin). James' brother Bob had been impressed by Bruce's martial arts prowess during demonstrations at the Chinese association dances, so James asked Allen to look Bruce up when visiting Seattle.

The Hotel Monticello, where Allen stayed in Seattle, was only a few blocks away from Ruby Chow's restaurant where Bruce worked and lived. Bruce was out for the evening, so Allen waited for him while having a couple rounds of Scotch. Around 10 p.m., in walked a well-dressed young man in a gray flannel suit; it was Bruce. Allen thought he looked more like a model than a gung fu man. Bruce was a little cautious when first approaching Allen, but as soon as he mentioned Bob and James Lee, Bruce loosened up and relaxed.

After Bruce ran upstairs to his room to change out of his suit, they walked to the hotel to meet Allen's wife and family. Bruce then asked Allen to join him for a late-night hamburger and root beer. While walking to the restaurant, he asked Allen to show him some of the gung fu he had learned, so Allen demonstrated some of the saam seen kune and Bruce thought it looked pretty good. He then asked Allen to throw a

punch at him, and when he did, he found Bruce *lop sao*-ing him (grabbing his arm) all over the place: "When he lop sao-ed me, he jerked my shoulder so hard that might be why my socket is still sore today." It was the beginning of a great friendship! At the restaurant, Bruce showed Allen some of his gung fu notes and drawings.

When Allen returned to the Bay Area, he called James and told him that Bruce was for real. James subsequently contacted Bruce and they began visiting each other from time to time. James was already an accomplished

Allen Joe, Bruce Lee and James Yimm Lee

gung fu practitioner and author of some of the earliest books on Chinese martial arts, including his series on iron and poison hand training, but he was impressed with Bruce. With his book publishing experience, James helped Bruce get started writing his first book, *Chinese Gung Fu: The Philosophical Art of Self-Defense,* published in 1963.

James Yimm Lee, Bruce Lee and Al Novak on the covers of martial arts books

Bruce intentionally wrote this introductory book about Chinese gung fu for those in America, which included very little of the wing chun gung fu that he had been practicing and teaching. The book illustrated a more basic, generalized approach and primer to the theories of gung fu, including much of the classical approach Bruce later criticized. While Bruce showed a glimmer of his eventual unconventional approach to martial arts, he expressed himself in this book from a traditional approach. At the same time, he showed how Chinese philosophy played a key role in gung fu with his introduction to the notion of yin and yang. Bruce took the photos for this book with some of his students in Seattle, including Taky Kimura, Jesse Glover, James DeMile and Charlie Woo.

In *Chinese Gung Fu*, James Yimm Lee claimed to have changed all his "Gung Fu techniques to his [Bruce Lee's] method. When he demonstrated his type of striking, which is based on inner energy, I found it much more powerful than the power I had developed from previous Iron Hand training." [9] Allen substantiates this remark to show that James was really sold on Bruce and his approach to martial arts: "He [James] had been searching for the ultimate in martial arts for all those years, studying Sil Lum Gung Fu, and he discovered it from a man half his age!"

Bruce planned to follow up with another book, entitled *The Tao of Gung Fu*, which he never finished. In that manuscript, the reader sees Bruce's continued deep research into Chinese martial arts and its many

---

[9] *Chinese Gung Fu: The Philosophical Art of Self Defense.* p. 2.

masters over the last couple of hundred years. He also planned to present some of the wing chun gung fu he had been practicing. Although Bruce had already taken a nonclassical approach to martial arts, he found value in introducing the rich, vast history of traditional systems in China, including internal and external systems such as tai chi and iron palm training to the Western world.

Linda, Bruce, James and Ed Parker and son

At the end of 1963, Bruce and Linda traveled to Pasadena, California, ostensibly to watch the University of Washington Huskies in the Rose Bowl, but the real reason was to stay with Ed Parker, a prominent *kenpo* karate teacher whom Bruce met through James Lee. Linda says, "We drove down to Oakland to pick up James Lee, then the three of us went down to Ed Parker's house in Pasadena and spent several days with Ed." Ed was planning his first International Karate Championships at the time.

With James' encouragement, Bruce began to contemplate establishing a chain of gung fu schools. According to Linda, James convinced Bruce that not much was going on in the Pacific Northwest as far as martial arts were concerned and he needed to "find himself" in California. During the summer of 1964, Bruce decided to move to Oakland to train James and establish the Oakland Branch of the Jun Fan Gung Fu Institute. Linda and Bruce were married that summer, and they stayed with James and his family in Oakland. Tragically, James' wife contracted a fast-acting cancer and died shortly after the Lees moved in. Linda became a surrogate mother to James' two young children, Karena and Greglon.

Allen Joe: An Inspiration for Health and Fitness

Allen Joe was born on July 31, 1923, and raised in Oakland, California. His mother, a seamstress, raised Allen and his brother as a single parent, since the boys' father left the family when the children were young. Allen remembered the days of broken sidewalks caused by the horses and buggies. He also remembered the *tong* (hatchet-men) associations: "When something happened, my mother always made me pull the shades. When the town crier said that somebody hanged himself, rumor was he owed an unpaid gambling debt, and the departed would rather hang himself instead of being chopped up." As he became older, Allen found out the tong were gung fu men. That was the first time he recalls asking, "What is gung fu?"

As a youngster, Allen periodically came across the tong when visiting his good friend James Lee and his family's shrimp business in Oakland's Chinatown, which actually served as a gambling joint in the backroom: "I ran into some of these people; they were always into Chinese lottery tickets."

James Lee was a few years older than Allen, and everyone looked up to James, who was voted class president by the students in elementary school. Allen and James went to Chinese school together, but while James learned how to read and write Chinese very well, Allen goofed off. They became lifelong friends.

As a teenager, Allen moved to Berkeley, where he worked as

a butcher at a grocery store. During this time, an acquaintance showed young Allen some weight training as well as some ring work, leading to his eventually becoming a member of the high school tumbling team. He remembers the first thing he bought for strength training was the Charles Atlas training springs from the "97-pound weakling" advertisement. Eventually, he went to the foundry to buy his first 80-pound set.

Allen was very fortunate that James knew Ed Yarick, who became Allen's weight training mentor. A huge Swede at 6 feet 4 inches and 245 pounds, Ed motivated young Allen, who was the only Chinese person lifting at the time. After the bombing of Pearl Harbor, before his 21st birthday, Allen found himself drafted into the service. Ed sent him letters of encouragement during his years in the Army, even when he was overseas.

In preparation for D-Day, during basic training in Atlantic City, Allen assisted the drill instructor in demonstrating the hand-to-hand combat drills because he was in pretty good shape. Before he knew it, Allen was shipped out of San Francisco on a big ship bound for the Pacific theater. He landed in New Guinea, Okinawa, Palau, the Philippines and, eventually, Japan. He made sure he continued his weight training while in the service, improvising with Jeep parts serving as weight plates.

Prior to serving in the military, Allen had decided against marrying his high school sweetheart, Annie, because he did not want to make her a young widow should he not return from the war, but as soon as he returned in 1946, they were married. Their honeymoon included a train trip to Los Angeles, and lo and behold, Ed Yarick was on the same train going down to Muscle Beach for a competition! Allen says, "It was just a coincidence—then he bought us our wedding breakfast."

Ed became a legendary trainer of bodybuilding champions. A contemporary of Jack LaLanne, Ed produced four Mr. America champions: Steve Reeves, who was best known for his role as Hercules in the movies of the day; Clarence "Clancy" Ross; Roy Hilligenn; and Jack Delinger. Ed also trained Tommy Kono, an Olympic weight lifting champion from Hawaii. (Kono had spent time at the same internment camp as Taky Kimura in Tule Lake.)

Ed continued to encourage Allen to compete in bodybuilding contests, although Allen never thought he had a chance to win, due to the discrimination prevalent at the time. Finally, in 1946, at a contest at the Berkeley YMCA, with Jack LaLanne as one of the judges, Allen won the Mr. Northern California title in his height division. He was the first Asian to do so. In fact, this contest featured winners in each height class who were white, black and Chinese. Allen eventually became a coach himself, mentoring many young, up-and-coming Chinese bodybuilders.

It was James Lee who suggested that "Tiger" (his nickname for Allen) look up this "cat" (Bruce Lee) in Seattle. After his visit, Allen told "Killer" (his nickname for James Lee) that this young man, Bruce Lee, was unbelievable!

Allen Joe (left) and Jack Delinger accept awards at the 1946 Mr. Northern California contest

When Bruce Lee began weight training seriously, Allen Joe saw the results during occasional visits to Los Angeles. Bruce developed some tremendous strength; Allen recalls Bruce being able to extend a 45-pound Olympic bar with one arm. Allen remembers visiting Bruce around the time Shannon was born and noting "his body looked terrific." During that visit, Bruce had Allen hold a wooden board that he broke with a kick; Allen could feel the vibration from the kick all the way up his arm!

Photos courtesy of Allen Joe

According to James Lee's first student, Al Novak, the first Jun Fan Gung Fu Institute in the San Francisco Bay Area was established in Hayward, California, then the Oakland school was subsequently opened. A business was slowly beginning to grow, with Linda processing orders for *Chinese Gung Fu: The Philosophical Art of Self-Defense*. Allen also had a stack of the books for sale at his grocery store, and he helped set up demonstrations for Bruce at the Wah Sung Club, where Bruce impressed the association members with his strength when James stood on Bruce's outstretched arms.

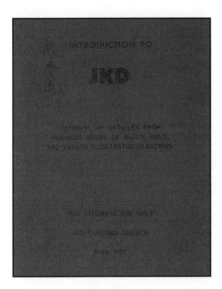
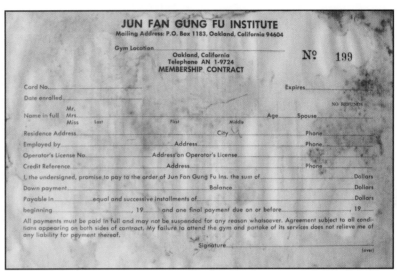

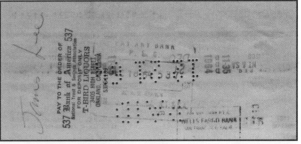
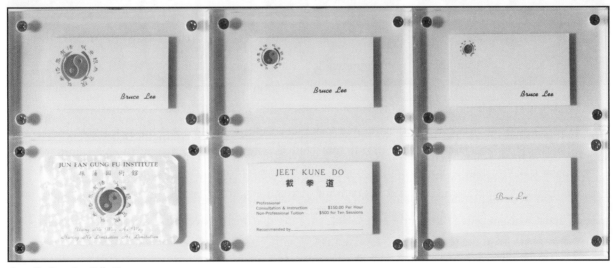

From the Perry Lee Collection

During his stay in Oakland, Bruce developed some very close friendships with prominent martial artists in the San Francisco Bay Area, including Wally Jay from the judo and jujitsu world as well as Ralph Castro from kenpo karate. Along with Ed Parker in Southern California, these men were progressive in their approaches to martial arts, and they spurred Bruce on to continue his nonclassical path. Although James was old enough to be Bruce's father, he recognized Bruce's tremendous talent and greatly respected him. With Bruce living at his house, James spent countless hours learning from Bruce and refining his skills.

Bruce Lee, James Yimm Lee, Ed Parker and Ralph Castro

Some of the earlier students at the Oakland and Hayward schools included Allen Joe, George Lee, Al Novak, Bob Baker (who portrayed the Russian villain in *Fist of Fury,* aka *The Chinese Connection*), Leo Fong, Fred Meredith, Tom and Jan De Laura, and Felix Macias Sr. Many others taught JKD from the Oakland years during the Jun Fan jeet kune do/Bruce Lee educational years, including James' son Greglon Yimm Lee, Gary Cagaanan, Dave Cox, Gary Dill, Allen and Mario Magdangal, and Howard Williams.

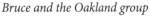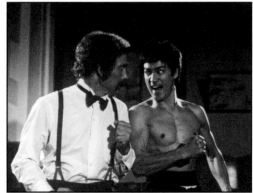

Bruce and the Oakland group *Bob Baker and Bruce*

During the summer, Ed Parker organized the first international karate tournament. Bruce attended to support Ed. Many excellent demonstrations were given of different styles from prominent martial artists, including Tak Kubota, Jhoon Rhee and Ben Largusa. Kali Grandmaster Largusa was the next-to-last martial artist to demonstrate, just before Bruce. He recalled that each performer was sure to top the martial artist who preceded him, and Largusa was sure to raise the bar over all the earlier performers, "but left some room at the top for Bruce to take the top spot." As the last performer, Bruce was expected

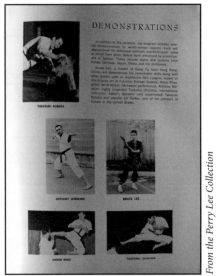

From the Perry Lee Collection

to top the rest. He did not disappoint. His demonstration of two-finger pushups, speed punching, blindfolded chi sao with Taky, and the one-inch punch were crowd pleasers to say the least. It was during this tournament that Bruce met Dan Inosanto for the first time. Dan was one of Ed Parker's black belts in kenpo, and he was assigned to help Bruce during the tournament. Shortly after, he served as a demo partner for Bruce when Taky was unable to spend any extra time in California.

Word got around about this young dynamo named Bruce Lee. Ed Parker captured Bruce's performance on film and showed it to Jay Sebring, a hairstylist to the Hollywood stars. Jay mentioned it to William Dozier, a producer for 20th Century Fox, while cutting his hair. Dozier was looking for an actor to be Charlie Chan's son for a proposed series called *Number One Son*. Sebring told Dozier how dynamic Bruce was, full of personality and charisma. A day or two after the demonstration, Linda was in Oakland when she received a call from Dozier's office. When Bruce came home, Linda told him, "This guy, this producer from Hollywood, called you and wants to talk to you."

From the time they first met in Seattle to their move to Oakland, Linda recalls that Bruce did not have any aspirations to become an actor: "There was never a mention of going into a film career." During the Seattle years, "Bruce had a plan to teach gung fu because his students loved it and he thought that would be his career." But things were about to change radically for the young couple. Although *Number One Son* did not materialize, Dozier was also producing the TV series *Batman* and working on a follow-up, *The Green Hornet*. Dozier needed an Asian actor to play the Green Hornet's sidekick, Kato.

The Turning Point: The Genesis of Jeet Kune Do

In late 1964, Bruce began to teach gung fu to students in a small studio on Broadway Street in Oakland. As in Seattle, he took on students of all colors and ethnicities: white, black, Chinese, Filipino, etc. This inclusiveness did not sit well with the staunch traditionalists of Chinese gung fu in San Francisco. Coming out of China's isolation from imperialism in the 1800s and the Boxer Rebellion in the early 1900s, when Chinese martial artists could not contend with Western bullets, it was decided Chinese martial arts should be just for the Chinese and it became taboo to teach them to Westerners. Allen Joe remembers that it was common for Chinese martial artists to not openly teach gung fu to "outsiders." Bruce did not take well to this antiquated idea, contending that he would teach anyone he wanted. Bruce was also outspoken about his nonclassical approach to martial arts, ruffling feathers when he criticized classical martial artists who taught techniques, forms and training methods to their students that were not practical for real combat or self-defense.

In late 1964, a Chinese martial artist from San Francisco appeared with several men at the Oakland studio to issue Bruce a challenge. Linda was present and eight months pregnant with Brandon. An ultimatum written in Chinese was presented to Bruce; if he were to lose the fight, he would discontinue teaching gung fu to non-Chinese. Bruce accepted the challenge and the gym was cleared, with only a small group of people remaining to witness the fight, including Linda and James Lee. Dressed in a traditional gung fu outfit, the challenger wanted to discuss the rules of the fight (no finger jabbing to the eyes, no hits below the belt, etc.), but Bruce responded, "No, you came to my school to challenge me and now you want to set the rules? As far as I am concerned, it's no holds barred. There are no rules!" After some 50 years, the event was still burned in Linda's memory, as she recalled:

> They did not exactly bow to each other, more like a nod, but not a bow or formal salutation. My recollection is that Bruce did a very quick hand movement and began straight blasting his opponent, and almost immediately, the challenger backed away and then he began to run, running about 15 feet, entering this door, going through this dressing room and emerging from the other door, and they must have run around like that five times with Bruce chasing him. The challenger turned around and backpedaled at some point and tried to do something, then turned and ran. Then they engaged again in the middle, with some techniques exchanged, but almost immediately then, Bruce got him down on the ground and was standing over him saying, 'Do you give up! Do you give up?!' And he said, 'Yes.' The entire engagement lasted about three minutes. There was very little combat or connecting blows. Nobody got banged up; there were no black eyes or anything like that. After the incident, the challenger and his entourage quietly left the gym.

Linda noted the significance of the challenge fight in Bruce's development as a martial artist:

> But now that was the beginning of something else, because Bruce said nothing and went out to the back of the building and sat on the steps of the back porch of the studio, breathing heavily for several minutes with his chin in his hand. I remember going next to him and asking him, 'Is everything okay?' And he said, 'It shouldn't have been like that.' Instead of feelings of elation, he was so disappointed with his performance because the whole thing had taken about three minutes. He said it should've been over much faster, 'I should've had a way to stop him. I'm out of breath because of all this running.' This was the beginning; this was the birth of what would become JKD and his increased physical fitness. This was when he started doing aerobic training, weight training and developing techniques that were suitable for him. Because the challenger fought a different style, Bruce realized he needed to have techniques that would work against any type of style, not just with another wing chun person. Bruce had to employ some techniques that he was not accustomed to, getting him down on the ground. Some grappling techniques came into play that he had not really been practicing before. He began to go beyond his training. He began his research, reading and training with other people outside of wing chun, and developed his way of martial arts, which he eventually called jeet kune do.

To be fair to Bruce's original style, the fight had more to do with his rigid adherence to wing chun than the system itself, according to Linda:

> The fact that the fight did not go the way Bruce wanted it to go was what initiated the idea that he should not be stuck on the system that he had learned in wing chun, so he came to realize that

he depended on those techniques that he had been taught in class and that he practiced for years. And here he was in a situation where some of those techniques did not work as effectively as he would have wanted them to. He realized that he had become stuck to those techniques and that he needed to broaden his array of skills to deal with a situation as it is unfolding. You cannot predict what is going to happen in a fight; you cannot have a set of techniques that you are going to do.... You have to just react to what is presented to you.... You just have to be able to flow with the situation. And that was part of Bruce's broadening, both philosophically and technically.

While the incident was a wake-up call for Bruce, he was already on a path of excellence and self-exploration. Linda concludes:

I would say in Oakland, after the fight, he began to express those qualities which he had within himself before this time: the desire to be the best he could be, the desire to expand in all directions, always aimed at knowing himself better and being the best person he could be. The big change occurred in Oakland, but it was not black and white, but more a graying matter; he already had these qualities in Seattle, the desire to explore, the desire to find the best within himself. He had this passion within himself, and he was going to do something with it. After Oakland, we begin to see this come to fruition.

Linda recalled that Bruce reviewed the fight with the gung fu man in his head constantly, especially in the initial aftermath. While in Hong Kong, Bruce wrote to James Lee on August 7, 1965:

As for the "runner's" gung fu school, it's just another waste of time with a little bit more to offer—calisthenics! The more I think of him to have fought me without getting blasted bad, the more I'm pissed off! If I just took my time, anger screwed me up—that bum is nothing!

Linda agreed:

The fact that the challenger and his elder Chinese gung fu men had the nerve to challenge him and to demand that he stop teaching non-Chinese made Bruce very angry, he was beside himself. He went into that fight with this big anger within himself. He was very upset afterwards that during the entire fight he was feeling this anger so much, and he didn't just let go of that anger and defeat the opponent, just blast him. That was also a philosophical lesson that he learned from that fight, that if you have anger inside of you, it defeats itself. So you have to be able to let go of those emotions and react to "what is," what is going on at the moment and how the fight is going, and not get tied up with all these emotions.

Transitions: Brandon Is Born,
Lee Hoi Chuen Passes

Shortly after the challenge fight, on February 1, 1965, Bruce and Linda became the proud parents of a baby boy, Brandon. A week after Brandon's birth, Bruce's father, Lee Hoi Chuen, passed away in Hong Kong. Around the same time, William Dozier showed interest in Bruce for the Kato role in *The Green Hornet*, so Bruce traveled to Los Angeles for a screen test. Because production of *The Green Hornet* was delayed, Dozier signed Bruce to an option that prevented him from taking other movie roles for 18 months, paying him an $1,800 retainer fee. Linda recalls, "This was the first inkling that Bruce might have a career in show business." With that money, Bruce was able to take the whole family to Hong Kong for four months and Linda was able to meet Bruce's family for the first time.

After their visit to Hong Kong, Bruce and the family returned to the U.S. and stayed in Seattle for another four months, living with Linda's mother before briefly returning to Oakland to check in on the school. By that time, *The Green Hornet* was given the green light, so Bruce was preparing to move to Los Angeles.

From the Perry Lee Collection

Years later, Bruce reached a conclusion about the exclusionary practice of not sharing Chinese martial arts with non-Chinese when he explained to Ted Wong that a Caucasian "would not need gung fu to beat up a Chinaman." Instead of concealing it, Bruce would introduce Westerners to Chinese gung fu, and as a result of understanding and appreciating the beauty of the art, they would in turn appreciate all the other things Chinese culture had to offer. *The Green Hornet* television series, featuring Bruce and his dynamic martial arts, was an excellent venue to reach out to the masses.

Martial Art: Tao of Chinese Gung Fu

Early on in the Oakland period, while Bruce maintained the core of his teaching to his modified wing chun training, "Oakland still had a lot of wing chun," Allen recalls. However, Bruce was definitely on a path of exploration, seeking out what worked well for him and what didn't. Bruce was always looking for ways to improve his skill and power, but the fight in Oakland pushed the issue. Winning that fight was not enough. He knew the fight should have lasted only a few seconds instead of a few minutes. As a result, Bruce delved deeper into boxing with its rich history and scientific approach to delivering punches as well as fencing for speed development and attacking methodology such as the five ways of attack, and this knowledge began to be reflected in his training. The following shows Bruce's vast breadth of research from a variety of sources during this time, continuing to refine his wing chun while at the same time developing more skill in kicking and researching how to generate more power. He didn't have a name for it, but he expressed this personal approach as "The Tao of Chinese Gung Fu," similar to what he was going to entitle his second book and emboss on the certificates he issued to those deserving students who had been personally taught by him.

BRUCE LEE'S
TAO OF
CHINESE GUNG FU
振 藩 拳 道

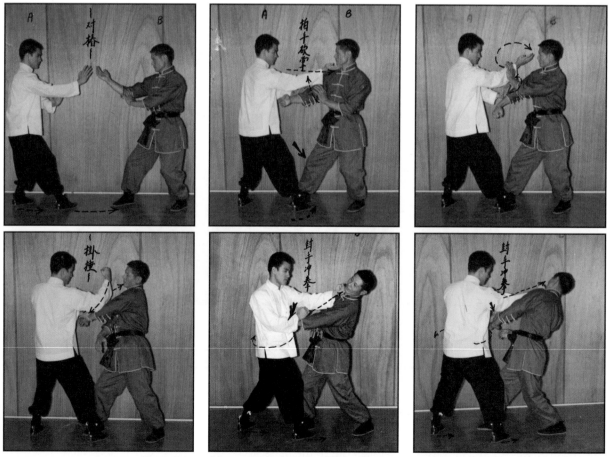

Bruce Lee and James Yimm Lee in a classical wing chun sequence

Principles

Springing Energy

One of the basic principles from wing chun gung fu is to cultivate springing energy in your arms to ensure the centerline is protected. An opponent may pull, push or slap your arm in an attempt to create an opening and attack your centerline. By automatically springing the arm back to a proper defensive position, you have a better chance of continually protecting the centerline.

"Short-Cutting" the Technique

Bruce modified his practice of wing chun techniques by simplifying them. He would cut two movements down to one, concentrate on straight-line movements (versus circular or disengagement), and insert illusive punches between trapping movements, thereby making a technique more efficient and effective. Allen Joe and George Lee described this process as "short-cutting" the technique because Bruce reduced a technique down to its bare essence. Bruce liked to describe his art as "a sophisticated fighting style stripped to its essentials."

Sticking vs. Non-Sticking

While the touch sensitivity developed in the arms as a result of chi sao training was important to Bruce Lee, the ability to read the opponent's intentions without being in contact with the opponent became just as critical. Without sticking to the opponent's arms, there is less stimuli to sense the opponent's movement and intentions, so distance, positioning and visual cues were used to control the fight. As Lee began to develop more speed in his movement, he had less need to attach himself to his opponent. With a fast-penetrating attack, Lee could bypass an opponent's defenses, and therefore not require any "sticking."

Trapping: A Byproduct of Hitting

Lee's view on trapping evolved during these years in Oakland. While trapping, being the central theme, may have been viewed more as an "end" early on, it definitely became a "means to an end" later when boxing and mobility were emphasized. In light of what boxing brought to the table, trapping became a byproduct of hitting.

Boxing Influence

Lee had already been exposed to Western boxing in many ways on his martial arts journey. His senior wing chun brother Wong Shun Leung was a boxer and had a lot of respect for the sport and its fighters. Lee also won the high school boxing tournament in Hong Kong and many of his Seattle-era students were boxers. However, during the Oakland period, he took a deeper look at boxing, reading numerous books about its techniques and methodology. He discovered it was an efficient means of fighting, albeit as sport with rules in a confined ring, but the development of punching power, evasive movement and fighting strategy gave weight to the refined approach to the art of pugilism. Ted Wong believed Lee was attracted to boxing because of its simplicity. Boxing only has a few different types of punches, yet it is so versatile that each boxer develops his own "style."

Lee was highly influenced by books written by boxers and coaches such as Jack Dempsey, Joe Louis, Jim Driscoll, Edwin Haislet and Thomas Inch, among many others. When meeting Senator John Tunney, whose father was the great boxer Gene Tunney who beat Jack Dempsey, Lee impressed the senator when he told him he had read his father's boxing books. Lee was especially inspired by Muhammad Ali, whose hand speed, footwork and movement, as well as his long-range fighting tactics, gave him much success in the ring at the time. James Lee, a former amateur boxer with street-fighting experience and an eye for practicality, mentored Bruce on what worked in and out of the ring. Bruce found similarities and differences between his previous wing chun training and what he discovered from boxing, so he had to decide what was useful to him and what was not. Below are the boxing techniques and principles Bruce Lee considered useful.

Stance—Leading with the Strong Side vs. Weak Side

Boxing emphasized balance as one of the most critical components of a fighting stance, and balance is achieved only through correct body alignment of the feet, legs, trunk and head. With the arms and hands serving only as the "vehicles of bodily force," it is the body's center or core that ultimately generates power. According to Haislet, the fundamental position in boxing is the "most favorable to the mechanical execution of the techniques and skills" with its "muscle tonus most favorable to quick reaction time." [10]

While Lee took the study of boxing seriously, he continued to compose his stance with the strong or dominant side forward. Most conventional boxers lead with their left or "weak" hand and foot, jabbing or probing with the lead hand, while preserving the rear (or dominant) hand for power punches such as the cross. The strong-side forward stance from JKD appears to be a southpaw stance since it leads with the right side for right-handers, but he chose it for many other reasons. Whereas a southpaw boxer is placing

---

[10] Haislet, Edwin L. *Boxing*. New York, NY: A.S. Barnes & Co. 1940. p. 1.

his weak or "right" side in the front since he is left-handed, the JKD man actually places his dominant hand in the front.

With the emphasis on speed, Lee believed the hand primarily used to attack should be the closest to the opponent, so it has less distance to travel, and with some practice, can be difficult to defend against. Since Lee also used his feet as weapons, this principle became twice as important as 80 to 90 percent of his punching and kicking came from the front hand and foot.

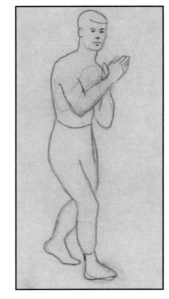 

Also, while boxing is a battle of attrition between two fighters in the ring, one of its objectives is to preserve energy and deliver maximum power in its punches over many rounds during a boxing contest. Today, championship fights are 12 rounds, but in the past, there were many more rounds. In a self-defense situation, the goal is to end the confrontation as quickly as possible, expending a tremendous amount of energy and delivering as much power as possible over a few seconds.

Since Lee chose to use the strong-side forward stance, he marked up his books to understand more easily the mechanics of boxing applied to a stance in that configuration, such as a jab being delivered with the right hand in JKD (the left in boxing) or that one moves to the left when slipping an opponent's right jab. Lee also watched many boxing films, and he would either watch the projection from a mirror or turn the film the other way around in the projector, so the boxers appeared to be fighting from a right-hand stance.

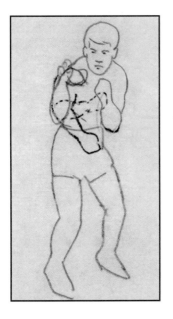

When training his students, Lee insisted they first exclusively cultivate their lead-side tools. The power that could be generated early on from the rear hand was enticing. It took much longer to develop power from the lead hand, so if one were tempted by the power from the rear, he was more likely to give up on the lead tools: "Complete use of the right hand and right leg are taught before the left hand or leg are developed at all (generally).... Cultivation of the lead tools, develop coordination and strength before being wooed with the rear tools."

Mobility through Footwork and Lateral Motion

Through the study of boxing footwork, Lee realized that "the essence of fighting is the art of moving at the right time" and that "maintaining balance while constantly shifting bodyweight is an art few ever acquire." And "to move just enough, 1) will make an opponent miss and 2) will deliver a counter blow more effectively." [11]

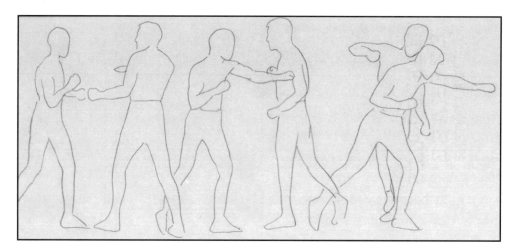

According to Bobby Neil's *Instructions to Young Boxers*, boxing is 60 percent footwork, since it provides the foundation, putting your feet in the correct position to use your hands effectively. Because it is balanced, it is firm but with movement, it is a highly mobile base.

Lee wrote in his seven notebooks comprising his *Commentaries on the Martial Way*:

> *The object of footwork is to enable a boxer:*
> a. *to move about with his opponent rapidly and*
> b. *at the same time always keep the right distance from him, and*
> c. *retain a suitable stance for resisting blows from all angles, and*
> d. *always maintain such a position as to enable him, while just keeping out of range, to be yet near enough to instantaneously take an opening should his opponent leave one, and this is quite impossible unless a boxer has learned to be able to move with equal facility in all directions.*

Some of the basic steps include stepping forward, stepping back and circling left or right. As a result, Lee modified the way he performed the sidestep by first moving the foot closest to the intended direction. Earlier, he stressed the importance of protecting the groin and centerline, but later mobility and speedy foot movement were emphasized. He remarked:

> *Sidestepping is not only one of the prettiest things in boxing, but a method of escaping all kinds of attacks and countering an opponent when he least expects it. It consists of avoiding a lead or a rush by moving out of the line of attack by taking a quick step either to the left or right, much after the fashion of a toreador escaping the charging bull.*

---

[11] From Bruce Lee's personal notes at the beginning of the chapter on fundamental footwork in his copy of Haislet's *Boxing*.

Punching, Boxing-Style

Powerline

While many other boxing coaches recommended hitting with the first two knuckles, Lee found that heavyweight boxer Jack Dempsey advocated hitting with the bottom three knuckles of the vertical fist, similar to his previous wing chun training. Dempsey, one of the greatest heavyweight boxers of the early 20th century, had in his prime weighed no more than 180 pounds.

In his book, *Championship Fighting*, Dempsey presented a very thorough breakdown of the many different elements contributing to knockout punching, including the "powerline," which, when a lead punch is properly aligned, runs from the shoulder down the length of the arm to the bottom knuckles of the fist. According to Ted Wong, Lee had students place their vertical fists on a wall to feel the powerline as Dempsey illustrated in the book.

Also similar to his previous wing chun training, Lee found many boxing authors professed the effectiveness of straight punching, which had been all but lost in the 1900s when boxers preferred to throw swinging punches—more brawling than boxing. According to Driscoll, historically, modern-day boxing got its start from fencing masters, "so early boxing was like sword fencing without the sword," using rapier-like punches. However, the refined art and scientific method of straight punching lost ground to the crowd-pleasing brawling and subsequent knockouts. Straight punching was more difficult to master, while swinging punches were easier to cultivate, but the mark of a master boxer was a swift, stiff jab.

Ted Wong and Bruce Lee

Boxing coaches knew that straight punches were more efficient and accurate than swinging punches. Like their wing chun counterparts, they saw that straight punches gave the boxer the inside line, and therefore, the advantage in most instances. Unlike their wing chun counterparts, boxing coaches saw that straight punches allowed their boxers to fight from the outside, and then they could close the distance and deliver punishing hooks and uppercuts. Fighting from the outside could also avoid potential clinching or wrestling when in close proximity to the opponent.

Following are Lee's scribbled notes in his copy of Haislet's *Boxing* regarding the subject:

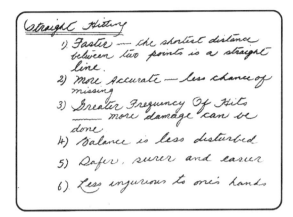

> Straight Hitting
> 1) Faster — the shortest distance between two points is a straight line.
> 2) More Accurate — less chance of missing
> 3) Greater Frequency Of Hits — more damage can be done
> 4) Balance is less disturbed
> 5) Safer, surer and easier
> 6) Less injurious to one's hands

Since the balance is less disturbed when throwing straight punches, recovery is quicker and multiple punches can be delivered. Also, straight punching is less injurious to the hands, since the bones in the hand and the wrist are better aligned than with a hooking punch, especially with a glancing blow. Lee appreciated the economy of the straight punch from boxing because of its efficiency. The balance between obtaining maximum power with a minimum of movement is achieved with the straight punch. But while the principle of straight punching was shared between wing chun gung fu and boxing, its execution was different.

Power: Leverage and Timing

Lee found knockout punches were largely a result of a combination of leverage and timing. Boxers are warned not to punch just with the arms. They are taught how to transfer their body weight, snapping their waists and whirling their shoulders when punching. This body weight transference is in contrast to Lee's previous wing chun, which typically maintains the body weight to the rear and keeping the shoulders square so that both hands can be used equally.

As Lee advised: "In jeet kune do you never strike your opponent with your fist only, you strike him with your whole body. In other words, you should not hit with just arm power, your arms are there as a means to transmit great force from the correct timing of feet, waist, shoulder and wrist motion—at great speed."

The timing involved with punching is twofold: the proper coordination of the parts of the body working together and the ability to hit the opponent at the right time, like when he is rushing in, creating the head-on collision effect. The opponent could also be lured off-balance or his attention drawn away from the power punch so that the strike is doubly effective. As Thomas Inch wrote: "Correct timing is one of the great secrets of severe hitting with little effort." [12]

---

[12] Inch, Thomas. *Spalding's Book on Boxing and Physical Culture*, "Art of Hitting." Aldershot, UK: Gale & Polden, 1945. p. 146.

Lee wrote:

> *An action, although technically perfect, can be frustrated by the opponent's preventive hits. Therefore, it is absolutely essential to time the attack at exactly the right moment, psychologically or physically, when the opponent cannot avoid being hit.*
>
> *Thus, timing means the ability to recognize the right moment and seize the opportunity for an action. Timing can be analyzed through its physical, physiological and psychological aspects.* [13]

Footwork for Power

Some of the best boxers and coaches use footwork to enhance punching power. By forcefully stepping in, the body is propelled into the target and all the momentum generated is transferred when the punch is delivered. Even if one can only take a very short step, one is encouraged to step in with the straight punch. Dempsey's advice for punching power put all of the elements together: "Exploding bodyweight is the most important weapon in fist-fighting or in boxing." [14] Dempsey used the stepping-straight jolt (versus a simple jab) because there was more footwork and body involvement in this devastating lead punch. It is likely that the stepping-straight jolt was the prototype for Lee's straight-lead punch. (The effect of using footwork when punching is analyzed in later chapters.)

Lee wrote about the importance of footwork for power in his notes:

---

[13] Lee, Bruce. *Tao of Jeet Kune Do.* Valencia, CA: Black Belt Communications, 1975. p. 61.

[14] Dempsey, Jack. *Championship Fighting: Explosive Punching and Aggressive Defense.* New York, NY: Prentice Hall, 1950. p. 3.

The Role of the Feet

In advancing to attack, the right foot should not land before the fist makes contact or the bodyweight will end up on the floor instead of behind the right punch.

Remember to take up power from the ground by pushing off from the left foot.

Follow-Through/Penetration

In order to deliver punches with tremendous impact, the arms and fists must not buckle upon contact. Through follow-through or penetration, power is achieved. While the entire body is to be loose and relaxed throughout the delivery of a punch, at the moment of impact it becomes rigid to add force to the blow.

The fist must be clenched tightly, with the forearm, extended arm and shoulder held rigidly as one solid piece during impact. With this battering-ram effect, the fighter is able to penetrate and hit through the target. Lee paraphrased Haislet in his notes: "A blow is never hit at a mark. It is driven through a mark." [15]

[15] Lee, Bruce. Annotation in Haislet's *Boxing*. p. 16.

OAKLAND: REJECT WHAT IS USELESS

Lee underlined Dempsey's instruction in *Championship Fighting*: "As the relaxed hand approaches its target, it convulsively closes in a grab, so that the fist, arm and shoulder is frozen steel-hard, creating an explosive follow-through." [16] Lee summarized:

> *Follow-through generally refers to continuation of a high rate of movement, or even acceleration from the instant of contact, until the ceasing of contact. In boxing, for example, the athlete is taught to "strike through" the opponent to maintain or increase the rate of movement during the contact so that the "explosive push" carries through farther and changes the opponent's position more sharply.*

> *Relaxation is essential for faster and more powerful punching. Let your right punch shoot out loosely and easily, do not tighten up or clench the fist until the moment of impact. All punches should end with a snap "several inches behind the target." Thus you punch through the opponent instead of at him.*

> *Make up your mind that you'll hit as hard as you possibly can with every ounce of your bodily strength, with every fiber of your mental determination, and also that you'll keep on hitting harder and harder as you progress through the object.* [17]

Power of the Hook and Straight Rear

Through his study of boxing, Lee learned more about its other diverse punches such as the straight rear and hook punches, which perfectly complement the straight lead. With the straight rear punch, the same logic applies as in the straight lead punch, but the rotation is in the opposite direction, transferring even more power since the punch is coming from the rear, with the waist, shoulders and arm in perfect alignment.

---

[16] *Championship Fighting.* p. 46–47.

[17] *Tao of Jeet Kune Do.* p. 96.

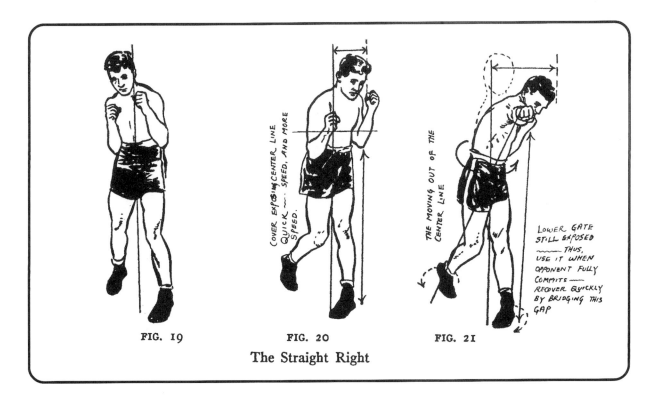

COVER EXPOSING CENTER LINE. QUICK —— SPEED, AND MORE SPEED.

THE MOVING OUT OF THE CENTER LINE

LOWER GATE STILL EXPOSED —— THUS, USE IT WHEN OPPONENT FULLY COMMITS —— RECOVER QUICKLY BY BRIDGING THIS GAP

FIG. 19   FIG. 20   FIG. 21

The Straight Right

Dempsey wrote that the hook punch is the perfect whirling punch, with one shoulder whipping forward while the other one whips back. The more loop, the more explosive the punch. Also, the tighter the hook punch, the more powerful it becomes.

Thomas Inch wrote in *Boxing: The Secret of the Knock-out*:

> *The two best knock-out punches are left hook to the jaw and right hand to jaw used either straight or otherwise according to circumstance…. Jaw punches must be slightly to the side of the point of the chin. This gives the leverage which produces slight concussion; the stunned effect necessary to keep a man down for the count of ten…. Snap, velocity, whip-lash effect are what are needed.* [18]

Lee wrote in his notes about the straight rear: "Remember, the secret of power in the straight rear cross (or thrust) is using the lead side of the body as a hinge and allowing the rear side of the body to swing free."[19] And about the hook, Lee said, "Against a clever defensive fighter, the lead hook is sometimes the only way you can penetrate his defense or force him to vary it so that you can find openings for other types of punches" [20] and "A hook is a deceptive punch, especially when preceded by feints. Unlike a straight punch that comes straight, a hook comes from the side, outside the range of vision and scores by sneaking around the opponent's guard. It is a powerful blow, but oftentimes the practitioners get carried away and turn it into a swing."

---

[18] Inch, Thomas. *Boxing: The Secret of the Knock-out*. Surrey, UK: The World's Work Ltd., 1953. p. 24, 11.

[19] *Tao of Jeet Kune Do*. p. 102.

[20] Ibid. p. 106.

Lee realized having a small arsenal of diverse tools enhanced his fighting ability; since they offer more powerful counters and finishing blows, they can open up the opponent's defense, they allow for more possible combinations and their flexibility presents more angles of attack. In this way, the right type of punch is used depending on the range.

Punching Combinations

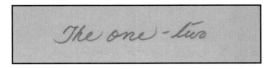

Some of the most devastating knockouts in boxing are the results of perfectly timing a series of blows to the opponent. While they could be a combination of straight and hook punches or from high to low angles, they are designed to deliver the maximum power. Sometimes they are setups in that the first punch is delivered to distract the opponent:

The one-two which means sending in first a comparatively light left to the face, not a hard punch, sufficient to throw your man off balance and perhaps to interfere with his vision. The second, KO punch follows likes lightning. They land almost at the same time, but the right-hander is sent in with terrific force and good step in to make sure that body weight helps without, however, turning the punch into a push of any kind. [21]

Set Up: a series of blows delivered in a natural sequence. The object is to maneuver the opponent into such a position or create such an opening, that the final blow of the series will find a vulnerable spot thus rendering the opponent helpless and setting him up for the finishing or knockout blow.... The difference between an expert and a novice is that the expert makes use of each opportunity and follows up each opening. He delivers his blows in a well-planned series, each opening creating another, until a clean shot is obtained. [22]

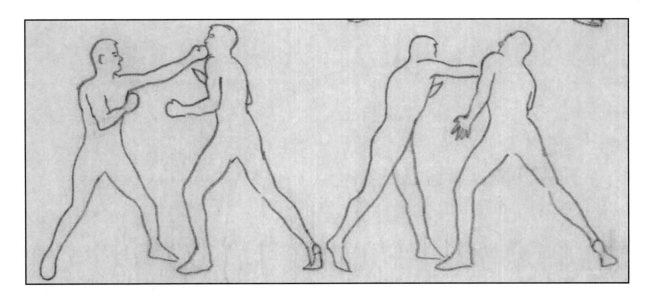

---

[21] *Boxing: The Secret of the Knock-out.* p. 37.

[22] *Spalding's Book on Boxing and Physical Culture.* p. 85.

Lee liked boxing combinations because they could be used as setups or to deliver maximum power though proper body mechanics: "A good Western boxer hits from every angle. Each punch sets him in position to deliver another punch. He is always on center, never off-balance. The more effective combinations a fighter has, the more different types of opponents he will be able to defeat." [23]

Offensive Defense and Evasive Movement

Lee found similarities between wing chun and boxing when it came to an offensive defense to the opponent's attack. With wing chun gung fu there is the simultaneous attack and defense. In *Championship Fighting*, Dempsey said that the best defense is an aggressive one in that nearly every defensive move should be accompanied by a simultaneous or delayed counterpunch.

 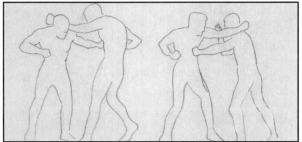

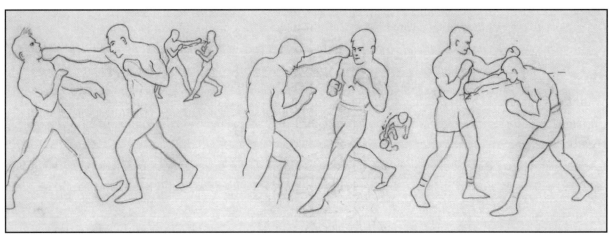

Lee found the way boxers parry a punch—based on timing rather than force when blocking a punch—much more efficient. And by parrying at the last moment, the boxer gives less chance for the opponent to react to a counterattack: "Parrying is a sudden movement of the hand from the inside or outside onto an oncoming blow, to deflect the blow from its original path. It is a light, easy movement depending on timing rather than force. A blow is never parried until the last moment and always when close to the body." [24]

Lee especially liked boxing's use of evasive movement, allowing both hands to deliver punishing punches instead of one hand being used defensively. When slipping a punch, snapping back from a head attack, or bobbing and weaving, the boxer can also deliver a counter punch, another form of simultaneous defense

[23] *Tao of Jeet Kune Do.* p. 114.

[24] Ibid. p. 132.

Bruce Lee and Dan Inosanto

and attack. Even more, evasive movements allow the boxer to evade attacks without moving the body out of range while continuing to pummel the opponent. In the event that a boxer is actually struck, he is taught to roll with a punch by moving with its force to nullify its damage: "Slipping is a most valuable technique, leaving both hands free to counter. It is the real basis of counter-fighting and is performed by the expert." [25] Lee continued, "The art of swaying [bobbing and weaving] renders the fighter more difficult to hit and gives him more power, particularly with the hook." [26]

Attacks and Counters

By studying boxing, Lee learned about its basic attacking methods such as leading, feinting, drawing and infighting. The success of an attack depends on proper strategy, speed, deception, timing and judgment. Selecting the right type of attack depends on the opponent's movements and reactions.

While Lee was able to execute a speedy leading attack, he was very interested in the deceptive methods of feinting and drawing an attack. When a boxer feints or fakes an attack, the opponent attempts to block the attack, creating an opening, which provides the final or ultimate line of attack. In this way, the opponent's opening is created by reacting to your false attack. The fighter may also use broken or irregular rhythm to create an opening. Changing the rhythm of a movement can throw off the opponent's timing, especially when the opponent becomes motor-set with an established rhythm.

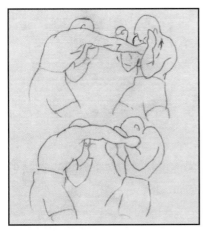
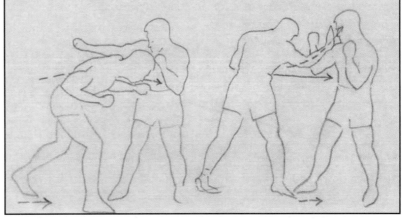

[25] Ibid. p. 154.

[26] Ibid. p. 157.

Deceptive movements are indirect attacks used to create openings in tight defenses and are considered a mark of the master boxer. Drawing an opponent's attack is the epitome of the counterattack, since the boxer is planting the angle of attack into his opponent's mind, and when attacked, the proper counter movement is already prepared.

Ringcraft (Adaptability in the Ring)

Haislet described ringcraft as "the ability to meet and successfully solve problems as they arise in the ring," "the faculty to successfully adapt oneself to the opponent's style" and "the ability to out-smart and out-think the opponent in the ring." He also defines ring generalship as "the general plan of battle throughout an advance of the bout, which attempts to nullify the opponent's strength and take advantage of his weakness." [27] Strategies are formed to deal with a tall opponent, a boxer, a slugger, the rusher, the southpaw, the counterfighter, etc.

Lee also found boxing to be very much a mental game in the ring, taking on some of the nature of Chinese philosophy, such as "no-mindedness." From Haislet:

> *Boxing should be done with the head, not with the hands. It is true that during the time of actual boxing one does not think of how to box but rather of the weakness or strength of the opponent, of possible opening and opportunities. Boxing will never reach the stage of a true art unless performance of skill is made automatic and the cortex freed to think and to associate, to make plans and to judge.* [28]

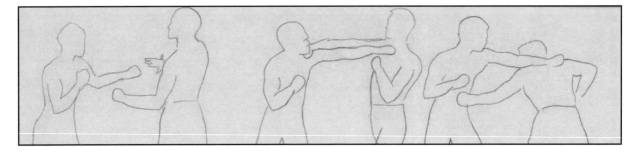

Finally, from reading Joe Louis' book *How to Box*, Lee learned that mind discipline is developed in a boxer by being more patient, yet having the will and determination to succeed, some of the very qualities he needed to reach his own goals.

---

[27] *Boxing.* p. 94.

[28] Ibid. p. 73.

Training Methodology

Physical Training

Lee's physical conditioning and confidence in his ability were challenged during the fight in Oakland. During that confrontation, though he bested his opponent, he literally had to chase him across the gym floor for several minutes at full speed, finding himself winded and running out of gas. Day-planner entries from 1965 show Lee spending much more time developing his abdominals and endurance along with a regular regimen of working his forearms and punching routines. They also illustrate his integration of wing chun with boxing techniques such as the hook, punching combinations and kicks. Described here are the many physical training methods he employed during this time in Oakland.

Aerobic Conditioning

Emanating from the Oakland fight, Lee became concerned with his endurance. His stamina had not been tested earlier since his incredible hand speed and quick reflexes allowed him to end confrontations rapidly. However, in Oakland he found himself in an unexpected circumstance with a retreating opponent, which nullified his punches. Lee's endurance was tested and did not meet the high standards he set for himself. His weakest attribute was exposed, and although he came out victorious, he learned a valuable lesson. And he was going to do something about it. He rededicated himself to increasing his physical capacity through rigorous exercise, raising the intensity of his physical conditioning with much emphasis on his cardiovascular system. He added cardio exercises such as running and skipping rope to his regimen. He was influenced by boxers, so roadwork and shadowboxing would further enhance his

endurance. When running, Lee was sure to attack hills and perform interval training, as well as integrate some of his martial arts footwork into the routine. And while he had developed some foot agility from cha-cha dancing, skipping rope enhanced his footwork, putting a bounce in his step.

Strength Training with Weights

When spending time in Oakland, Bruce Lee began to develop his body musculature. James Yimm Lee and Allen Joe were pioneers during the very early era of weight training and bodybuilding alongside such luminaries as Jack LaLanne and *Hercules* actor Steve Reeves. Bruce was influenced by these men who were twice his age with built-up muscular bodies. They helped him get started by showing him some of the basic lifts and general exercises with weights. With his prominent large forearms and well-developed lats already in tow, Bruce took that training and began seriously to apply himself to developing the rest of his body.

Allen Joe

Bruce Lee

Photo courtesy of Allen Joe

But as Allen Joe states, "Bruce used the weight training according to what worked for him. James and I were into heavy weight training, but Bruce's idea was that you might be strong, but you don't have the speed or power. So he went with the lighter weights with higher repetitions."

During his stay in Hong Kong, Bruce Lee continued his physical training with a lot of running and weight training. Until that point, most of Lee's regimen consisted of practicing gung fu with some supplemental weight training. But now he doubled the amount of weight training time between practicing skills along with a rigorous supplementary training program. In Hong Kong, he joined a fitness club to do some weightlifting. Linda recalls: "By the time we went to HK [in 1965], he already decided a path for himself: getting into shape, learning more about different types of martial arts at this time. And he started to do the weight training during that time. He was doing weight training before, but more intensely after the fight."

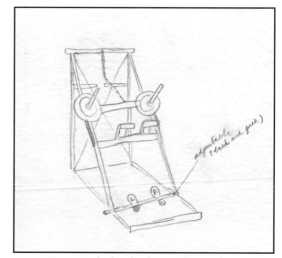

Bruce Lee's sketch of a weight machine

Iron Rings

At the same time, Bruce's curiosity brought him to continue his research into ancient ways of training as illustrated in Bruce's letter of August 13, 1965, to James Yimm Lee about training with iron arm rings:

James Yimm Lee

For better results in sil lum tao I advocate iron rings on forearms while doing "open hand" and "close hand" as the weight gives the actual resistance of the opponents… More resistance can be provided by wearing more iron rings. This is an alive way of building "long bridge force" without getting the hands rigid. This is a kind of modernized progressive weight method that is effective. Anything for the betterment of wing chun.

Bruce wrote in personal notes that he preferred iron rings to dumbbells since "you can keep your fingers and wrists relaxed, as they need to be in chi sao" and that they "provide the necessary resistance when the practitioner directs his energy outward without tensing his fingers and wrists." There is not much evidence that Bruce continued the practice with iron rings, but it illustrates Bruce's way of looking to the modern and the ancient in his attempt to better himself.

Training with Equipment

Bruce Lee used many different, unique training methods in his practice of gung fu.

Heavy Bag

As he became more aware of boxing's training methods, Lee started to integrate some of its methods, such as the heavy bag, into developing proper coordination, skill and power in his punches and kicks.

The bigger and heavier the bag, the more challenging it is to move it when hitting, sort of like a form of resistance training, only that one wants to make it move by punching, not pushing. While in Los Angeles, Lee was given a 300-pound bag as a gag, but he worked with it.

As he got more acquainted with its use, Lee also began to see certain limitations with the heavy bag. He cautioned his students in Los Angeles against using the heavy bag too much, continually attempting to kick or punch the bag for power, since good form can be compromised. That, in fact, working the heavy bag over and over with the wrong mindset can retard one's speed, since one continues trying harder and harder to hit the bag for power instead of working on proper body mechanics and leverage:

On hitting the heavy bag

- *The fact that the bag can't strike you back—"perfecting faults."*
- *Always keep well covered and never leave yourself open for one movement.*
- *The power of the punch and kick comes not, as so many people imagine, from the vigor with which the blow is struck, but by correct contact at the right spot at the right moment, and with feet and body correctly in position and balanced.*
- *Remember that the body is an integral part of the kick and punch, it is not only the leg and arm that delivers them.*
- *A definite routine of kicks and blows—practice first for form, then for power.*

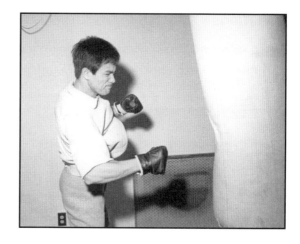

Hanging Paper Training

Lee ensured he approached his training from a balanced perspective, so while developing power in his punches and kicks was important, developing proper distance and penetration without the constant focus on power allowed more precision and accuracy in the strikes. He desired to perfect everything about his punches or kicks, so he cultivated proper distance and timing by using a suspended piece of paper. Punching paper also helped to develop snap and penetration in the punch without the resistance of a heavy target. Speed and finesse were developed when "popping the paper" as he snapped his punches and kicks.

Unique Training Devices

James Yimm Lee was a welder by trade, and he invented many unique training devices that Bruce Lee used. They were often built out of steel parts and heavy springs so they would spring back after being struck or released. These were ingeniously designed to move and withstand the full brunt of a kick or punch.

Some notable pieces James created were a face-shaped finger-jabbing device in which the eye target sprang back when released from a finger jab; a padded bobbing head target that moved when struck; a headlocking device that contained a heavy spring that worked the arms in a headlock position; multiple leg apparatuses made of steel and springs for kicking at the knee or shin at full power; and his "thousand way dummy"—his own rendition of a full-sized training dummy similar to the wing chun wooden dummy, but made of heavy car springs so it would give and spring back when being punched or kicked. James often built copies of the smaller devices and sent them to Taky to be used at the Seattle branch.

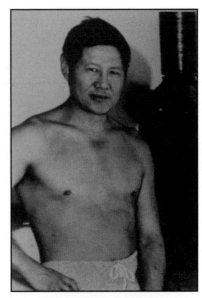

James Yimm Lee

From the Perry Lee Collection

Finger-jabbing device

Another of Bruce's close students in Oakland was George Lee, who was a machinist. His valuable contributions to Bruce began when he built a small box that Bruce could store his school receipts in. Soon George's master craftsmanship was recognized. Even after Bruce moved to Los Angeles, he continued to ask George to build items for him.

To develop kicks on something solid yet mobile, Bruce asked George to build a kicking shield. Supported by a wooden board with handles on the back for a partner to hold, the kicking surface consisted of dense foam rubber. The rubber gave a great feeling when kicking the shield, so it became one of Bruce's prized training devices. Since George painted and stenciled the back of the shield, students were reticent to kick it because it looked like a piece of art, but Bruce used it in developing his art.

From the Perry Lee Collection

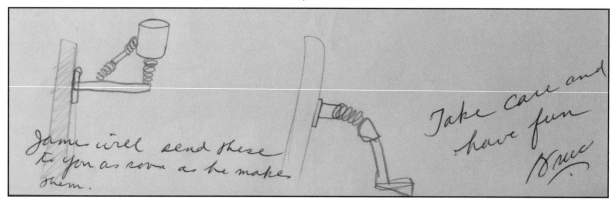

Hand Conditioning

Bruce was influenced by James and his iron and poison hand training, so he sought to toughen up his hands to withstand the brunt of the tremendous power and impact he could generate in his punches. However, there was a time when Bruce desired to develop calluses on his knuckles, which was different from James' approach. James' hands were known to have no calluses or scars despite his being a master brick-breaker since he took great care of his hands and judiciously used Iron Hand Liniment, an herbal formula used for skin conditioning.

Bruce asked George to make a few devices to help develop these calluses. Of course, since Bruce punched with a vertical fist, the calluses were to be on his last three knuckles instead of the first two knuckles like karate practitioners. George built a beautiful container with a dragon design to hold the sand or mung beans that Bruce punched to toughen up his hands. George also made small canvas bags that Bruce placed on the fence for hand conditioning. He filled these bags with different materials, resulting in each having a different level of hardness. Being a practical joker, Bruce would fool visitors into hitting the hardest bag at full force.

To build his grip and forearm strength, Bruce had George build a hand-gripping device that included weightlifting plates to provide resistance. This device helped Bruce further develop his forearms, so his fists, wrists and forearms would be able to withstand the tremendous force he could eventually deliver in his punches.

Suffice to say, Bruce began to experiment with all kinds of devices to enhance his martial arts performance. Whether it was to develop punching and kicking power, speed and timing, or hand and forearm conditioning, Bruce's equipment training was highly specialized and revolutionary even by today's standards.

Realistic Training

While Bruce initially practiced and performed classical forms for demonstrations, he began to take a dim view of them because he wanted realism in his training. Instead of punching or kicking the air, he trained by hitting the devices previously described. Moreover, he was reticent about forms training, since their reliance became a crutch for the forms practitioner. As the practitioner becomes more technically proficient with forms, that skill can become like a "disease" because he begins to lose his grip on reality. Instead of reacting to "what is," the person begins to deal in the "what ifs" or "what should be." Bruce believed in dealing with the reality of things, which are alive and constantly changing. He wanted his students to cultivate awareness, quick thinking and spontaneity.

Boxing contained much of the training Bruce was looking for, since it attempted to prepare the boxer to assimilate to actual conditions in the ring. The ultimate training tool was sparring with a training partner. Instead of continually missing the training partner's face by striking an inch or two short or to the side of the target as in some earlier martial arts training, in boxing, training partners actually hit each other. The robotic modes of stance training, practicing forms, even one- or three-step sparring were not enough for Bruce since they were not alive. They only partially prepared competitors for actual combat. He didn't want to test his skills against a static wooden dummy, but something that moved, such as a living human being who could react to his movement and even hit back.

As a result, Bruce and his training partners began to wear protective gear to understand the realistic distance and orientation when truly delivering a strike or kick to the opponent. Bruce wrote to George on December 18, 1965: "The protective equipment is the most important invention in gung fu. It will raise the standard of gung fu to unbelievable heights. In order for gung fu to remain supreme over the other systems, the protective equipment is a must."

1964 International Karate Championships full-contact sparring demonstration

Philosophy: Letters Expressing the Formless Form

Moving Toward Personal Freedom

While still in Seattle, before moving to Oakland, Bruce Lee called his approach to martial arts "nonclassical." In a letter to Taky on September 18, 1964, before the incident in Oakland, Bruce expressed his new approach, which he would later call jeet kune do:

> *I am beginning to form a structure of my own principle using wing chun as foundation and my boundary lines as the skeleton—the method will be "freedom within boundary and beyond the boundary." I am going to invent these forms as the structure of my own school, the first will be concentrating on ELIMINATION—to move within boundary, the second will be simplicity of attack/defense and finally the third, which will be the all in one and the one in all—the grand harmony of sticking and non-sticking. In other words, the third will be the training of freedom in which everything flows within and beyond the boundary using no limitation as limitation and no way as way. Wing chun is very good but needs to be transcribed—to bring it out from the nutshell…. Together with sticking hand, this method will form two halves of one whole and I can only say this—it will be most surging.*

According to Linda, the fight in Oakland was definitely the beginning of Bruce developing his own way of martial arts, which he refused to call a style, because the word "style" put it into a box. He expressed it as "his way," much more diverse, well-rounded, bringing different elements into it and finding the very best way for him. However, as evidenced in the letter above, he was already on a path of personal freedom using "no limitation" as limitation and "no way" as the way. He acknowledged wing chun as a critical starting point and continued to recognize the value of chi sao training, but he was blazing the path to his own destiny, exploration and evolution.

In the time following Brandon's birth and his father's death, Bruce was between Oakland, Hong Kong and Seattle, and he wrote his close confidants Taky and James, describing the directions he was taking with his martial arts and devoting himself to discovering more training ideas.

Totality, Simplicity, Broken Rhythm

In a letter to Taky in February 1965, Bruce wrote:

> *My mind is made up to start a system of my own—I mean a system of totality, embracing all but yet guided with simplicity. It will concentrate on the root of things—rhythm, timing, distance—and embrace the five ways of attack. This is by far the most effective method I've ever encountered or will encounter. Anything beyond this has to be super-fantastic. Wing chun is the starting point, chi sao is the nucleus, and supplemented by the FIVE WAYS. The whole system will concentrate on irregular rhythm and how to disturb and intercept the opponent's rhythm*

the fastest and most efficient way. Above all, this system is not confined to straight line or curved line, but is content to stand in the middle of the circle without attachment. This way one can meet any lines without being familiar with them. Wait till I assemble everything.

Simplicity with "No Limit" Limitation

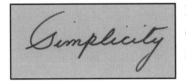

In another letter to Taky dated May 28, 1965, he wrote, "I, too, am working on my transformation of simplicity to yet another more free-flowing movement of no limit limitation."

A Way of "No Way"

And on June 7, 1965, he wrote to Taky again:

Talking about method, my style has formed, but have to see you personally to explain. The idea can be summed up as this—just as it is difficult to come in on an opponent with no bai-jong [by-jong] (thus, no guided lines or boundary) it is more difficult to a method with no exact style or method (yet governed by an immovable FIRST PRINCIPLE). TIMING and DISTANCE are the basic stuffs, but wing chun principle is the nucleus (the most important foundation).

Using No Way as Way; Having No Limitation as Limitation

It was probably during the later stages of Seattle or very early stages of Oakland that Bruce Lee came up with these phrases. He found them so important in describing his ideals in the martial arts that he used the Chinese phrases to surround the yin/yang symbol with the arrows: "Using no way as way" and "Having no limitation as limitation" (Cantonese, *Yee mo faat wai yao faat* and *Yee mo haan wai yao haan,* respectively). The first statement stipulates that the martial artist is to approach combat without any preconceived notions and simply respond to "what is." In this way, the martial artist is adaptable and pliable, fitting in with the opponent and situation instantaneously, using no particular or set way that was preconditioned. "No-mindedness" is the ideal state or condition, but it is difficult to attain. The JKD practitioner attempts to "be like water" when using this "no way" approach. Water automatically assumes the container that it is poured into; therefore, the practitioner constantly fits in with the opponent and adapts to the situation ultimately to defeat the opponent.

By having no limitation as the only limitation, the martial artist can transcend artificial boundaries set by style, tradition, race, individual preferences, etc. Lee gave the JKD man the freedom to explore and think "outside the box." Furthermore, Lee wanted his followers to search deep within themselves to find what works best for them. No longer were they dependent on the teachings of particular styles or teachers. By taking an honest assessment of their own strengths and weaknesses, they could improve not only their martial arts skills but also their daily lives. Like he said, "Knowledge ultimately means self-knowledge." With this freedom, a JKD man is able to express himself with honesty.

Over the years, these phrases have been misinterpreted, as Ted Wong noted:

> *Having no way as way. I can do anything I want, it's okay. I can do anything I want, it's my way. No limit, I can learn anything, any art, put them together, join them together, flow from art to art. I don't think really Bruce Lee intended it that way. Basically, I think he meant don't be hung up on any particular way or not to be boxed in to any certain way, so if any situation comes up, you only have one solution. So now you should be able to adapt to what the situation calls for. That is what I think he meant. Don't limit yourself to a certain way, find a better way to do things. Don't limit to just one thing.*

Wing Chun, Fencing and Boxing

In a letter to James Lee dated July 31, 1965, Bruce mentioned a new attack method and his new formulation of martial arts:

> *In my formation of a more complete wing chun I've added on an INDIRECT PROGRESSIVE ATTACK to the original chi sao, which is close quarter combat. Indirect Progressive Attack is the link to achieve chi sao.*

> *Indirect Progressive Attack is used against an opponent whose self-defense is right and fast enough to deal with Simple Attacks like Straight Blast, Finger Jab and Trapping Hit….*

> *I'm having a gung fu system drawn up—this system is a combination of chiefly wing chun, fencing and boxing.*

"Organized Despair": A Reflection on Classical Styles

On April 18, 1966, Bruce Lee eloquently made his case to Taky Kimura to avoid the "organized despair" of classical styles. Even if a practitioner is proficient in his movement, he is not fully prepared if he is not free and fluid, adapting to the situation at hand:

> *The more I observe the prevalent karate men here, the more I'm amazed at the public that ignorantly eats up such impractical mess [without] at least analyzing karate with their more alive [and] certainly more practical sport boxing. If you want to excel in gung fu, you have to throw away all classical junk and face combat in its suchness, which is simple and direct. Forms and classical techniques…are "organized despair" that serve only to distort and cramp his students and distract them from actual reality of combat. Such means of practice (a form of paralysis) solidify and condition what was once free and fluid. Throw away mysticism and B.S., it is really nothing but a blind devotion to the systematic uselessness of practicing routines and stunts that lead to nowhere. Even a man that moves classically fast and snappy is really not to be praised— you see he is trying to set up a rhythm not to adjust [to] broken rhythm, which is the thing that will happen in actual combat. Then you have to take reactional speed, etc. into consideration. Most of the self-defensive systems are "dead" because the classical techniques are futile attempts to "arrest" or "fix" the ever changing movement in combat and to dissect and analyze them like a corpse, when you come down to it, real combat is not fixed and is definitely very much "alive."*

Returning to Original Freedom

On May 23, 1966, Lee wrote to Kimura of his respect for the wing chun system, but in his move to personal expression, he shed himself from its boundaries and limitation:

> *First of all, our school's name is "Jun Fan" Gung Fu, after my Chinese name. Though I'm grateful for wing chun, the fact remains that the Jun Fan is yet several steps ahead of the wing chun system. Where wing chun ends, Jun Fan starts—not to add on, but to see the* isness *with freedom and in its totality. One thing must be stressed that without wing chun, I would never have arrived at this stage. The three basic structures of the Jun Fan system are—(1) Sticking to the nucleus—wing chun idea, though I've expand [sic] on it. (2) Liberation from the nucleus—my ideas of non-confinement, to see things totally. (3) Returning to original freedom—the circle without circumference—direct expression.*

> *The system will be "it"—not in the past four thousand years had there been a "live" system of totality without any classical confinement. The Jun Fan consists of all roots of all systems yet having a unique characteristic of its own.*

While Lee was experiencing this radical departure from his earlier training, he still considered his training with Yip Man as a very precious time in his life. According to Linda: "When I first went to Hong Kong, we were married; then, it was 1965, he introduced me to Yip Man with the greatest of reverence. He loved Yip Man and felt very indebted to him for the training that he had. Yip Man was definitely the most influential person in Bruce's growing years in martial arts." Lee was also sure to credit his early training in wing chun: "I would like to stress the fact that though my present style is more totally alive and efficient, I owe my achievement to my previous training in the wing chun style, a great style." [29] But at this stage in his life, he would have to walk the path alone, becoming self-sufficient and relying on combat science as his teacher.

The Seeds of JKD Planted

While the time Lee spent in Oakland was the shortest period in comparison to Seattle and Los Angeles, it was very significant for him and the eventual development of jeet kune do. In many ways, Oakland is the birthplace of JKD. Much of what was to become jeet kune do began in Oakland. He discovered the nonclassical approach as early as Seattle and discovered a way of "no way" early on in Oakland. But after the incident in Oakland, his thoughts and actions springboarded toward totality and simplicity, backed by science, in leaps and bounds. While these seeds were planted in Lee, the time spent in Oakland was just too short. The fruits of his labor in Oakland would really begin to blossom in Los Angeles.

George Lee, Bruce Lee, James Yimm Lee and Allen Joe

---

[29] Pollard, Maxwell. "In Kato's Gung-Fu Action Is Instant." *Black Belt Magazine,* November 1967. Reprinted in *The Legendary Bruce Lee.* Burbank, CA: Ohara Publications, 1986. p. 44.

Note: The following is a list of techniques and principles that a coalition of students from the Oakland school compiled for the First Annual Jun Fan Jeet Kune Do Seminar. Much appreciation to the following for compiling this list: Allen Joe, George Lee, Gary Cagaanan, Dave Cox, Greglon Yimm Lee, Allen and Mario Magdangal and Howard Williams. The Oakland school curriculum displays the transition from Jun Fan gung fu and jeet kune do, as Bruce was updating James Lee on his innovations.

Oakland Branch Curriculum

1) Salutation

2) Kicking drills
    a) Five-corner kicking: alternating kicks between left and right foot
    b) Five-corner kicking: from low to high
    c) Clockwork kicking: real-time kicking with the closest weapon
    d) Combination clockwork kicking and hitting: advanced
Key: These are real-time, no hesitation; closest weapon to closest target

3) Stance (by-jong)
    a) Lead stance: shuffle, front, rear, side
    b) Form is the essence, balanced, smooth, feet stay on the ground (skating)
    c) Strictly lower body movements; each movement is independent
    d) Lively, natural bounce, not rigid or stiff while hopping or jumping
    e) Shuffle to various strikes and kicks
Key: Be alive and comfortable

4) Evasive maneuvers
    a) Evade various strikes (some exaggerated to make easier)
    b) Evade various kicks
    c) Evade various combinations of strikes and kicks
    d) Minimal movement to make opponent miss
    e) Evade and counter: after learning the above
Keys: Know the safest position and distance
    Individualize and adapt to the size and reach of the opponent
    Better to miss by an inch than to block by a mile (to block is to get hit)
    Don't engage the opponent, disengage him (e.g., don't get tangled in blocking and trapping movements)
    Intercept the opponent's physical and emotional intent to do harm

5) Classical versus new (modern)

    a) Sil lum tao: performed the classical way

    b) Regarding trapping: cut the movement in half for realism

    c) Hook punch: closer to the body than in boxing (elbow next to the rib, tight and compact)

    d) Rear heel kick: tighter, more centered

Keys: In trapping, concentrate on speed, efficiency and economy of motion

    For the hook punch, use centerline theory (from the center, not outside or wide) and take the skin (or paint) off your ribs; for the rear heel kick, take the skin (or paint) off the inside of your legs

6) Separate punching and kicking drills

    a) Centerline punching (rapid): straight-line blast with closing footwork

    b) Two aspects for improved kicking:

        1) Power: water in the hose analogy for transfer of force through target

        2) Speed: whip analogy for speed of recovery (e.g., shoelaces pop, kicking a gnat out of the air)

    c) Combine, blend power with speed drills; make adjustments

Keys: Delivery system—instant, fast, relaxed

    Hand before foot

    Non-telegraphic (no pre-steps or stutter steps); in punching, no flinching

    Emphasize speed and economy of motion

    Conservation of motion

    Clean and sharp as a two-edged sword, pure Chinese kung fu

    Power comes with time, sometimes years

    Speed comes with accuracy

    Proper form and body alignment with balance

    Footwork should be light and easy, not jumping around stiff; relaxed and smooth without deliberation; angular and instant

7) Basic trapping

    a) Pak sao

    b) Lop sao

      c) Gong sao

      d) Jut sao

      e) Tan sao

      f) Bong sao

      g) Economy of motion: cut these movements in half

      h) One-hand trap

      i) Two-hand trap

Keys: Trapping is only a by-product

      Hit, hit and more hits; not trap, trap and hit

      While engaging an opponent, if there's emptiness…hit

      Skim and glide with friction but let the *chi* flow

8) Line drills (quiet awareness)

      Sensitivity: Touch versus non-touch

9) Distance: measure your distance

      a) Safe

      b) No-man's land

      c) Gates, body positions and zones

Keys: Put yourself where you are safe and the opponent is not

      Circle to the outside of the strong side, away from the rear hand

      Immobilize the lead leg or hand, after you hit, not before

10) Practice drills (attack and defense)

Key: Stun the opponent first, before obstruction, to break his rhythm of forward momentum

11) Apparatus training

      a) Finger jab

      b) Straight blast

      c) Side kick: shin, knee target

      d) Side kick: power through target

      e) Strikes to traps

      f) Kicks to traps

      g) Bridging the gap

      h) Basic wing chun traps

      i) Strike to hand immobilization to takedown

      j) Kick to leg immobilization to takedown

      k) Backfist (high to low, low to high)

Keys: All trapping concludes in hitting

> Don't punch and kick at an opponent—kick and punch through him
>
> Use broken rhythm (don't be predictable)
>
> Incorporate the stop-kick in footwork using it as a jab (e.g., be loose, fluid, Ali-like)

12) Burning step (hand-to-foot impetus)

13) Pendulum (avoidance, then following back swiftly and instantaneously)

14) Basic and primary goals: each student must find his own

> a) Identify the tools
>
> b) Use the tools
>
> c) Sharpen the tools
>
> d) Dissolve the tools

> The three phases in adapting to the opponent:
>
> a) Ice: solid, unchanging, rigid
>
> b) Water: liquid, flowing
>
> c) Steam: gaseous, focused pressure

BRUCE LEE'S
JEET KUNE DO
截拳道

以無限

以無法

LOS ANGELES ERA

Los Angeles: Add What Is Specifically Your Own (The Culmination)

Hip in Hollywood

By mid-1966, *The Green Hornet* television series was greenlighted, so Lee moved the family to Los Angeles. When walking through Chinatown looking for a place to live, he ran into fellow gung fu practitioner Tony Hum, whom he had met earlier in Vancouver, Canada, while performing at a demonstration. Hum had immigrated to the United States and settled in Los Angeles. While *The Green Hornet* was being filmed, Lee privately trained Dan Inosanto, Tony Hum and Wayne Chan in the back of Chan's pharmacy in Los Angeles' Chinatown.

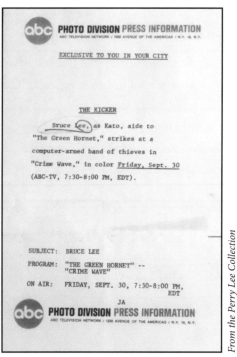

From the Perry Lee Collection

On one occasion, Oakland students James Lee, Allen Joe and George Lee visited the set of *The Green Hornet*. Joe recalls watching them do a lot of scenes in the Black Beauty (the car driven by Kato, the character Bruce Lee portrayed) that day, and then having lunch with Adam West and Burt Ward, aka Batman and Robin, in the cafeteria. During his time on *The Green Hornet*, Lee maximized the opportunity by learning all he could about filmmaking, which paid off when he took this knowledge with him to Hong Kong a few years later. Lee moved so fast that *The Green Hornet* producers asked him to slow down and/or exaggerate his movements so they could be captured on film. This issue was exacerbated by dark lighting on the set and the black uniform Lee wore when portraying Kato.

During media interviews, Lee introduced the mass audience to gung fu: "They are making me the weapon. I'll be doing all the fighting."[30] He explained to the reporters how his martial art was more offensive than the more defensive style of karate. Lee also interjected philosophy when describing his approach to martial arts to the press. Linda kept a scrapbook of news clippings: "I try to live freely from moment to moment, letting things happen and adjusting to them."[31] "The main thing is teaching a man to do his thing, just be himself. The individual is more important than style. If a person is awkward he should not try to be agile. I'm against trying to impose a style on a man. This is an art, an expression of a man's own self."[32] "Karate has become patternized, organized. I favor moving like a boxer; jeet kune do offers more freedom, more self-expression."[33]

Chinatown School

The Green Hornet started airing that fall, but was not renewed, so at the encouragement of his students, Lee opened another school in Los Angeles' Chinatown on February 5, 1967. Inosanto, the assistant instructor, recruited many students from Ed Parker's school, where he was also an assistant. Early students included Dan Lee, Jerry Poteet, Steve Golden, Bob Bremer, Pete Jacobs, Tony Luna and Larry Hartsell. Some others joined the school as well, such as Ted Wong, Herb Jackson, Pete Rosas, Alfred and Curt Haber and Richard Bustillo.

Opening day at the Los Angeles Chinatown school

[30] Aarons, Leroy F. "Batman's Boy Has Black Belt Rival." *The Washington Post.* August 30, 1966.

[31] "Gung Fu Is Serious Business to Kato, The Green Hornet's Muscular Aid." *Springfield Union News.* July 5, 1967.

[32] Wister, Emery. "Judo Expert Calls Hand Chop 'Stunt.'" *Charlotte News.* October 23, 1969.

[33] Glass, Ian. "Chop Talk With An Actor: Mayhem Up His Sleeve." *Miami News, Florida Report.* October 24, 1969.

The Los Angeles school was still called the Jun Fan Gung Fu Institute and its curriculum was very similar to the Seattle and Oakland branches, although it included more mobility, footwork, kicking and sparring, reflecting some of the new directions Lee was moving toward in martial arts. Ted Wong recalled the school was still "pretty much wing chun, with a lot of trapping and straight blast punching a piece of

The Los Angeles Chinatown school class

newspaper the partner held moving across the gym floor." He estimated the curriculum in Los Angeles to be approximately 60 percent wing chun (versus 80 percent wing chun in Seattle), with the balance composed of punching and kicking. Lee wrote in his notes about the Chinatown school: "No sign— door locked—no affiliation—no ties." This exemplified his movement toward personal fluidity and the development of the individual, denying the systemized classical approach to martial arts.

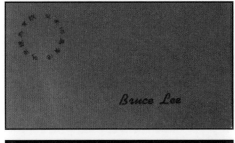

Training in the Backyard

Lee also began to offer private training sessions at his home, and on Wednesday nights, students such as Ted Wong, Dan Lee, Jerry Poteet and Herb Jackson went for training in chi sao, which was not taught at the school early on. Those training sessions died out after a brief period, so Lee ended up training only a few select students at his home. According to Linda, Wong probably spent as much, if not more, time than anyone else with Bruce Lee during this period (1967–1971). Some others who spent time at the Lee home were Jackson, Bob Bremer and Peter Chin.

Lee, Peter Chin and Ted Wong

Wong considered himself very lucky to have witnessed Lee's evolution as it was happening, since he observed not only what was taught at the Chinatown school, but also what Lee was working on in the backyard. While the modified trapping taught at the school was already more functional, fluid and alive than his earlier wing chun training, what Lee was developing at home was very different. One particular departure was that they hardly practiced any trapping in the backyard. Instead, individual kicks and punches were honed and combinations were practiced and then applied in sparring. While Lee had already moved away from his earlier wing chun training in 1967, the school continued to retain many of the earlier teachings, but he was working on new things at home on his own. Although the school had a prescribed curriculum, private training in the backyard took on a more experimental and free-form approach based on what Lee was developing.

At the same time, Wong points out, Lee continued to practice chi sao with him in the backyard. Several years after Lee's death, Wong questioned himself, "Why [was Bruce] still doing chi sao?" After becoming acquainted with some wing chun teachers over the years, Lee found that chi sao tested one's skill. Since no ranking existed in Yip Man's wing chun school, the only way to measure one's achievement in wing chun was to perform chi sao with another. So while he minimized the amount of time spent on trapping, he continued to practice chi sao to maintain his close-range fighting skills: sensitivity in the arms, a constant flow of energy and "being like water" by harmonizing with the opponent and flowing

Lee with Wong

moment to moment while keeping the mind free. During those years, Lee continued to modify the way he performed chi sao, such as placing one foot ahead of the other to be better balanced when the partner attacked. Wong recalled simplified, efficient movements from Lee when "rolling" with him later on. He did not realize how much Bruce modified his practice of chi sao until he rolled with some wing chun people many years later and noticed how differently Lee performed it.

Nevertheless, while wing chun was burned into Lee's neuromuscular system after thousands of hours honing these skills, he was now moving in directions that would exploit his strengths and natural abilities, including physical speed, footwork and mobility.

Kicking

While in Los Angeles, Lee placed much more emphasis on developing his kicking technique. Instead of just using it as a distraction when closing the distance to end a fight with the hands, he made himself more versatile with powerful kicks. After observing martial artists who specialized in kicking, Lee recognized the devastating effects of powerful kicks when used as primary weapons, so he focused his training to develop further his kicking ability. When student Peter Chin asked him why the emphasis on kicking, Lee bent over and placed his arm next to his leg and asked, "Which do you think is going to be more devastating?" Because the leg is longer, one's offensive capabilities are increased; and since the leg is heavier, the damage inflicted by a kick is much more devastating than a punch. Lee wrote: "Given a

choice I would always choose the leg. It is longer than the arm and can deal a heavier blow, and it is much more powerful."

Lee ran every day not only to increase his endurance, but also to strengthen his legs. He took a very practical view of kicks.

Lead Shin/Knee Kick

A simple kick this is, but no style thoroughly made use of it quite like jeet kune do, and a lot of scientific study is put into this most efficient and simple kick.

The leading shin kick is a potent weapon both in offense and defense. It is a giant killer. This shin kick is equivalent to a jab in Western boxing except it is longer and much harder to defend against. This kick is the spearhead of your attack and its effectiveness is simply the adhering to the principle of using the longest against the closest. And with a pair of shoes on, the effect can be quite devastating. Your opponent will find this simple shin kick a constant threat.

The old slogan of a Chinese fighter is "first kick your opponent in the groin," but in jeet kune do, the practitioner knows better.

Footwork and Mobility

More than ever before, Lee put emphasis on footwork and mobility, not just for the sake of movement, but tactically in "controlling the distance" and "bridging the gap." Footwork also enhanced the power of his kicks and strikes by fully using his bodyweight. He showed a Newton's cradle (below) to Peter Chin to illustrate how proper kicking was to be performed. With proper timing and mechanics, footwork puts the body in motion, and the additional momentum contributes to the overall impact, resulting in devastating kicks.

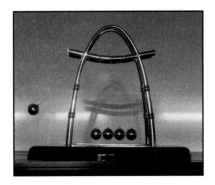  

Lee was much more alive and mobile with his footwork, kicking and punching. This mobility was evident during his demonstration at Ed Parker's International Karate Championships in the summer of 1967, where he sparred full contact wearing boxing gloves, headgear, body armor and shin pads. Allen Joe recalls visiting Lee in Los Angeles and seeing a big difference in his training with more boxing, jump roping, running and lifting weights.

Although Lee was changing his art, the process was slow. From day-to-day, it was hard to notice the changes. But over a few weeks or a month, they were more obvious. Wong described this process as "a move toward simplification, refining what he had, making it better, faster, more powerful. It was not new techniques, but refining the same techniques for more speed or power, or better timing when sparring." He recalled Lee specifically working on the side kick for almost three months, "breaking down the technique and looking into what muscles were used in executing the technique and working them. When he worked on certain things, he would work on it with just one technique until he was satisfied with his improvement. During those workouts, he would try to find a way to do it better. I remember one time I was holding a shield for him to hit, and he kept asking me how this kick felt, or how that kick felt, so more like a sounding board. He would try different ways coming in or whatever, so he would just work on it until the technique got better."

Jeet Kune Do: Naming His Style of "No Style"

As a result of this radical departure from rigidly adhering to any style or system, Lee searched for a name to give his new approach in martial arts. In his day planners, we see the term "jeet kune do" for the first time on July 9, 1967. Wong remembered it was during the summer of 1967, when they were in the parking lot across from the Chinatown school where they often talked after class. Lee told him he was going to name his own style jeet kune do. "In fact the name was in Chinese first, and then he said he would go to UCLA, because he knew a professor there, I think he was a linguistic professor, he [Lee] said, 'I will ask him to have the exact pronunciation in English.' 'The way of the intercepting fist' was the result of the translation into English." Linda recalls: "Because he had been forming his thoughts, and his physical movements, and putting it all together, this was his way of expression. And he came up with jeet kune do because it had meaning to him."

Lee based the term on the stop-hit technique from fencing and its intercepting qualities. To intercept an opponent's attack, the practitioner needs a high level of proficiency and refined skill. Timing and distance must be perfect, not necessarily with anticipating the opponent's attack, but being in the moment with the opponent and adapting to the situation. There is no preparation, hesitation or thinking. In this way, there is a lot of fencing in JKD. Wong explained: "Jeet kune do is more related to fencing than boxing. In fact, you read a lot of his notes that he put together, a lot of fencing terms there. So I can see that jeet kune do is really fighting like a fencer. A lot of techniques come from boxing, but the way you think, the way you apply your technique, is more like a fencer. That's why I can see that in fencing there is a lot of intercepting; that's why he picked the name."

Ted Wong: The Eternal Student of Jeet Kune Do

Ted Wong was born on November 5, 1937, in Hong Kong. By the time he was three, the Japanese had occupied Hong Kong, so the family moved to China. Over the next seven years, the family moved around a lot throughout China, even sleeping in the hills and fields, as World War II was taking place. After the war, the family settled in Canton, where his mother passed away when he was 10 years old. When the Communists took over China in 1949, the family moved back to Hong Kong and eventually immigrated to the United States in 1953. Wong spent his first year in America living in San Francisco with his aunt, a "boxing nut" as he liked to describe her, since she loved to watch boxing on television every Wednesday and Friday night. Actually, this is where he developed his love for boxing, watching the championship fights of the day with fighters like Sugar Ray Robinson, Carl "Bobo" Olson, Archie Moore and Rocky Marciano.

During his stay in San Francisco, Wong worked in the evenings for a Chinese newspaper and he often stopped at the nearby gung fu school to watch the students practice "as Bruce Lee called it: unrealistic horse stances and punching from the hip." This classical way of training was a stark contrast from what he saw in the boxers on television, who actually hit their opponents and knocked them out, so he never had any deep desire to learn gung fu. When later moving to San Diego with his family, Wong started buying all the boxing magazines he could. He was so into boxing that he "could name each champion and who took the title away from him and who came along to take the title from another champion."

After returning from serving in the U.S. Army, Wong moved to Los Angeles' Chinatown. His roommate, Raymond Huang, told him that Lee Siu Loong, the actor who was playing Kato on *The Green Hornet*, was about to open a gung fu school. The first episode Wong watched was "The Preying Mantis" and he was duly impressed with Lee. When the Chinatown school opened early the following year, it turned out that its location at 626 College Street was only three blocks from his apartment, so he signed up as a student. When he saw Lee demonstrate and explain gung fu that opening day, Wong knew this was the guy he wanted to learn from. He was impressed with Lee's knowledge, energy and openness: "He was able to explain things. You go to any martial arts school, I watched them, they never tell you something, just do it and you mimic, and that's just about it. No science in there. But when he [Lee] talked, even though it was the first time I met him, he talked about the speed, he talked about the angling."

Photos courtesy of the Ted Wong family

Wong was already 30 years old when he began training at the Chinatown school, and he had a heck of a time preparing his body. But he fought a lot when he was young and "the instinctive 'throw-a-punch,' whatever, when I was a little kid, that was ingrained in my mind….When you fight as a little kid, you don't know about fighting; you just fight. You have no obstructions in your mind, you have no style." So although he was not physically prepared when he started training, Wong's mind was there and Lee could see what he had up there.

As a youth, Wong recalls his father grabbing him by the collar and telling him never to run away from a fight, even when there were three attackers. (His father stipulated to the three that they would have to fight young Ted one at a time, at which they promptly ran off.) More than 20 years later, Wong recalled that after a rough sparring session with fellow student Dan Lee early on in his training, he got frustrated and turned and walked away from the session. Later on, Bruce Lee came up to him and said, "When you get hurt, don't show it. Don't run away from a fight."

When Lee took Wong as a private student and training partner, one of the first things Lee told him was that "he needed some basic requirements," which meant muscle. Lee took him to a weightlifting place to buy a weight set and crash weight-gain powders to build up his body. Within three months, Wong went from 132 pounds to 147 pounds. But it was too difficult for him to maintain the weight.

Lee also recognized the wealth of boxing history Wong had in his mind. He could answer Lee's questions about boxers' fight histories and even their nicknames. Wong credits his love of boxing with preparing him to observe Lee in the backyard: "Half of what I learned from Bruce Lee was through observation, while the other half [was] through direct instruction." Many of those who personally knew Wong know how fortunate the world was in having a student with a keen sense of observation to pass on his knowledge to the next generation. Wong said, "When I look at Bruce Lee's movement, I captured it in my mind like a video, and today I still vividly see him kick, performing the movement, the footwork, how he moved."

After Lee passed away in 1973, Wong continued to train in the backyard with fellow student Herb Jackson, refining his skills. During that time, Robert Lee, Bruce's brother, joined the group for a couple of years. Wong found that he had to rely on himself to understand JKD better: "It really took me 15 years, 15 years to understand what is jeet kune do." When more of Lee's personal writings became available during the late 1990s, Wong began his own journey of getting into Lee's head: "Most of the things I learned were after he passed away. I realized that I was still learning from him; even though he passed away, he's still teaching me because he left behind so much material."

The eternal student of JKD, Wong noticed that while Lee studied many combative arts, he was drawn to certain ones and utilized only certain aspects of an art: "And that is jeet kune do to me, so intriguing and so exciting, even today, 40 years after that. I think about it. I tell you jeet kune do is incredible."

On one particular occasion, Lee was involved with an article for *Black Belt* magazine and they needed to take some photos. Lee wanted a person supporting a heavy bag so he could truly feel the full power of his kick. Typically, when one holds the bag for another to kick it, he braces it against the shoulder and can see when the kick is coming. But Lee didn't want the holder to brace for the full impact, so he had Wong turn around, facing the opposite direction. "When he [Lee] kicked me, that particular shot, I had a few shots before, but that particular shot…when he faced the camera, I tell you, he increased 2,000 percent. When he kicked me, it was just like getting hit by a freight train, heading right toward the wall. What stopped me was 'boom' (hands up in front of his face). Right there, you see my hair, like Don King, okay. I used a heavy duty hair spray, so I tell you, the air wouldn't lift up my hair, but that kick did!" According to Mito Uyehara in *Bruce Lee: The Incomparable Fighter,* he saw Wong a few days later wearing a neck brace as a result of the kick.

Wong couldn't help being reminded of that kick, since the neck injury he sustained never completely healed. "In fact, one time, I went to a chiropractor to take X-rays, and he said, 'Boy, have you had a big accident before, someone hit you from behind?' I said, 'I never had a car accident.'" But when reminded of the various injuries, aches and pains resulting from his time training with Lee over the years, Wong said, "If I had to do it all over again, would I change anything? No!"

Lean Years in Los Angeles

The years following *The Green Hornet* were lean financially for Lee and the family. It was hard for him to get regular work in Hollywood. He was given a few guest parts in television shows such as *Ironside*, *Here Come the Brides* and *Blondie*. Lee was also in the movie *Marlowe*, starring James Garner, and was hired to choreograph fight scenes on movies such as *A Walk in the Spring Rain* (with martial arts student Stirling Silliphant as screenwriter) and *The Wrecking Crew* with Dean Martin, Elke Sommer, Sharon Tate and Nancy Kwan, but the pay barely covered the bills.

On set with Dean Martin

Filming with Sharon Tate and Nancy Kwan

In addition to opening the Chinatown school, Lee took advantage of the fan base created by *The Green Hornet*. In actuality, as a result of playing Kato in the television series, Lee was probably the most recognized martial artist in the United States. He was a draw, so he started where he left off before *The Green Hornet*—demonstrating his art. He demonstrated at Ed Parker's International Karate Championships in 1967 where record crowds came to see him perform. Lee was the headlining performer, and as soon as he completed his demonstration, the crowds quickly dispersed, leaving the rest of the tournament rather empty of onlookers. Lee's celebrity got him invited as a special guest at Jhoon Rhee's National Karate Championships in Washington, D.C., for many consecutive years, and he was also invited to the United States Karate Tournament at Madison Square Garden in New York City.

Bruce Lee, Van Williams and Jhoon Rhee

Some martial artists sought Lee out either to train with him or so they could drop his name to further their own careers. And there were businessmen who approached him to develop a nationwide chain of gung fu schools. Never one to prostitute the art, Lee refused such proposals to franchise his fame for commercial purposes. He could have made a lot of money riding his *Green Hornet* fame, but he rejected such offers, feeling they were rip-offs. He knew his high standards for teaching could not be matched on a mass level and the students would suffer.

From the Perry Lee Collection

In an attempt to make ends meet, Lee started working on several book projects, including a book about wing chun gung fu and another about jeet kune do. Wong states, "In the fall of 1967, Bruce said that he would do a book about jeet kune do, only make 200 copies, very exclusive, that's it." Lee hired UPI sports photographer Oliver Pang to shoot hundreds, if not thousands, of photos of Lee demonstrating the core techniques of his art with Wong and Dan Inosanto. But he eventually decided against publishing the book. The volumes of these photos formed the primary basis for the *Bruce Lee's Fighting Method* series of books published after Lee's death. Photos speak volumes and the world was extremely fortunate the founder demonstrated his art.

While *Wing Chun Kung-Fu* listed James Lee as its author, the book was actually written by Bruce, according to Wong, who posed with James for the book's photos. Bruce no longer wanted to be connected with the book since he had already moved away from wing chun. Wong recalled the photos being taken around 1968 or '69, but before the book was completed, Bruce decided to shelve it. However, in 1972, when James Lee contracted cancer and needed the money to cover medical costs, Bruce took the book to Mito Uyehara and asked him to publish it right away and give the advance to James.

Bruce became close friends with Mito, who was not only a book publisher but also the founder and editor of *Black Belt* magazine. Mito featured Bruce in many articles during this time. According to Linda: "He allowed Bruce some free range back then, where he could write articles that really went against the current thinking in martial arts showing Bruce's freethinking way of martial arts. Mito was really integral to Bruce's philosophy and techniques being publicized so they were exposed to other people practicing martial arts, creating a lot of interest in what he was doing."

The Martial Arts Community

During the late 1960s, Bruce Lee was recognized as one of the best martial artists, and while living in Los Angeles, he worked with some of the top karate competitors of the day. Chief among them were Chuck Norris, Joe Lewis and Mike Stone. Linda recalls: "All three of these men came to study with Bruce because they had such high regard for his way of martial arts and wanted to learn from him. They were frequent visitors to our home. It's sometimes been phrased that they were just exchanging techniques, but really they came to Bruce to learn what he could teach them." Louis Delgado was another competitor from the East Coast who trained with Lee. A very talented martial artist in his own right, Delgado once called Lee "quite baffling, almost as though he had ESP," since it seemed like Lee could read Delgado's mind when they sparred against one another.

Lee and karate champion Joe Lewis

Sometimes, these men ended up winning their weight division at tournaments: Lewis in the heavyweight division, Norris as the middleweight champ and Delgado being the lightweight champion, with the grand champion being determined in a fight-off between all three champions. According to Wong, Lee had a lot of influence on Lewis: "Bruce helped revamp his [Lewis'] original Okinawan-style karate, which was more rigid with big horse stances and Joe's trademark reverse punch-side kick techniques." Lee taught Lewis a lot about mobility and developing more speed in his strikes and kicks. As a result, Lewis became even more dominant and considered by many as the best karate competitor of the era. Lee had Mike Stone double for Dean Martin in *The Wrecking Crew*, which was Chuck Norris' first movie role as an extra. Norris and fellow karate man Bob Wall became became Lee's opponents in his motion pictures later on.

Chuck Norris with Lee; Lee, Bob Wall and Norris in Hong Kong for the filming of The Way of the Dragon

Also, Lee came across martial artists from various disciplines such as Jhoon Rhee (father of American *taekwondo*), Hayward Nishioka from judo and professional wrestler Gene LeBell. Lee was like a sponge with these people, absorbing what was useful to him, rejecting what was useless and adding specifically what was his own. Linda recalls him having high regard for LeBell and his abilities as a world-class wrestler. Bruce had not studied wrestling extensively and learned some of his grappling techniques from LeBell. Nishioka, the 1967 Pan-American Games gold medalist in judo as well as a karate practitioner, wrote an article comparing the rear punch from karate to the straight lead from JKD. (Using kinesiology, subjects were wired with electrodes to measure the amount of muscle activity between both arts. The result? Because the JKD punch had less antagonistic muscle activity when delivered, it was faster and had more effective striking power.) Lee met Rhee first at the Long Beach Internationals in

Lee and Jhoon Rhee

Hayward Nishioka, Lee and Norris

1964, and they developed a very close friendship. Rhee stayed at Lee's home when visiting Los Angeles, and Lee stayed at Rhee's home when performing at the National Karate Championships in D.C. Rhee also visited Lee in Hong Kong in late 1972, along with Wong and Herb Jackson, for the premiere of *The Way of the Dragon* (released as *Return of the Dragon* in America). Lee introduced Rhee to Mito Uyehara, who published a series of taekwondo books for him. Lee also introduced Rhee to the movie community and got him started in a couple of movies in Hong Kong.

Hollywood Celebrity Students

According to Linda, it was Charles Fitzsimmons, *The Green Hornet's* producer, who counseled Lee on teaching gung fu to celebrities. Fitzsimmons told him, "If you sell a hot dog for $2, nobody will think it

is special, but if you charge $8.50, people are going to think there is something special about it, and they will buy it if they can afford it. Applying the same idea to teaching, if you charge more for lessons, there will be a certain group of people who will equate it with value." Lee thought it was a good idea: celebrities could afford it, they would think it was valuable, so he initially charged $150 an hour.

Bruce Lee's

JEET KUNE DO

截 拳 道

Professional
Consultation & Instruction..........$275 per Hour
Ten Sessions Course $1000
Instruction Overseas $1000 a week plus expenses

Among the most notable of these celebrity students were Steve McQueen and James Coburn. McQueen was an avid student of Lee's for several years and a very good friend. It was McQueen's adviser who counseled Bruce and Linda to buy the home in Bel-Air, and their dog Riff (a schnauzer) was from McQueen's dog's litter. Linda recalled they really connected, "because they were the same kind of guy, rough and tumble coming from similar backgrounds." Wong went with Lee to McQueen's house a couple of times for private lessons. McQueen's tough-guy image onscreen was for real. Wong recalled when McQueen tripped on his rough cobblestone courtyard barefoot and a hunk of skin almost thumb-size was torn from the ball of his foot. He was bleeding and Lee said, "You better stop now," but McQueen said, "No, no, no, keep going."

On the other hand, James Coburn was more of a philosopher, talking about ideas and ways of thinking or living. In many ways, the mellow Coburn was to yin what McQueen was to yang. It was through Hollywood screenwriter Stirling Silliphant that Coburn got acquainted with Lee. Silliphant was Lee's avid student, which led to a writing collaboration between Lee, Coburn and Silliphant in developing *The Silent Flute* script.

Lee with James Coburn and other crew members

According to Linda, "Bruce had written this story about a martial artist finding his way, finding his nirvana, or finding the ideal martial arts, and the travels and travails he goes through to do that." They had weekly or biweekly sessions to develop the script. The screenplay was optioned by Warner Bros., which sent Lee, Coburn and Silliphant to India to scout locations for the film since it had some rupees that had to be spent in India. Linda recalls, "Bruce was so high on this because this was now about 1970 or so, when Bruce had not been working regularly on TV or film, and this was going to be the big project that would bring him attention in Hollywood." However, Silliphant and Coburn didn't think India was going to work, so the film was nixed. Linda remembers that Bruce was tremendously disappointed, but that experience brought him in touch with Ted Ashley, the president of Warner Bros., who also became Lee's student. That relationship eventually led to the production of *Enter the Dragon*.

Lee with Stirling Silliphant

In India for The Silent Flute

Others Lee taught were James Garner, writer Joe Hyams and director Roman Polanski, who was married to Sharon Tate, the actress who was murdered along with hair stylist Jay Sebring and others by the Manson family in 1969. The most famous athlete Lee taught was Kareem Abdul-Jabbar, the 7-foot-2-inch center for the UCLA Bruins basketball team and later the Los Angeles Lakers. Abdul-Jabbar was interested in martial arts and he came to Lee's house to train. Linda recalled Bruce thought it was such an interesting exercise to spar with a guy who had legs that were 5 feet long! Kimura remembers that Lee once told him that practicing chi sao with Abdul-Jabbar was very difficult: "One day he called me and said that chi sao wasn't it anymore, doing it with a guy 7 feet 2 inches, looking at his bellybutton. He

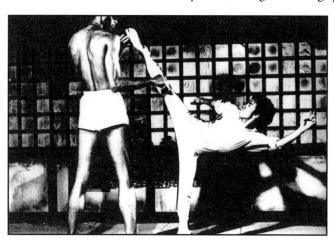

had a helluva time getting in. Sticking hands is still part of the beginning, the grounded first stage of the martial way. Anytime you have to connect yourself, you sort of ground yourself in that regard. That isn't where the real fighting is, but if you do get into close range, then it becomes very effective." Lee's friendship with Abdul-Jabbar continued after Lee left for Hong Kong, with Abdul-Jabbar traveling there to be in the fight finale of *Game of Death*.

Hazardous to Your Health

Lee's demonstrations of speed and power became legendary. On set, cameramen adjusted their equipment to capture his movements, or he would end up just a blur on celluloid.

At martial arts demonstrations, Lee often asked someone out of the crowd simply to block his punch. He started 5 or 6 feet away from the person, then explosively closed the distance, tapping the person on the forehead and withdrawing his hand before the person could touch his hand! Another trick Lee played on unsuspecting victims was having a person place a dime in his hand, with Lee snatching it out of the person's hand before he could close it. During the last attempt, Lee appeared to have failed, since the person could feel the coin in his hand, but when opening the hand, the person discovered a penny in place of the dime! Lee performed this trick countless times.

Many folks underestimated the amount of force Lee could generate with his kicks. When he was doing fight choreography for the movie *A Walk in the Spring Rain,* Lee had to prove his worthiness to the large American stuntmen. He made believers out of them by having them hold an air shield for him to kick. In a sense he "baptized" them by kicking them into a swimming pool.

The power of Lee's strikes was equally impressive, if not more so. With his unique one-inch punch, he placed his fist on his partner's chest, and with what appeared to be a twist of the hips, the partner was propelled in the air, landing on a properly positioned chair. This technique was so explosive when Lee did

it on Oakland student Bob Baker during the 1967 International Karate Championships that Baker found himself with chest pains the day after. On another occasion, when Lee was visiting the *Black Belt* magazine office, he asked a staff member to hold a focus mitt for him to punch. Lee's hook punch was so devastating that he dislocated the staffer's shoulder.

Since "boards don't hit back," Lee did not believe that board-breaking demonstrations displayed real skill. However, he did demonstrate some board breaking later on, but with a few twists. He had a partner hold a board rather loosely with one hand, instead of the typical way of fully supporting the board and not allowing any "give." This made it more difficult to break the board, so speed and power were both required. Lee also broke boards that were suspended in the air, holding a board with his hand at shoulder height, and then letting it fall and breaking it with a side kick before it hit the ground. During a Hong Kong television show appearance, not wanting to be outdone by others who broke multiple boards, Lee taped five boards together, breaking all but one. In private training, his students witnessed him breaking seven two-inch boards with a side kick.

When Allen Joe visited Lee in Los Angeles, Lee wanted to demonstrate a new kick on him, so they got some sofa cushions for Joe to hold up against his chest and Lee lashed out with a kick. Like Bob Baker, Joe was in such pain he ended up going to the doctor: "It hurt me so bad when I went home, my wife made me go to the doctor for X-rays." When James Coburn bought a new heavy bag, Lee thought it was too hard, so he said, "Let me soften it up." When he kicked it, the heavy chain holding the bag broke off and the bag flew into the backyard. Retrieving the bag, they discovered a hole in the canvas of the bag where Lee had kicked. Mentioned earlier was the incident when Lee wanted the "perfect photo" with Wong standing behind the heavy bag and being launched when Lee kicked it. Wong received quite a whiplash with that kick, but the photo (and the one on page 105) captured the action for posterity.

Karate competitor Louis Delgado actually wised up when he came to Lee's house for a lesson. Lee held the air shield for Delgado to kick, but he would not do it. When asked why, Delgado said he would kick only on the condition that he would not have to hold the shield for Lee. Apparently, Chuck Norris had warned Delgado, so he was not going to have anything to do with holding the shield for Lee. Lee chuckled and told him to kick it anyway; he would not have to hold it.

A New Aim and a New Addition to the Family

By 1969, Lee was being influenced by "how-to" books written by Dale Carnegie, Norman Vincent Peale and others, which motivated him to put down in writing what he wanted to accomplish in life. That year, his family's financial circumstances were dire, so Lee was looking for a means to improve the situation. Linda recalls, "He wrote his Definite Chief Aim [as suggested by Napoleon Hill in *Think and Grow Rich*], which he dated January 1969, and he said he was going to be the highest paid Chinese actor in the United States, starting in 1970, in return for which he would give the most exciting performance and be worth it."

SECRET

My Definite Chief Aim

I, Bruce Lee, will be the first highest paid Oriental super Star in the United States. In return I will give the most exciting performances and render the best of quality in the capacity of an actor. Starting 1970 I will achieve world fame and from then onward till the end of 1980 I will have in my possession $10,000,000. I will live the way I please and achieve inner harmony and happiness.

Bruce Lee
Jan. 1969

SECRET

During the spring of that year, Bruce and Linda were blessed with a daughter, Shannon, born on April 19. But the hard times continued, and eventually, Linda had to get a job. Her working was a secret kept within the family, "since Bruce was very embarrassed that his wife had to go to work. And he didn't tell anyone since he hated it so much." Linda worked from 3 p.m. to midnight at a telephone company. "At the same time," Linda recalls, "it was a great time, since Bruce had to take care of the children before they went to bed, and he was a great father to the kids."

By 1970, Lee returned to Hong Kong with son Brandon and discovered *The Green Hornet* was being aired on television there. It became known as "the Kato show," since the people of Hong Kong recognized the child actor who had supposedly "made it big" in America. While visiting Hong Kong, Lee appeared in a few television interviews, which led to some interest among movie producers later on.

Setback with a Severe Back Injury

On August 13, 1970, Lee suffered a severe back injury while attempting some heavy weightlifting before warming up properly. Linda describes it: "He picked up a 125-pound barbell [positioning it on his shoulder] and bent over from the waist without any warm-up, and something snapped in his lower back. He wasn't totally aware of it at that moment, but he knew something happened. That turned into a severe injury, taking a lot of tests, where it was discovered he damaged the fourth sacral nerve [in his spine]."

When Lee asked when he would be able to resume his martial arts training, the doctors said he would be lucky to walk normally again. Lee was prescribed complete rest, three months on his back followed by three months of just moving around the house. This injury put everything on hold and was a big turning point in his life. Linda recalls, "It affected him tremendously, mentally, especially with the dire forecast the doctors were giving him: You'll never kick high. They wouldn't allow him to do any martial arts. This was really a time of inner questioning for Bruce: 'Where do I go from here? Martial arts is my whole life; martial arts was the way I was going to realize My Definite Chief Aim. What do I do now?'"

Obviously, during this period, Lee was quite depressed. According to Linda, "He was not his cheerful, charismatic self. He was really down, really considering where his life was going to go now, and now he had two small children. But at the same time, he found it important to write down his thoughts, and he was considering at that time publishing his notes. He also wrote many script ideas, especially during this period. Luckily for the world, he did a lot of writing in his seven journals of ideas about martial arts, philosophy, psychology, about life in general." The world was fortunate during this quiet period in Lee's life since he started to pen his *Commentaries on the Martial Way* in these seven journals, which largely became the basis for the posthumously published *Tao of Jeet Kune Do*, providing a glimpse into the genius of Bruce Lee.

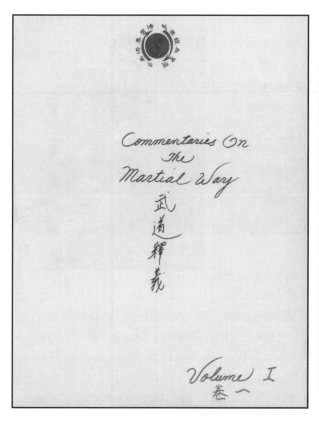

With a solid foundation in Chinese philosophy, Lee began to formulate his philosophical approach from 1965–1971. Linda recalls, "Bruce had a lot of time to think about the evolution of his philosophy and how it was integrated with his martial arts. He didn't have a regular job every day, so he had the time to think about life. He read widely: [Jiddu] Krishnamurti, [Hermann] Hesse, Joseph Campbell. And he borrowed phrases from these philosophers to express them in a way that was his own." The culmination of his philosophical walk was realized in his 1971 *Black Belt* magazine article, "Liberate Yourself from Classical Karate," most likely penned when he was still recovering from his back injury. According to Linda:

> *These were Bruce's core beliefs in his evolution in JKD and why it doesn't apply to a lot of classical martial arts. There was always backlash against Bruce. He was not respected by traditionalists. But Bruce had great respect for tradition as well; it was just certain aspects of doing things the same way that had been done for centuries he wanted to break free of. He felt that martial arts were so segmented into styles that people in one style were just blind to seeing things in another style or to see any other way to do something. He felt he had liberated himself from that kind of thinking, and that he could think freely about martial arts, not be stuck. He wanted to explain this. Some people felt this was going outside the bounds of tradition and they didn't like it. They've come around in the 35 years since.*

Lee slowly worked his way back physically by first walking, then trying "a little bit of this or that, using some resistance training to a small degree, to strengthen the muscles that had been lying in bed for a while," Linda states. "He also utilized some Eastern medicine, like acupuncture." In fact, it was during this recovery period that some of the famous backyard video footage was shot, with Lee telling Linda, "I look terrible" while she is in the background saying, "Not that bad." According to Ted Wong, after a short time, it seemed like everything came back.

A Big Comeback

After Lee recovered from his back injury, he almost immediately went into high gear, filming episodes of the *Longstreet* television series, with the premiere episode entitled

James Francisco with Lee in Longstreet

"The Way of the Intercepting Fist," written by Stirling Silliphant. This episode showcased Lee bridging the physical and philosophical dimensions in martial arts by simply being himself, as he later explained in his interview in 1971 on *The Pierre Berton Show*.

Soon after, Lee found himself in Hong Kong and Thailand doing his first feature film, *The Big Boss*, followed by *Fist of Fury, The Way of the Dragon*, filming fight scenes for *Game of Death*, followed by *Enter the Dragon*, all within a two-year span. Yet with all of this, Lee never considered himself

at a conclusion. As Linda said, "He was always 'in the process of becoming,' never reaching the top or the height of being, always in the process." Even in the middle of making all the films in Hong Kong, Lee kept growing in the martial arts. Wong recalls when he visited Lee in December 1972 that Lee showed him a kick he was working on that changed directions three times before hitting its target.

According to Linda, when Bruce returned to Hong Kong, he spoke to Yip Man and he explained the way his martial arts development had gone, how he had developed what he called jeet kune do, and that it contained elements from wing chun,

but he had expanded from there. Yip Man was very understanding, gracious and congratulatory to Lee because it was all part of the training Yip Man had given to him: One must think for one's self and develop one's self, not just copy what is given to him. So he appreciated the road Lee was on.

Although many may think Lee reached a zenith in the development of jeet kune do for himself, if he had lived longer, there is no doubt he would have continued to grow and progress, but in what direction, we will never know. With that, we must remember what he left behind.

Martial Art: Jeet Kune Do

During the JFJKD Nucleus years in the late 1990s, a handwritten note by Lee was discovered in one of his books. It said, "What is the Root of JKD?" with a short list describing this root. Conventional martial artists might guess Lee started his list with a trademark knockout punch like the one-inch punch, his devastating side kick or his blinding speed. But no, the list began with "On-Guard Position, Footwork, Mobility, Body Alignment, Coordination, etc." Lee found the essence of fighting distilled into these essentials, the foundational building blocks everything else rests upon, the support system for the physical art.

Lee's efforts to discover the essence of fighting came together while he lived in Los Angeles. He continued his research into sports such as boxing and fencing for their physical execution and their use of tactics. He also looked to sciences such as kinesiology, physiology and physical training to understand the science of motion. Lee referred to jeet kune do as a devastating combination of speed, power and broken rhythm. Speed and power were developed by understanding how to cultivate these qualities, combined with the physical work to develop them; broken rhythm represented the tactics used against an opponent.

Lee had limited knowledge of the grappling arts, so he increased his knowledge by studying numerous books and experimenting with Hayward Nishioka and Gene LeBell. Although he did not formalize his grappling knowledge in what he taught his students, Lee shared it from time to time, and he used many of the skills in his movies.

Lee liked to refer to jeet kune do as a sophisticated form of street fighting or scientific street fighting. The application of science to optimize the performance of techniques, combined with the no-holds-barred approach and cunning of a seasoned street fighter, demanded JKD be functional, practical and suited to the individual. Jeet kune do was a very personal form of self-expression for Lee. Once he was beyond systems and was transcending traditions, Lee was much freer to express himself physically and realized the need to encourage his students to find their own personal expressions: "I can give you the tools, but you have to develop your own way of using them."

Principles

Three Stages of a Technique

Lee wrote that when one begins to learn a technique, one must first learn the proper execution and mechanics. During training, the mind and body are molded to execute the technique correctly, and then refined to perform it with speed and power. Once this is achieved, one learns how to apply the technique with the proper distance and timing to use it successfully against an opponent. Learning to apply it involves sparring, where circumstances are ever-changing and one must sense the right opportunity to execute the technique. The following descriptions are from Lee's handwritten notes:

Stage I (Synchronization of Self)

a) Correct form

b) Precision

c) Synchronization of the whole

} *augmenting speed progressively*

Stage II (Synchronization with Opponent)

a) Timing—the ability to seize an opportunity when given

b) Distance—correct maintenance of

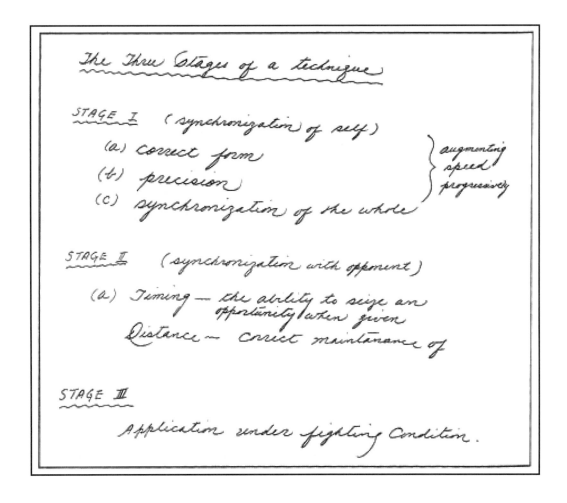

Stage III (Application Under Fighting Condition)

a) Mobility

b) The physical ability to lengthen movements of arms and legs, in other words to increase reach

c) Resistance to fatigue, i.e., stamina

d) Spring and resilience

e) Physical and mental alertness

f) Imagination and anticipation

g) Courage to take chances

h) Speed progression

i) Strength progression

Understanding and Fully Using Your Tools

"There should be no method of fighting. There should only be tools to use as effectively as possible."

Lee took time to understand fully his tools and how they could be used: offensively in an attack, defensively as a counter, high line, low line, in combination with other tools, against an opponent in right versus left stance and how to counter the technique should it be used against him. In this way, by applying this approach to every technique he contemplated using, he extracted all he could from it.

In the same way, Lee applied this thinking to how he would counter a technique, should an opponent attack him.

What is my counter for...

1) before or during initiation?

2) [when] it's coming?

3) [when] it's snapped?

As he told Dan Lee in a phone conversation regarding the sharpening of tools: "Here it is: if you can move with your tools from any angle, then you can adapt to whatever the object is in front of you. And the clumsier, the more limited the object, the easier for you to potshot it."

Lee and Wong

Fighting as a Stage of True Art

Once the tools have been sharpened and their use well understood, the JKD man then must fit in with the opponent and react to "what is." After hours and hours of training, the practitioner begins to trust his instincts to make the right move so that action and reaction are spontaneous:

The highest skill operates on an almost unconscious level.

Fighting should be done with the head, not with the hands or feet. It is true that during the time of actual fighting one does not think how to fight but rather of the weakness or strength of the opponent, or possible openings and opportunities. Fighting will never reach the stage of a true art unless performance of skill is made automatic and the cortex is freed to think and to associate, to make plans and to judge. The higher nerve centers always retain control and will act when necessary. It is like pressing a button to start or stop a machine.

Fencing Influence

Lee received inspiration from fencing early on. His brother Peter was an accomplished fencer and demonstrated how extreme speed and solid footwork contributed to a fencer's success. But these early, influential years were more like seeds planted in Lee's mind. He was still coming into his own as a teenager in Hong Kong, so the insights from fencing didn't bear fruit until he had moved to America and explored fencing more deeply.

Lee made notes in his many fencing books and
he applied fencing's theories to martial arts
techniques. He was highly influenced by fencing
authors Aldo Nadi, Julio Martinez Castello and his
sons Hugo and James, and Roger Crosnier.

Finger Jab

The finger jab is analogous to the single straight
thrust from fencing. It is the longest hand weapon
and the fastest. Lee noted:

> Like a fencer's sword that is always in line,
> the leading finger jab is a constant threat to
> your opponent. Basically, it is Western sword
> fighting without a sword and the primary
> target is your opponent's eyes. [34]

> Faced with the choice of socking your
> opponent in the head and poking him in the
> eyes, you go for the eyes every time.

Dan Lee with Bruce Lee

Straight Lead Punch

The straight lead punch is more versatile than the finger jab, and Lee transmitted a lot of what he learned
from fencing into this unique strike. Much of what Lee writes about the straight lead encapsulates the art
of jeet kune do:

> It is a potent offensive and defensive weapon because of its advanced position—it is halfway to
> the target before starting.

> No preparatory or get-set postures before delivery. Every blow just shoots from wherever [the]
> hands happen to be at the moment. This will add speed (no wasted motion) and deception (no
> give away preceding movement) to your punch. [35]

The on-guard stance, with its raised heel for pushing off the arch of the foot, was the platform from which
Lee exploded off the blocks, covering distance and creating momentum by propelling the body forward.
Moving the hand before the foot in a straight-line trajectory made it non-telegraphic and accurate.
When snapping the hips and shoulders in sequence so the body is aligned at the moment of impact, then

---

[34] *Tao of Jeet Kune Do.* p. 100.

[35] Lee, Bruce. n.d. "Chinese Boxing." Papers. Jun Fan Gung Fu Institute.

hitting with the last three knuckles of the vertical fist, the body's structural alignment creates the power line—the line of force that travels through the body to transmit and absorb force. At the same time, while keeping the body relaxed until the moment of impact, the fist lands before the front foot lands to preserve the body's momentum and the body is braced for tremendous impact and penetration several inches behind the target. Lee stated that "the leading right punch is the backbone of all punching in jeet kune do." However:

No any one punch, not even the efficient straight right lead, can be an end in itself, though there are styles that use nothing but straight line punching. The straight right is used as a means to an end and definitely should be reinforced and supported by the other angle punches (and kicks), making your weapons more flexible without confinement to any one line. After all, a good man should be able to strike from all angles, and with either hand (or leg), to take advantage of the moment.

Tactics and Strategy

"Total Offense—Lack of Passive Defense"

Lee studied fencing's rich history of attacking theory and its robust approach to tactics developed over centuries. Much of his knowledge on attacking came from fencing, where proper timing and exact distance are essential. Fencers believe in the premise that the best defense is not allowing the opponent to attack by keeping him on the defensive. A fencer might also wait for the opponent's attack so he can counter or stop-hit the offensive action: "In attack you must study the adversary's weakness and strength, and take advantage of the former while avoiding the latter." [36]

Lee learned in fencing, depending on the opponent's tendencies, one must come up with the proper way of attack to succeed: "In any form of attack, the final choice of stroke should be based on the observation of your opponent's reactions, habits, and preferences. Thus, observe, deduce, and apply. . . . Different style demands different method to cope with—The FIVE WAYS." [37]

---

[36] Lee, Bruce. Paraphrased passage from Julio Martinez Castello's *The Theory and Practice of Fencing.* New York, NY: Charles Scribner Sons, 1933. p. 60–61.

[37] Lee, Bruce. Notes written in his copy of Roger Crosnier's *Fencing with the Epee.* New York, NY: A.S. Barnes and Company, 1968.

Five Ways of Attack

Lee distilled the variety of tactics and strategies from fencing and other martial arts into five ways of attack. It served to encompass the many different methodologies into a simplified approach that looked to the root of combat.

<u>The Five Ways Of Attack</u>

(✓) <u>Simple Angle Attack</u> (S.A.A.)

       check the eight basic blocking positions

     1.) leading with the right, guarding with left, while moving to right

     2.) leading right time stop kick---target-groin, shin, knee

     3.) broken timing angle attack (B.T.A.A.)

(✗) <u>Hand Immobilizing Attack</u> (H.I.A.)

     --close own boundaries while closing distance
     --watch out for opponent's stop hit or kick
     --be ready to angle strike when opponent opens or
     backs up
     --feinting before immobilizing is recommended for
     double safety and success

> add ⁽⁵⁾ Leg immobilizing attack (L I A)
⁽⁶⁾ -hair immobilization head

(1) 虚攻下門疾手封　(四) 搪椿掛摟封
(2) 變位封外門鈎手　(五) 標指問手封
(3) 虚腿疾手封

(✗) <u>Progressive Indirect Attack</u> (P.I.A.)

     --whenever possible move out of line or sudden
     change of level----for added safety and surprise
     --boundaries close accordingly

   1) <u>High to Low</u>

       a) r. str. to low r. jolt
       b) r. str. to r. groin toe kick
       c) r. str. to l. str. or kick
       d) l. str. to r. str. or kick

   2) <u>Low to High</u>

       a) r. str. to high r. jolt or hook
       b) r. groin kick to high r. str.
       c) r. groin kick to high hook kick
       d) l. str. to high jolt or hook

   3) <u>Left/Right or Right/Left</u>

       a) r. str. to r. hook
       b) l. thr. to r. thr.
       c) tangle leading hand with r. and l. cross
       d) r. lead draw snap back and cross

5) attack by draw (see blocking picture)

(✗) <u>Attack By Combination</u> (A.B.C.)

     tight boundaries---speed and surprise---determination

       a) the o-n-e two   b) the o-n-e two-hook
       c) r-body r-jaw l-jaw   d) the straight high/low
       e) r-jaw hook-jaw l-jaw

(Continue in P I A)

1) Simple Angle Attack (SAA)

All direct or indirect attacks are called "simple" because their object is to get to the target by the most direct route.

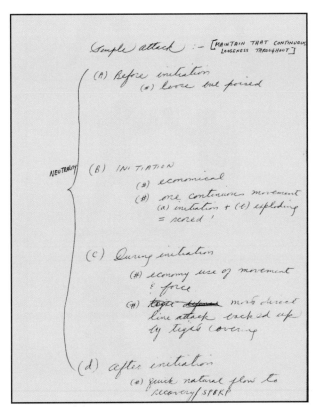

In its purest form, a simple attack is one that zips directly to its target, with superior speed as the main ingredient for success. The practitioner may have caught the opponent when vulnerable, either mentally or physically, so the straight-line attack is successful. He may also deliver an attack at an unconventional angle that the opponent may not expect. However, the practitioner may require variable timing to throw off the opponent, which is what broken rhythm accomplishes.

Theory of Broken Rhythm

According to Lee:

> *A broken-time attack—making a pause before delivering the final movement, can be very effective in deceiving the opponent as to the attacker's intention.*

When implementing broken rhythm, speed is no longer the sole determinant. Lee found much value in using broken rhythm and, in his notes, he paraphrased Julio Martinez Castello from his book *The Theory and Practice of Fencing*:

When rhythm is broken, speed is no longer the primary element in the success of the attack or counter attack of the man who had broken the rhythm. If the rhythm has been well established, there is a tendency to continue in the sequence of the movement. In other words, each man is "motorset" to continue the sequence. The man who can break this rhythm by a slight hesitation or an unexpected movement can now score an attack or counterattack with only moderate speed; his opponent is motorset to continue with the previous rhythm and before he can adjust himself to the change, he has been hit.[38]

Lee also underlines sections of other books regarding the subject, such as this passage from Crosnier's *Fencing with the Sabre*:

A very effective change of cadence is to slow down, instead of speed up, the final action of a compound attack or riposte…This form of delivery is known as attacking, or riposting, in "broken-time," and is very often successful.[39]

When the practitioner uses a variety of speedy attacks and broken rhythm, the opponent is challenged to predict what the practitioner will do. Lee summarized the two approaches this way:

Two Effective Means of Simple Attack

Fighting is a game of timing, tactics, and bluff. Two of the most effective means to this end are:

The Simple Attack from Immobility

This will often surprise the opponent especially after a series of false attacks and feints have been executed, so that the defender [opponent] is subconsciously expecting a preparation or more complex movement and fails to react in time to the swift and unannounced simple movement.

---

[38] *Tao of Jeet Kune Do.* p. 62.

[39] Crosnier, Roger. *Fencing with the Sabre.* New York, NY: A.S. Barnes and Company, 1949.

The Variation of Rhythm or Cadence

Made prior to, or during, an attack. This may achieve the same element of surprise. For example, a series of judiciously slowed-down feints to the leg and slow gaining and breaking ground may be used (to "put the opponent to sleep").

A final simple movement which suddenly erupts at highest speed will often take him unaware. Again, some rapid feints followed by a deliberately slowed-down or broken-time final movement will often disconnect a vigilant opponent. Sometimes a number of feints in the high lines can pave the way for sudden disengagement to the knee.

2) Hand Immobilization Attack (HIA)

Lee listed the immobilization attacks as:
      hand immobilization,
      leg immobilization and
      head and/or hair immobilization.

Lee applied the "trapping hands" knowledge from his wing chun training to the general category of HIA, but expanded the concept to include trapping the leg and immobilizing the head or grabbing the opponent's hair. After bridging the gap on an opponent, HIA serves as an effective close-range system for follow-up, but it is more a byproduct of hitting.

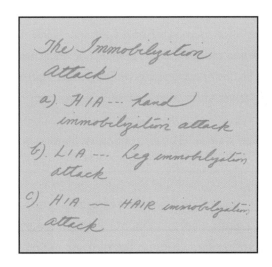

The Immobilization Attack
a). HIA --- hand immobilization attack
b). LIA --- Leg immobilization attack
c). HIA --- HAIR immobilization attack

3) Progressive Indirect Attack (PIA)

Progressive (to gain distance) Indirect (to gain time) Attack (to move ahead of opponent's defense)

Used against opponents with strong defenses who can react to the suddenness of a simple attack, PIA is used to gain distance and time on an opponent by faking an attack, then subsequently attacking the line that is opened as a result of the opponent's reaction. The pattern of movement can be high to low, low to high, left to right, or right to left. While in Hand Immobilization Attack, one may crash the line of engagement, in Progressive Indirect Attack, one evades the line or engagement.

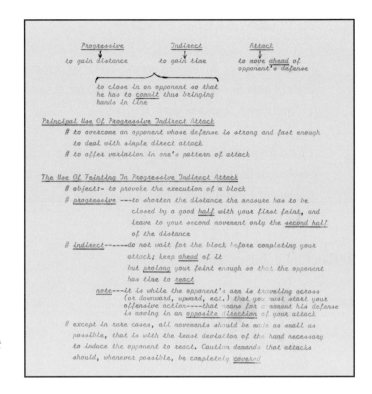

Lee stated: "HIA moves toward hand, while PIA moves away from hand."

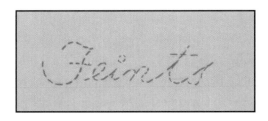

Critically important to the success of a PIA is that the feint must appear to be a real attack in order to compel the opponent to react and create an opening. This can be established with several real simple attacks to establish the pattern in the opponent's defensive movements.

PIA is indicative of Lee's departure from his original wing chun training in that while wing chun tends to crash the line in a very aggressive manner, Lee begins to integrate the more refined elements of feinting and evading the opponent's movement. Bear in mind that Lee implemented PIA with his hands *and* feet.

4) Attack by Combination (ABC)

An attack by combination is a succession of punches or kicks that are typically thrown at multiple target areas of the opponent. They generally follow a natural sequence, taking advantage of body mechanics and optimal positioning. This type of attack implemented the many punching combinations Lee found in Western boxing. In an attempt to set up an opponent, boxers throw combinations to great effect, resulting in damaging or knockout blows. Lee emphasized maintaining good balance when throwing combinations because, if balance is lost, subsequent blows will have little effect on an opponent. Of course, Lee implemented his kicks, trapping hands and grappling techniques to expand this type of attack.

However, Lee did not robotically execute a prescribed set of techniques against his opponents. When attacking, Lee assessed his opponent's reaction after each movement to determine his next move. For instance, instead of simply executing a jab-cross-hook punching combination at his opponent, after throwing the first punch, Lee studied his opponent and determined his next move; Lee processed this information at such lightning speeds that it appeared he was attacking by combination. This process of assessing the situation to determine the optimal move was referred to as "stop action" in Joe Hyams' book *Zen in the Martial Arts*. Hyams, along with Silliphant, studied with Lee. Silliphant recalled Lee referring to stop action as "playing between the notes" in that the silence between the notes in a song is as important as the notes themselves. For Lee, the split seconds between moves and countermoves were the "silence" between each move in the symphony of a fight.

5) Attack by Drawing (ABD)

An attack by drawing is a form of counterattack that sets up the opponent into launching an attack on an apparent opening, then countering the opponent by attacking the opening created by his movement. Another ABD strategy is to lure the opponent to counter an initial attack, and then countering his counter.

To perform an effective counterattack, a practitioner must have foreknowledge of openings that result from an opponent's movements, whether offensive or defensive oriented. When the opponent moves, he exposes certain targets, and the key is to become familiar with these movements and the associated target areas. Lee wrote: "The counterattack is not a defensive action but a method of 'using the opponent's offense as a means of the successful completion of one's own attack.' The counterattack is an advanced

phase of offense…. It is the greatest art in fighting, the art of the champion."

It is advantageous for a practitioner to draw an opponent's attack, because once the opponent has committed his movement, his intentions are a certainty. The opponent has not only committed himself physically but also mentally. As a result, he will be unable to alter his position and handle the counterattack. By falsely exposing certain targets to lure an opponent to attack, the martial artist is dictating the terms of the fight and thereby controlling the opponent.

One of the most efficient counterattack methods is the stop-hit, which is a timed counter made against an opponent's attack. In many ways, the stop-hit is akin to a simultaneous defense and attack, and it can have a demoralizing effect on an aggressive opponent. Anticipating the opponent's moves and stopping him in his tracks are extremely effective. Moreover, being able to draw the opponent's attack or counterattack with a preliminary movement puts the practitioner in complete control of the fight. Lee particularly liked the stop-hit. Jeet kune do (the way of the intercepting fist) is based on the stop-hit.

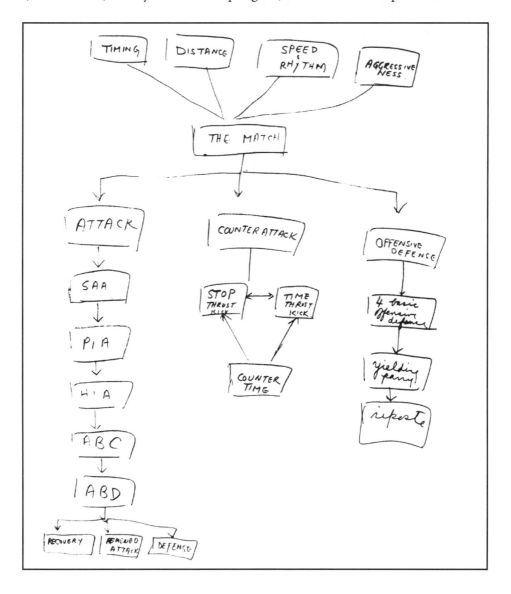

Making an Attack Work

According to Lee, who paraphrased from Crosnier's *Fencing with the Epee*, there are three factors in a successful attack:

1) *A fine sense of timing*
2) *A perfect judgment of distance*
3) *A correct application of cadence*

Lee learned that an attack must be executed at the right time with the proper tactic suited to the opponent's reactions and tendencies. The golden principle, he said, was that each movement of the practitioner must correspond to the opponent's. Proper timing, distance and regulated speed are cultivated through sparring, so the practitioner learns how to launch attacks effectively against a variety of opponents. At the same time, if those attacks are unsuccessful, the practitioner must be able to adapt and change the plan of attack—and be wary of the novice who may do what is unexpected. Nevertheless, keep it simple:

A fighter who is observant will not carry on, stubbornly, with strokes which are no longer the right ones. So many fighters put down the failure of an offensive stroke to lack of speed, rather than to the incorrect choice of the stroke—difference between a pro and an amateur. [40]

It is all right to change one's style to adapt to various circumstances, but remember not to change your basic form. By changing style, I mean switching your plan of attack. [41]

Dealing with the Novice
The novice is often much more difficult to deal with because he may make un-coordinated movements and fail to respond normally (or at all) to orthodox feints or other forms of attack.

A golden rule is never to use more complex movements than are necessary to achieve the desired result. Start with simple movements and only introduce compound ones when you cannot otherwise succeed. [42]

---

[40] Lee, Bruce. Paraphrased from Crosnier's *Fencing with the Sabre*.

[41] *Tao of Jeet Kune Do*. p. 54.

[42] Ibid. p. 190.

Commentaries on
Hand - to - Hand Combat

①   The right beginning — ᵃ⁾ Kris. ᵇ⁾ emptiness - Zen.

②   Aliveness →   being so of itself

③   Economy :- simplicity : non - telegraphic
See ↑ paper.
      use   ⎰ a). stance   b). attacking: ⁽¹⁾ feet ⁽²⁾ hand
   progressive ⎱
      chart   c). Counter   d). defense.

④   Footwork. :-

⑤   The basic weapons.
            a). feet
            b). hand
            c). grappling

⑥   Some combination :-
            a). long range — progressive chart
            b). Close range / grappling

⑦   Broken Rhythm & Rhythm., cadence, timing,
      speed, distance.

⑧   The Five ways of ATTACK:
            a) H I A
            b). P I A   NOTE :- in each technique
            c). S A A   comments on :-
            d). A BC   1). general idea behind
            e). A B D   each technique
                                  2). itemized details
                                      as to; a) economy starting
                                      b). progressive detail
                                      c). Counter to watch
                                          for. ⎰ Ex. :- Counter :- remember the
                                                  R. Lead   simple done right
                                                               has no counter :-
                                                               xxxx :- strong sticky
                                                                        etc. etc.

⑨). Counters —— list counter to
                    every attack and counter
                    time to Counter.

Speed

While he already had tremendous physical speed, Lee did all he could to further increase it, such as using a fighting stance that put his primary tools in front and following the principle of putting the longest weapon closest to the target. He also looked into lengthening his opponent's reactions and finding the optimal time to launch an attack. Lee discovered that fencing broke speed down into mental and physical components, or rather reaction and movement, resulting in five types of speed:

Perceptual Speed—Quickness of eye to see openings and to discourage the opponent, confusing him and slowing him down.

Mental Speed—Quickness of mind to select the right move to frustrate and counter the opponent.

Initiation Speed— Economical starting from the right posture and with the correct mental attitude.

Performance Speed— Quickness of movement in carrying the chosen move into effect. Involves actual muscle contraction speed.

Alteration Speed—The ability to change direction midstream. Involves control of balance and inertia. (Use small phasic bent-knee stance). [43]

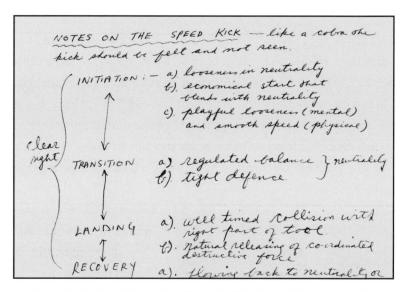

The practitioner must first have the ability to see and quickly recognize what is happening before determining what to do. Awareness

---

[43] Ibid. p. 56–57.

and visual recognition drills are used to enhance perceptual speed. Once the situation is assessed, the practitioner must have mental speed to quickly decide on a course of action. The more choices there are, the slower the reaction time, so the aim is to minimize choice reactions, yielding more instinctive reactions that are more efficient.

The principle of moving the hand before the foot came from the straight-thrust technique in fencing, one of the speediest movements in all sports. Nontelegraphic motion and swift footwork were aspects of initiation speed. Further, an explosive movement was not only physical, but also mental/emotional—having a fighting spirit was important for successfully launching an attack.

Lee developed the on-guard position as the platform from which to launch his techniques quickly. Through the study of human motion, he looked at the proper sequence and timing for executing techniques effectively. It turned out that additional impact and power resulted, since speed and power go hand-in-hand. Finally, Lee studied the muscle groups involved in executing particular techniques, and he found ways to increase their performance by developing them, either by strength- or speed-training.

Relaxation is a key to moving quickly and speed is power. But Lee also realized there had to be a balance between speed and power. He used the water and the whip principle to cultivate the full spectrum within a single technique. Snapping a kick was more like a whip, cultivating speed without much depth; while kicking for deep penetration and rigidly locking out the leg developed the opposite quality. By cultivating both extremes, Lee was able to shift his balance between speed and power as required.

A review of the different types of speed shows they are largely a mental process, requiring cultivation of the mind. The practitioner first perceives the situation (perceptual), then decides what action to take (mental), initiates and executes the physical motion (initiation and performance), followed by perceiving the result to decide the next course of action (perceptual). Keeping the body and mind relaxed are keys to maximum physical speed as well as quick mental reactions. The alteration speed involves modifying speed, path or target in the middle of executing a technique. It involves broken rhythm and feinting, regulating speed so a technique's timing will score.

Cadence: Speed must be regulated very carefully to fit in with the speed of execution of the opponent. The regulating of one's speed to correspond with that of the adversary is known as cadence.

Tempo: Ability to recognize the opportunity and seize the right moment for an action. The timing can be analyzed through its physical, physiological, and psychological aspects.

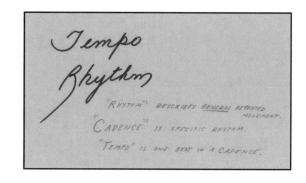

[It is] Essential to time the attack at exactly the right moment (psychologically or physically) when the opponent cannot avoid being hit.

From a psychological point of view, the moment of surprise and, from the physical point of view, the moment of helplessness are the right moments to attack. This is the true conception of tempo—choosing the exact psychological and physical moment of weakness in an opponent. [44]

Lee was truly a master when it came to reading his opponent. Through a highly refined level of awareness, Lee could sense his opponent's intentions and movements. As previously stated, karate fighter Louis Delgado thought Lee had ESP when sparring with him.

When Bob Bremer was a student training in Lee's backyard, Lee continually tapped Bremer on the forehead, and Bremer told him he was simply too fast. But Lee responded, "There's a split second when you are not with me and somehow I seem to know when that is." Bremer thought it had to do with hypnosis, which he knew a little about, so he willed himself not to let his concentration slip. They started again and Lee took his time dancing around until Bremer started to slip up mentally and bam! Lee hit him on the forehead.

The Triumvirate (Distance, Mobility, Footwork)

For Lee, distance, mobility and footwork formed a triumvirate. About the significance of distance, he stated:

<u>Distance</u>

The maintenance of the proper fighting distance has a decisive effect on the outcome of the fight—acquire the habit! … The art of successful kicking and hitting is the art of correct distance judging—strive to bridge for even a split second to attack. [45]

In fact, distance can be a type of aggressive deterrent during sparring.

Properly judging and controlling distance are essential qualities a successful fighter must have. No matter how quickly the fighter may react to an opponent's attack, if close enough, the attack will succeed. Once the practitioner is within this distance, known as "no man's land," one must do something: move by either

---

[44] Ibid. p. 64.

[45] Ibid. p. 139, 140.

increasing the distance or execute an attack. Likewise, the ability to bridge the gap and close the distance on an opponent during an attack requires careful judgment of distance.

> *It is essential that each man learn his own fighting measure. This means in a fight he must allow for relative agility and speed of himself and his opponent. That is, he should consistently stay out of distance in the sense that his opponent cannot reach him with a simple punch, but not so far that, with a short advance, he cannot regain the distance and be able to reach his opponent with his own powerful attack.* [46]

With effective footwork, Lee was able to lengthen the distance between himself and his opponent, which made him increasingly difficult to attack and allowed him more time to react. At the same time, since Lee developed effective gap-bridging skills with speedy footwork, he could score on his opponent. The distance was also increased to accommodate an extended kicking range. Lee's notes on distance sum up fighting altogether:

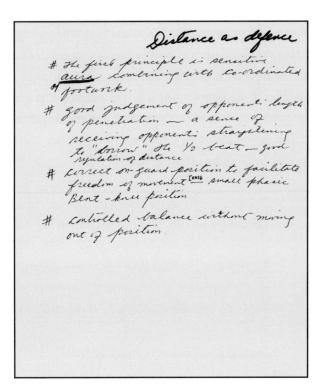

Mobility/Movement

According to Lee, when it comes to martial arts, it is all about motion. By moving, one becomes a hard target to track and hit. Movement tends to keep the opponent off-balance, making it more difficult for him to launch an effective attack. Lee insisted one must maintain balance while in motion, so one could immediately launch another attack given the opportunity.

> *The essence of fighting is the art of moving.*

---

[46] Ibid. p. 139.

Mobility is definitely stressed in jeet kune do because in combat it is a matter of motion, an operation of finding a target or of avoiding being a target…. In jeet kune do, one finds firmness in movement, which is real, easy and alive. [47]

To move just enough:
1) Will make an opponent miss
2) Will deliver a counter blow most effectively [48]

One should seek good balance in motion and not in stillness. [49]

Footwork

According to Ted Wong, "Footwork was the key for Bruce Lee." By using footwork, Lee increased his fighting measure, controlling distance and thereby controlling the fight. Footwork made him fluidly mobile, allowing him to adapt to the opponent, yet still retain his balance, so when an opportunity arose, he could immediately launch an attack or counter. His footwork enhanced his speed because he could cover distance quicker. It also improved his power because it put his entire bodyweight in motion: "Footwork can add weight and power to a punch or kick," and "Like a coiled spring one can release great power by pushing off the ground."

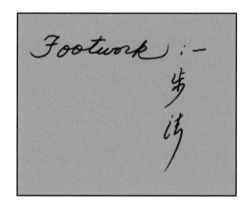

The quality of a man's technique depends on his footwork, for one cannot use his hands or kicks efficiently until his feet have put him in the desired position. [50]

Footwork in jeet kune do tends to aim toward simplification. Whatever you aim to do should be done with a minimum of movement. Economical footwork not only adds speed but by moving just enough to evade the opponent's attack, he is thus fully committed.

Footwork will beat any punch or kick.

Therefore, springiness and alertness of footwork is the theme, and in order to lighten the feet for increased speed and mobility, the rear left heel is slightly raised with the weight on the balls of the foot. Thus, unlike the traditional flat-footed practice, the left heel is raised and cocked ever-ready to pull the trigger and go into action.

The left heel is the spark plug, or better still, the piston, of the whole fighting machine.

---

[47] Ibid. p. 142.

[48] Lee, Bruce. Annotation in the margin of Haislet's *Boxing*.

[49] *Tao of Jeet Kune Do*. p. 49.

[50] Ibid. p. 142.

On-Guard Position

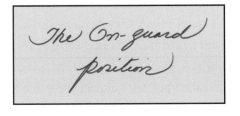

The primary purpose of JKD is kicking, hitting, and applying bodily force. Therefore, the use of the on-guard position is to obtain the most favorable position for the above-mentioned. . . . Because of their advanced position, your leading foot and hand constitute at least 80 percent of all kicking and striking (they are half-way to the target before starting). It is important that they can strike with speed and power singly or in combinations. Also, they must be reinforced by equal precision of the rear foot and hand. [51]

Lee recognized the basic fighting position used in his earlier wing chun training would not allow him to reach the potential he was looking to achieve:

> *Wing Chun Bai* [By-] *Jong: Elongated guard proves dangerous* [in] *both attack and defense*
> - *Attack: Necessitates withdrawing of arm, thus telegraphing (no coiled up spring); it needs preparation for hooks.*
> - *Defense: Uncovers lead side of body; the opponent "knows where it is," and can maneuver around it; extended arm offers HIA (thus, don't present your lead hand to a wing chun man).*

With the critical elements of distance, mobility and footwork in mind, Lee realized he needed a stance that enabled him to move swiftly and efficiently. Speed was enhanced by starting with the strong side forward, since the primary tools to kick and punch were already halfway to the target. The strong-side-forward stance also allowed Lee to use body alignment to support techniques, thereby delivering powerful blows more efficiently.

The on-guard position also allowed for constant balance while in motion. Based on the "small phasic bent-knee" position, small steps maintained controlled balance, and phasic facilitated imperceptible constant motion, and the bent-knee allowed mobility, ensuring readiness. The semi-crouch position with the rear heel slightly raised and cocked enabled Lee to overcome inertia and explode off the blocks when bridging the gap.

---

[51] Ibid. p. 34–35.

Utilize techniques that deviate less from the stance, for quick recovery and follow-up. A great deal of care will have to be taken to cut down to a minimum the amount of time spent on the loss of balance, which is the initial stage in the execution of the movement.

Lighten the stance so that the force of inertia to overcome will be less.

It is essential to preserve the balance and poise of the fighting turret carrying your artillery. No matter in what direction or at what speed you move, your aim is to retain the fundamental stance which has been found to be the most effective for fighting. Let the movable pedestal be as nimble as possible.

Training Methodology

Treating the Body as a Temple

Lee started to train fanatically when he moved to Los Angeles. While he believed he might be able to make a living teaching and demonstrating his martial arts, he also realized that through the medium of film and television he could show the masses what martial arts had to offer. To do so, he needed to be in the very best shape of his life, so he made training part of his job, referring to his hands and feet as the "tools of the trade," the instruments he would use to express his art. Even more, Lee knew he needed to be in peak physical condition to perform at the highest levels in martial arts. According to Peter Chin, Lee treated his body as his temple. Training was important, not only for the physical, but also for the mental and spiritual.

Lee's daily training schedule in 1968 showed his regular routine was working on his abdominals, grip and forearm strength, along with aerobic training such as running, cycling, skipping rope and bench stepping in the morning. These activities were followed by weight training (weights or isometrics) in the late afternoon or evening. Lee adhered to a weightlifter's routine of working muscle groups on alternate days for rest and recovery, combined with healthy doses of stretching for flexibility. All of this was, of course, coordinated with skill development of the upper- and lower-body techniques (punching and kicking) as well as his private lessons and group sessions with students.

By 1970, according to his day planner, Lee was working on his abdominals and flexibility every day, performing weight training and kicking routines on Tuesday, Thursday and Saturday, while practicing punching and hand conditioning on Monday, Wednesday and Friday. He also practiced some form of aerobic exercise every day (running, cycling, rope skipping). He kept his tools sharp by faithfully practicing his punches and kicks daily (averaging 500 punches and 500 finger jabs daily, completing 1,000 hand strikes a day).

Aerobics for the Cardiovascular System and Lower Body

Lee exercised his cardiovascular system in many different ways, such as riding the stationary bike, skipping rope and shadowboxing, but he really took to running. He ran the hills of Bel-Air near his home on a daily basis and, later, he ran in the streets of Hong Kong early in the morning to avoid the mob of movie fans. Running not only worked the heart but provided benefits to the whole body and Lee really enjoyed it, as he wrote in his personal notes: "Jogging is not only a form of exercise to me. It is also a form of relaxation. It is my own hour every morning when I can be alone with my own thoughts."

Lee even started to run with a weight belt and ankle weights so he could progressively increase the amount of work in his running, akin to progressive weight training. Also, by increasing his capacity for more taxing activities, Lee was in good condition to accommodate the effort involved with increased mobility, footwork and kicking.

Strength Training

By the time Lee moved to Los Angeles, the weight training he had been introduced to in Oakland began to take on a life of its own. Conventional thinking of the day was that weight training resulted in excess bulk and decreased flexibility, which would only result in slowing down the athlete. However, Lee found that certain types of training yielded functional strength, thereby enhancing his martial arts performance. Wong recalls Lee developing specific muscle groups to enhance his footwork, kicking and punching, such as the back and lat muscles, the shoulders and deltoids, and forearms for the wrist snapping motion in his one-inch punch. He put less emphasis on the chest and biceps. Of course, Lee's abdominal muscles were legendary and could only be developed by constant daily work, a forerunner of today's core training. Abdominal strength not only contributed to all-around movement, but also tremendous torque when snapping the hips for punching or kicking. As kicking became more integrated, Lee performed squats and calf work. Linda remembers that during this period, Lee was working out with heavier weights, obtaining a 300-pound Olympic barbell set.

Lee looked at many different ways to develop strength aside from weightlifting. He constantly experimented, modifying his routine until he found what yielded the best results. He did isometric training, positioning himself within a power rack to work against its fixed-position bar. He would get into a lifting posture and exert maximal muscular contractions against the immovable bar for approximately 10 seconds. This practice served to strengthen and tone the muscles, but Lee also modified the training so he could work the energy flow in his arms to enhance his chi sao practice. George Lee made a portable platform so Bruce could perform isometric contractions at home. He stood on the platform and attached a chain to it with a small bar at the end, so he could exert the pulling, pushing, curling and pressing actions.

Herb Jackson built a unique training device for Lee, which consisted of a board fitted with a shoulder harness made of seat-belt material and designed for isometric training. Lee used this one-of-a-kind item to condition the muscles involved with footwork. Using the harness, the practitioner stands on the board with the harness over his shoulders and the knees slightly bent. By pushing up against the harness while in the on-guard position (slightly forward, centered, slightly back), the practitioner works the quad and calf muscles using dynamic tension, while getting the proper feel in anchoring himself for a quick takeoff when launching an attack. This "footwork board" was evidence of Lee's training focus on footwork and speedy attacks.

Lee also developed explosive strength by performing certain lifts as quickly as possible, including partial bench presses and squats. He worked on initiation speed by snapping punches with dumbbells in his hands, a move not recommended for everyone because it can damage the elbows if not performed carefully.

Wong believed that by studying human anatomy, such as the fascia, muscles and tendon strength, Lee concluded that the connective tissue must be strong when hitting something. For instance, developing wrist and forearm strength made his fist and arm more solid upon impact, like a battering ram. Lee applied this logic to the shoulders, lats, back muscles and all the muscle groups used in making the body solid when coming into contact with an opponent. Wong recalls Lee used leverage training,

Ted Wong

including curls with extended arms and extending a barbell out in front of the body, stressing the joints to increase tendon strength.

Lee was also known to use an electro-stim machine to continue working his muscles via electricity. Karate champion Mike Stone, who learned about the device while teaching karate to Los Angeles Rams football players during the 1960s, introduced Lee to it. Although meant primarily for physical therapy to rehab injuries, Lee experimented with it to enhance muscular contractions.

Abdominal Training

Lee always believed that training the abdominals was important. A well-developed set of abs assists not only in general, all-around movement, but also in generating tremendous torque for punching and kicking. The amount of work Lee put into developing his abdominals is evident; they are still legendary even by today's standards when core training is better understood.

A Physique without Compare

Despite not focusing on bodybuilding, Lee's body began to develop and his musculature became spectacular, amazing even by modern-day standards. Lee shared his knowledge of strength training with his students when he created personal training routines for them to use in their supplementary training. For instance, as previously mentioned, Lee spent time with Wong to "develop some basic requirements." In other words, to build up the body by not only lifting weights but also taking protein powders for muscle growth.

Allen Joe, with his bodybuilding background, recognized the gains Lee was making when he visited him in 1969. He had not seen Lee for some time and was impressed by Lee's muscular achievement. Later in 1972 when Wong visited Lee in Hong Kong, he remembered the extreme muscle definition Lee had achieved. He recalled Lee stepping on a scale and being very proud of his 127 pounds of solid muscle. Although he had lost weight, Lee believed his punches and kicks were just as powerful as before.

On that same trip, Herb Jackson ordered and helped assemble the Marcy Circuit Trainer (multi-exercise weight-training machine) for Lee. By performing the different exercises on the multistation machine without rest, Lee integrated circuit training into his routine. This training for cardiovascular effect would further shape Lee's body with the impressive results highlighted in several scenes of *Enter the Dragon*.

Training with Specialized Equipment

As Lee started to increase the level of intensity in his practice, equipment had to be built to withstand the extreme punishment Lee inflicted on the items. While the wooden dummy could withstand the punishment, Lee was not enthused with it later on because it did not move like a live opponent. He wanted things to be alive and moving since he concluded that the essence of fighting was the art of moving. When he did work on the wooden dummy, Lee worked on it more "free form" than in a prescribed set or form, integrating some of the new techniques added to his arsenal.

Portable Kicking Equipment (Foam Pad)

Lee continued to use the heavy bag in his training, but he sought other ways to develop his kicks and punches. A good follow-up to the heavy bag was the air shield used as a blocking pad in American football. Whereas the heavy bag develops power because of its weight, the air shield develops speed and swift initiation. When someone held the shield, it was more alive than the heavy bag's "dead," swinging weight. It was more mobile in the sense that Lee could have someone hold it while he launched them into the air with a well-placed side kick.

Mentioned earlier, Lee especially liked the kicking shield George Lee built for him because it was solid yet mobile. The combination of dense foam rubber supported by the wooden backing provided a great "feel"

Bruce Lee and James Yimm Lee

Ted Wong

147

when kicking it. George and Los Angeles student Herb Jackson made similar pads with the dense foam rubber material for punching. Jackson also built a much larger (approximately 5 feet long) kicking shield that the partner strapped on with seat belts.

Lee recommended kicking a pad or shield rather than in the air to save wear and tear on the joints: "When you use the leg it is much better to use it to kick at the foam pad or something like that. Watch out with the side kick or air kicking too much because it's bad for the knee joint if you snap it too much without resistance at the end. Just think about economical movement."

Focus Mitt

Lee was taken by the focus mitts used in boxing. Lee liked them because they developed extreme accuracy and versatility in punching and kicking. The partner could hold a pad in each hand at different angles and heights so the practitioner reacted to the angle of the mitt. The partner could also check on the practitioner's defense by attacking with the mitts to be sure the practitioner remained aware. Finally, because of the pads' portability, the person holding them could test his partner's nontelegraphic motion and speed by making him miss the pad, moving it before the partner made contact.

Ted Wong and Lee with the focus mitt

Broken-Rhythm Ball

Jackson also developed another unique, yet simple piece of equipment for Lee. Jackson hung a plastic ball from a string and attached it to a heavy chain suspended from the ceiling. The ball moved erratically when struck. After the initial hit, one had to track the unpredictable movement of the "broken-rhythm ball" to hit it again.

Overall, Lee experimented with all kinds of devices to enhance his martial arts performance. Whether it was developing punching and kicking power, speed and timing, or hand and forearm conditioning, Lee's equipment training was highly specialized and revolutionary even by today's standards.

Realistic Training

Lee believed there had to be functional realism in training to reach the highest levels of martial arts. Although he referred to his hands and feet as the "tools of the trade," he also said, "actual sparring is the ultimate," and training was only a means to the ultimate. He referred to stance training, forms, even touch sparring as "idealistic dryland swimming":

> *No amount of idealistic land swimming will prepare you for the water. The best exercise for swimming is swimming. The best exercise for jeet kune do is actual sparring.* [52]

> *Only in free sparring, can a practitioner begin to learn broken rhythm and the exact timing and correct judgment of distance.*

---

[52] Pollard, Maxwell. "In Kato's Gung-Fu Action Is Instant." *Black Belt* magazine, November 1967. Reprinted in *The Legendary Bruce Lee*. Burbank, CA: Ohara Publications, 1986. p. 50.

Realism was important, so students wore protective equipment when sparring with each other. Linda recalls: "He used to say touch sparring was so unrealistic, that it was swimming on dry land. So he thought that his students should train with actual contact, so he had headgear, gloves, chest protectors, shin guards, all of that. And his students did go after it with each other, because he said you can't really train to fight unless you fight. He had done it to a certain degree earlier, so you can see these ideas blossoming in Los Angeles." In this way, students would understand what was important when sparring against a living, uncooperative opponent who was attempting to knock your block off. Only by sparring full-contact could one truly know whether he could apply what he had learned and whether he could adapt to an opponent.

During this period Lee kept in touch with some of his wing chun brothers, updating them on his advances and training methods. He wrote on January 4, 1969, to William Cheung, who had introduced Lee to wing chun:

> *William, I've lost faith in the Chinese classical arts—though I still call mine Chinese—because basically all styles are products of land swimming, even the wing chun school. So my line of training is more toward efficient street fighting with everything goes, wearing head gear, gloves, chest guard, shin/knee guards, etc. For the past five years now I've been training the hardest and for a purpose, not just dissipated hit-miss training. I'm running every day, sometimes up to six miles. I've named my style jeet kune do—reason for my not sticking to wing chun because I sincerely feel that this style has more to offer regarding efficiency.*

He also wrote on January 11, 1970, to Wong Shun Leung, his senior in wing chun, for whom Lee had high regard. Many say Wong Shun Leung put Lee on the path of pragmatism in the martial arts:

> *Since I started to practice realistically in 1966 (protectors, gloves, etc.), I feel that I had many prejudices before, and they are wrong. So I changed the name of the gist of my study to jeet kune do. Jeet kune do is only a name. The most important thing is to avoid having bias in training. Of course, I run every day, I practice my tools (punch, kick, throw, etc). I have to raise the basic conditions daily. Although the principle of boxing is important, practicality is ever more important. I thank you and Master [Yip Man] for teaching me the ways of wing chun in Hong Kong. Actually, I have to thank you for leading me to walk on the practical road.*

Here were Lee's pointers on sparring:

- *Require individuality rather than imitative repetition.*
- *Efficiency is anything that scores (in primary freedom one utilizes all ways and is bound by none, and likewise, any technique or means which serves its end).*
- *Simplicity of expression rather than complexity of form.*
- *Turn your sparring into play—but play seriously.*

- *Don't take your sparring too seriously.*
- *Totality rather than partiality.*
- *Dissolves like a thawing ice (it has form) into water (formless and capable to fit in with anything—nothingness cannot be confined…).*
- *When you have no form, you can be all form. When you have no style, you can fit with any style.*
- *In sparring there is no answer; truth has no future, it must be understood from moment to moment. You see, to that which is static, fixed, dead, there can be a way, a definite path but not to that which is moving and living. There is not conviction or method, but perception, a pliable and choiceless awareness.*
- *To have a choiceless awareness, one should have the totality, or emptiness—all lines, all angles.*
- *If one is isolated, he is frozen and paralyzed. To be alive is to be related. Action is our relationship with our opponent.*
- *Action is not a matter of right or wrong. It is only when action is partial, not total, that there is right and wrong.*

When sparring, the participant watches and observes the opponent, and being like water, must be flexible enough to adapt to the opponent's way of fighting to defeat him. A plan of attack or counterattack is formulated based on the strengths and weaknesses of the practitioner and the opponent. This does not necessarily mean to adopt the opponent's way of fighting, but to understand it and be resourceful in overcoming it.

Only after countless hours of training and sparring can the martial artist achieve no-mindedness (*mushin* or *wu-hsin*) and the mastery of nonaction (*wu-wei* or effortless action). Confidence increases when he can trust the unconscious mind to make the right move, which is much quicker since conscious decision-making is no longer taking place and allows the practitioner to perform without effort. In this way, "I do not hit. It hits all by itself," as Lee said to the elder priest in the opening scenes of *Enter the Dragon*.

Lee recognized a student quickly learns what works when sparring, and as a result, he begins to simplify his arsenal. No longer is there a need for more techniques, but rather the correct use of them:

Until the student begins to spar then he will stop searching for the accumulation of techniques; rather, he will devote the needed hours of practice to the simple techniques for its right execution. It is not how much one learns but how much one absorbs what he learns. The best techniques are the simple ones executed correctly. When sparring occurs, stress the above thought and the students themselves will realize it is futile to search for more and more new techniques. Rather, they will devote the needed hours on practicing the correct execution of simple techniques.

By sparring, the practitioner not only begins to understand his opponent, but more important, he begins to understand himself. Sparring against a partner gives the practitioner immediate feedback on his performance—not quick enough here, used the wrong strategy there, etc. But the learning process deepens as the practitioner begins to look inward at his tendencies, preferences, reactions, temperament and inner being. The knowledge gained from sparring ultimately becomes self-knowledge. As Lee said, you are no longer fighting your opponent, but rather yourself, your hang-ups, etc. This process can be very stressful since the student may not like what he finds initially; but once an honest assessment is made, he can move on to better himself.

During filming of Enter the Dragon

Adaptability

"Empty your mind. Be formless, shapeless—like water. If you put water into a cup, it becomes the cup. You put water into a bottle, it becomes the bottle. You put it in a teapot, it becomes the teapot. Now, water can flow, or it can crash. Be water, my friend."

Lee reiterated these words from a scene in the *Longstreet* television series when he was interviewed by Pierre Berton. He often referred to the nature of water to describe adaptability. To fit in with an opponent, the student must constantly adapt to the fluid "what is," which is constantly evolving: "In order to cope with 'what is,' one must have the awareness and flexibility of the styleless style. When I say 'styleless style,' I mean a style that has the totality without partiality; in short, it is a circle without circumference where every conceivable line is included."

A structured approach in dealing with "what is" does not work; that is precisely what a style or system attempts to do, which is fruitless. As Lee liked to say: "You can't organize truth. That's like trying to put a pound of water into wrapping paper and shaping it."

Ted Wong recalls Lee asking him, "What makes a good fighter?" Wong came up with all kinds of answers—he's tough, he can take a punch, he's fast, but Lee kept shaking his head saying, "No." Finally, Lee told Wong to think about it and come back with an answer. The next day, Wong came with a list, but all were the wrong answer. Finally, Wong asked, "What is it? I give up." Lee answered with one word: Adaptability. Wong never forgot that word. "That [was] ingrained in my mind; everything comes back to it. You read Bruce Lee's book, everything is adaptability." Wong recalled Lee saying, "If you cannot adapt, you are not a complete fighter."

All styles and fixed methods of combat simply lack adaptability. Lee said, "My followers in jeet kune do, do listen to this: All fixed, set patterns are incapable of adaptability or pliability. The truth is outside of all set patterns," and "Truth in combat is different for each individual in this style."

Adaptability is the key to jeet kune do.

Philosophy: The Liberation

Man, the living creature, the creating individual, is always more important than any established style.

In early 1967, when Lee was preparing the opening of his College Street school in Los Angeles' Chinatown, he asked his Oakland-era student, George Lee, to fabricate some items that would serve to communicate his thoughts on classical martial arts and the individual growth of the martial artist. These symbols of Bruce's genius endured long after he passed.

Miniature Tombstone

Philosophy always played a vital role in Bruce's approach to martial arts. In his January 31, 1967, letter to George requesting a miniature tombstone, Bruce mentioned it was to "dramatize the not too alive way of the so-called classical gung fu styles."

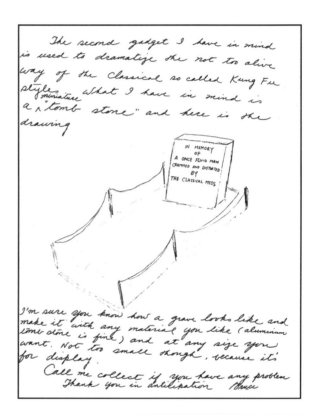

Ever reliable and loyal to Bruce, George masterfully fabricated a miniature-sized tombstone based on Bruce's drawing with the inscription: "In memory of a once fluid man, crammed and distorted by the classical mess." It represented the stifling traditions of styles and the formalities of the past causing the "death" of independent inquiry and the incomplete maturation of a martial artist. This was one of Bruce's fundamental messages on martial arts.

Bruce Lee wrote in his September 1971 landmark article for *Black Belt* magazine, "Liberate Yourself from Classical Karate," [53] that it was possible a martial artist had discovered some truth in combat while expressing his personal fluidity, and in fact, these teachings had been formalized and passed on to his students. However, when "the founder" passed away, elaborate rituals (organized despair as Lee called it) were created to preserve the teachings and the memory of the teacher. As a result, creativity is squelched, since the style and its traditions become more important than the individual. The student is then expected to fit into a mold and is not allowed to reach his full potential. Lee concluded: "In so doing, the well-meaning, loyal followers not only made this knowledge a holy shrine but also a tomb in which they buried the founder's wisdom." The miniature tombstone symbolized the death of the living, breathing

---

[53] Lee, Bruce. "Liberate Yourself from Classical Karate," *Black Belt* magazine, September 1971. Reprinted here in Appendix A.

Allen Joe, Bruce Lee, James Yimm Lee and George Lee

martial artist who is no longer permitted to challenge his intellectual capacity or exercise his creativity.

Lee placed the miniature tombstone at the entrance of the school to deliver another insightful message to his students. Linda says, "The small tombstone was to represent the stylistic way of martial arts that Bruce was opposed to, and going away from the non-fluidity of most martial arts, referring to the crammed and distorted type of martial arts [the classical mess]. He wanted to bury it, because this was not his way. So that tombstone represented that philosophy of the demise of organized despair." In other words, since Lee's teachings were not built on tradition, he was telling his students to throw away these notions and simply be free when they walked through the door of the school. Lee wrote: "It is when you are uninfluenced and 'die' to your conditioning of the classical response that you can be aware of something totally fresh, totally new," and "The function of jeet kune do is to liberate, not to bind."

Bruce Lee and Los Angeles-era students

Three Plaques

Bruce also asked George to make three plaques that would "illustrate the thought behind my system" and "the three stages of cultivation." A master craftsman by all accounts, George built the three plaques out of perfectly fitted, painted aluminum pieces fastened to lacquered wooden frames. Bruce treasured George's work and he displayed the plaques at the Los Angeles school.

On the first plaque, inscribed "Partiality: The Running to Extreme," the yin and yang symbols are drawn as separate independent entities, not interconnected. This image communicated Lee's belief that many martial artists viewed yin and yang as dualistic, not as one. Lee recognized extremism in martial arts: hard versus soft, external versus internal, striking versus kicking, striking versus grappling, etc. By design, he drew the yin and yang on this particular plaque without the small circles in each of the forces, to illustrate how rigid views ultimately resulted in isolation. A system and its followers tightly holding to their beliefs out of pride or for the sake of tradition act more like the rigid fir tree that cracks than the flexible bamboo reed that survives because of its suppleness.

 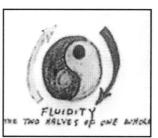 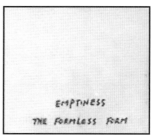

The second plaque, with the message "Fluidity: Two Halves of One Whole," illustrates the view of yin and yang as essentially one inseparable whole. The unceasing interplay of co-existing forces is illustrated by the arrows, while the small circle within each element communicates the balance that is to be achieved. With dualism eliminated, one takes on the nature of water in the sense that water can assume any form imposed on it. In this way, there is no "for" or "against":

> *JKD uses all ways and is bound by none and, likewise, uses any technique or means which serves its end.* [54]

> *To understand JKD, one ought to throw away all ideals, patterns, styles; in fact, he should throw away even the concepts of what is or isn't ideal in JKD.* [55]

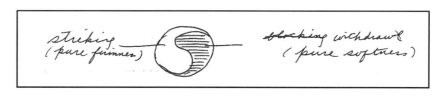

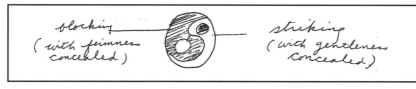

From an Eastern philosophical standpoint, to achieve totality, one aims to "have no technique" and be empty. The third plaque illustrates this concept. It's blank except for the words "Emptiness: The Formless Form." Being purposeless, letting go of oneself, and keeping the mind without thought, one achieves the state of no-mindedness, which can adapt to the situation at hand, resulting in autonomous responses:

---

[54] *Tao of Jeet Kune Do.* p. 24.

[55] Ibid. p. 11.

A JKD man should keep his mind always in the state of emptiness so that his freedom in action will never be obstructed. [56]

In JKD, all technique is to be forgotten and the unconscious is to be left alone to handle the situation. The technique will assert its wonders automatically or spontaneously. To float in totality, to have no technique, is to have all technique. [57]

Jeet kune do favors formlessness so that it can assume all forms and, since it has no style, JKD fits in with all styles. [58]

With all training thrown to the wind, with a mind perfectly unaware of its own working, with the self vanishing nowhere, anybody knows where, the art of JKD attains its perfection. [59]

Three Stages of Learning/Cultivation

Lee wrote about three stages in the development for the martial arts:

> *There are three stages in the cultivation of gung fu. Namely, the Primitive Stage, the Stage of Art, and the Stage of Artlessness. The Primitive Stage is the stage of ignorance in which a person knows nothing of the art of combat and in a fight he simply blocks and hits "instinctively." The second stage (the Stage of Art) begins when he starts his training in gung fu. In his lessons, he is taught the different ways of blocking and striking, the forms, the way to stand, to kick, etc. Unquestionably he has gained a scientific knowledge of combat, but his original "self" and sense of freedom are lost. His mind "stops" at various movements for intellectual analysis and calculation. His action no longer flows by itself. The third stage (the Stage of Artlessness) arrives when his training reaches maturity; his techniques are performed on an almost unconscious level without any interference from his mind. Instead of "I hit," it becomes "it hits!" This is the stage of cultivated ignorance. In other words, before I learned martial art, a punch was just like a punch, a kick just like a kick. After I learned martial art, a punch was no longer a punch, a kick no longer a kick. Finally, after I understood martial art, a punch is just like a punch, a kick just like a kick.*

---

[56] Ibid. p. 204.

[57] Ibid. p. 201.

[58] Ibid. p. 24.

[59] Ibid. p. 200.

Returning to "original freedom" is completely integrated with being. There is no effort to do something; simply flow and adapt to "what is." Having "no form" transcends the conventional.

The practitioner must progress through the first two stages to attain the third stage's personal freedom and enlightenment. Lee spent countless hours honing his skill, burning it into his neural pathways, so it became part of his essence, because without that foundation on which to build, structure collapses. Lee said, "When you perceive the truth in JKD, you are at an undifferentiated center of a circle that has no circumference." But without a base of hard work and discipline, wandering in a "circle with no circumference" leaves the martial artist feeling lost and subjected to the bondage of styles and tradition. He must learn the system, then not be bound by it: "The knowledge and skill you have achieved are meant to be 'forgotten' so you can float comfortably in emptiness, without obstruction. Learning is important but do not become its slave. Above all, do not harbor anything external or superfluous—the mind is primary." [60]

Lee made notes for students to guide them when making the jump from the stages of art to artlessness:

> *Your side kick is a very effective tool as far as the normal function of a tool is concerned. Your side kick has fulfilled magnificently the first function that is to destroy anything or anyone that opposes the will of its owner; however, the side kick's main function is to be directed toward oneself, to destroy all impulses of ego, the obstruction of our fluid mind. The latter should control and consecrate the former. Once you understand this, the tool is the embodiment of life and not of death.*
>
> *A decisive leap. In your case it was the side kick that caused you to lose your "presence of the primordial state." However, today your side kick became a tool to unlock a spiritual goal. There was spiritual loosening along with physical loosening, a sort of unconcerned immersion in oneself. The original sense of freedom was there. Congratulations! The side kick took the place of the ego.*

---

[60] Ibid. p. 201.

On separate occasions, Lee worked with Taky Kimura and Dan Inosanto, two of his closest friends and students, on developing emotional content when expressing their techniques. When trying to get them to kick harder, Lee surprised them by slapping their faces; out of anger they both forgot who Lee was for a couple of seconds. He got the reaction he wanted, telling them to kick with that kind of feeling. Controlled anger, putting emotions into physical motion, was approaching the epitome of merging the mind, body and spirit into one. According to Peter Chin, the Chinese phrase *sun yee hop yut* (unification of mind and body) is considered the highest achievement in martial arts.

Last, Lee designed a ranking system of "no rank" because he desired to liberate his students from the restrictions of style or system. When an individual student transcends a style that might have been imposed on him, he returns to his original freedom. Although a ranking system might have been used to motivate his students to work hard and improve themselves, Lee cleverly illustrated his notion of an individual progressing through the three stages with the ranking system. "The first rank is a blank circle which signifies original freedom." Ranks two through seven comprised the yin and yang symbol with arrows using different color combinations, similar to the colored belts of traditional martial arts systems. But the eighth rank, the highest, is again a blank circle, symbolizing the return to the beginning stage, or rather, original freedom. Instead of a ranking system in which the student attains higher levels, in jeet kune do, progressing is much more circular. In this way, the practitioner reaches the highest level of achievement when he is simply his true self.

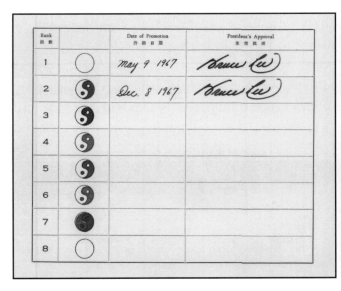 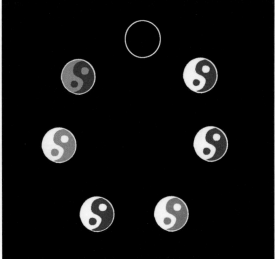

The three stages of cultivation became a self-fulfilling prophecy for Lee in his development as a martial artist. He wrote about the three stages before his fight in Oakland. After the confrontation, he discovered his own need to continue his path toward artlessness without any boundaries imposed from his previous training. He realized that the conditioning from his earlier classical training restricted his individual growth. The incident, therefore, springboarded Lee's leap to the stage of artlessness, which is simplicity!

Freedom

Toward achieving freedom, Lee wrote:

Learn the principle, abide by the principle, and then dissolve the principle. In short, enter a mold without being caged in it, and obey the principle without being bound by it.

Totality (circle without circumference)
1) Sticking to the nucleus
2) Liberation from the nucleus
3) Returning to original freedom

Conditioning is to limit a person within the framework of a particular system.
Man is constantly growing. And when he is bound by a set pattern of ideas or way of doing things, that's when he stops growing.

To be bound by traditional martial art style or styles is the way of the mindless, enslaved martial artist, but to be inspired by the traditional martial art and to achieve further heights is the way of genius.

In order to reach the highest stages, the student must have the ability to return to personal freedom. When learning a restrictive style, he is confined to that system, thus true learning cannot take place. He must be able to learn the system yet not be limited by it. Only in this way can he truly understand and express himself. Lee said, "One can function freely and totally when he is beyond system."

Lee was highly influenced by the writings of the Indian philosopher Jiddu Krishnamurti, who rebelled against the traditions of organized religions because their beliefs conditioned the minds of their followers. Krishnamurti wrote that knowledge as tradition is a hindrance if it restricts learning, eventually leading to dividing people. He concluded that one must avoid such fixed traditions, which only stifle personal freedom. Like the miniature tombstone, Lee said styles only served to solidify and condition what was once free and fluid, stifling and distorting the individual. Even a favorite technique can serve to hinder growth: "Any technique, however worthy and desirable, becomes a disease, when the mind is obsessed with it."

As a result, Lee wrote, each individual must find his own path to this freedom:

> *You must accept the fact that there is no help but self-help. For the same reason, I cannot tell you how to "gain" freedom, since freedom exists within you. I cannot tell you how to "gain" self-knowledge. While I can tell you what* not *to do, I cannot tell you what you* should *do, since that would be confining you to a particular approach. Formulas can only inhibit freedom, externally dictated prescriptions only squelch creativity and assure mediocrity. Bear in mind that the freedom that accrues from self-knowledge cannot be acquired through strict adherence to a formula; we do not suddenly "become" free, we simply "are" free.* [61]

When Lee realized he needed to be totally free of system in order to express himself fully, even his former training in wing chun was thrown to the wind. He no longer considered it the origins of his personal expression of jeet kune do as he wrote in his copy of Robert Powell's book *Crisis in Consciousness: Commentaries on Love, Life, and Death and Other Matter*:

> *Thus, wing chun becomes "non-nucleus"—the non-effecting base. Partial truth has become absolute laws.*

Powell writes that when having the critical "right beginning"—state of mind when undertaking anything—true creativity can be spontaneous, springing from a "non-beginning." Likewise, as yin and yang have no beginning, Lee concluded that there was no beginning or non-beginning in jeet kune do, so instead of wing chun being the nucleus as he expressed to Kimura in his letter, it was now the non-nucleus. Lee wrote that wing chun was a great style providing his initial foundation in martial arts, but now he was free and his true creativity emanated from his personal growth and self-expression: "Art is where absolute freedom lives, because where it is not, there can be no creativity." [62]

At the same time, Krishnamurti warned about taking the nonclassical approach as the gospel, "You have now started by denying something absolutely false—the traditional approach—but if you deny it as a

---

[61] Lee, Bruce. "Liberate Yourself from Classical Karate," *Black Belt* magazine, September 1971. p. 27. Reprinted here in Appendix A.

[62] *Tao of Jeet Kune Do.* p. 202.

reaction, you will have created another pattern in which you will be trapped." [63] Lee wrote: "Seeking the opposite of a system is to enter another conditioning" and "Do not deny the classical approach simply as a reaction, for you will have created another pattern and trapped yourself there." [64]

Constant Process

Following Krishnamurti's example, Lee was also adamant that learning is a constant process and is ever-fluid. He wrote in the margins of his copy of Krishnamurti's book *Think On These Things*: "Freedom lies in understanding yourself from moment to moment." When one reaches a conclusion, one has ceased learning. But life is constantly evolving, so one must be constantly learning and experiencing the moment-to-moment goings-on in life. Lee wrote:

> *Man is always in a learning process. Whereas "style" is a concluding, established, solidified something, you know? You cannot do that because you learn every day as you grow on, grow older.*
>
> *As soon as you have a way, there lies the limitation.*
>
> *Not mature, but maturing.*

Lee ultimately realized that all classical or traditional styles were essentially incomplete. Even his evolution toward jeet kune do would be dead if he stopped learning and growing. He told his Los Angeles student Dan Lee that he was not mature, but maturing and that what he believed today might, as a result, be different tomorrow: "Because I am changing as well as an ever-growing man, thus what I hold true a couple of months ago might not be the same now."

Scene from Fist of Fury

[63] Krishnamurti, Jiddu. *Freedom from the Known*. Hampshire, UK: Krishnamurti Foundation Trust Limited, 1969. p. 4.
[64] *Tao of Jeet Kune Do.* p. 25.

Simple, Direct and Nonclassical

Jeet kune do is training and discipline toward the ultimate reality in combat. The ULTIMATE REALITY is the RETURNING TO ONE'S PRIMARY FREEDOM which is SIMPLE, DIRECT and NONCLASSICAL.

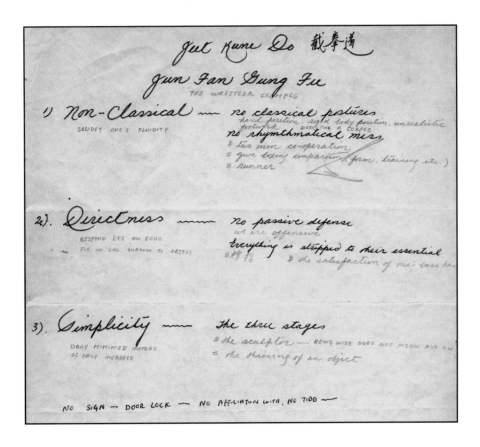

Nonclassical

JKD is nonclassical for all of the reasons mentioned previously (and illustrated by the miniature tombstone, the three plaques, etc.). The classical mess and organized despair (flowery forms and artificial techniques) of a fixed, rigid and confining style only serve to prevent the individual from honestly expressing himself. As Lee wrote: "Thus, instead of 'being' in combat, these practitioners are idealistically 'doing' something about combat." As styles become more and more entrenched in these views, extremism comes about, and these systems separate people, rather than unify them.

In contrast, by being nonclassical, the approach in JKD is never fixed or mechanical, but like water, a "formless form" that adapts to the ever-changing circumstances of combat. By not having bias in combat, the practitioner is alive and free to fit in with "what is." When Lee was asked once whether "Man, the living, creating individual, is always more important than any established style" [65] implied changing styles all the time, Lee clarified, saying it meant that, whereas a system or a style is an established and solidified thing, man is learning every day as he grows older.

---

[65] "Liberate Yourself from Classical Karate." p. 25.

Ted Wong characterized this phrase of Lee's as a nonclassical way of thinking: "My followers in jeet kune do, listen to this: All fixed, set patterns are incapable of pliability or adaptability. The truth is outside of all set pattern." In JKD, there are no classical postures or unrealistic movements, but rather a practical and functional arsenal that adapts to the situation. Instead of rhythmic practice with two-man cooperation, Lee reveled in the use of broken rhythm, which cannot be adapted to with a classical, fixed response. The martial artist must "fit in" and relate to his opponent in order to overcome him.

> *The usefulness of a cup is in its emptiness and the same can be said of a martial artist that has no form, and is therefore devoid of "style" because he had no preconceived prejudices with regard to combat, no likes or dislikes. As a result, he is fluid, adaptable and capable of transcending duality into one ultimate reality.*

Directness

In JKD, there is no passive defense such as a block followed by a counterstrike. In this way, the movements are most efficient. When being interviewed by Maxwell Pollard and explaining what he meant by directness, Lee tossed his wallet at Pollard, who simply raised his hand to catch it. Lee explained that Pollard

did not consciously think about how he should position himself and in what way he should catch the wallet; he allowed his unconscious mind to take over and merely catch the wallet. [66] In the same way, without the formalities of style, when the wrist is grabbed, the martial artist simply punches the opponent with the free hand. Cultivating "no-mindedness" allows the subconscious to react, and in this way, the body automatically responds so that "it" hits all by itself. In this way, everything is stripped to the bare essentials, as Lee said, so the martial artist can "respond like an echo, fit in like shadow to object."

Simplicity

> *It is basically a sophisticated fighting style stripped to its essentials.*

Lee continually stressed simplicity to his students, which was more difficult than it sounds since students often believe more complex techniques are a sign of achievement in martial arts. He wanted his followers to progress through the three stages, become self-sufficient and return to their original freedom so "a kick is just a kick and a punch is just a punch."

> *Gung-fu is training and discipline toward the ultimate reality in self-defense, the ultimate reality is simplicity.*

---

[66] Pollard, Maxwell. "In Kato's Gung-Fu Action Is Instant." *Black Belt* magazine, November 1967. In *The Legendary Bruce Lee.* Burbank, CA: Ohara Publications, 1986. p. 46.

To me the extraordinary aspect of martial arts lies in its simplicity. Martial art is simply the "direct expression" of one's feelings with the minimum of movements and energy.

Art is the expression of the self. The more complicated and restrictive a method is, the lesser the opportunity for the expression of one's original sense of freedom! The techniques, though they play an important role in the early stage, should not be too restrictive, complex or mechanical. If we cling to them we will be bound by their limitation.

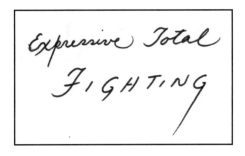

A Shedding Process—Peeling Off the Layers to Uncover True Self

Daily minimize instead of daily increase.

"Empty your cup so that it may be filled; become devoid to gain totality." [67]

For Lee, simplicity was a shedding process: "In JKD, one does not accumulate but eliminates. It is not daily increase, but daily decrease. The height of cultivation always runs to simplicity. It is the half way cultivation that runs to ornamentation." Bruce likened JKD to a sculptor who hacks away the unessentials so the truth is revealed without obstructions. One attains "totality" through simplification.

One may believe one must have knowledge of every style of martial arts to gain a totality of fighting, but that is impossible. Linda states of her husband's combination of martial arts:

He was very interested in all types of combative arts, armed and unarmed, Western and Eastern, ancient and modern. However, he adapted techniques to his own way of martial arts. I would say it is incorrect to say he just picked and chose from this type and that type and put them together into something. That was not really what Bruce was doing. He was researching; he was doing something through the scientific process, and then adapting it to his own way of martial arts, his own physicality, so that JKD was his way.

Lee researched various martial arts because he was curious about what others were doing. In his notes, he analyzed the "pros and cons" of Western boxing, Western fencing, wrestling, karate, *taekwondo,* judo, *kendo, aikido,* Thai boxing and Chinese techniques such as wing chun, *tai chi* and the southern styles. He did glean some effective principles from these forms of combat; however, his analysis was to gain insight into opponents, rather than looking for new techniques or training methodologies:

---

[67] *Tao of Jeet Kune Do.* p. 14.

The additive process is merely a cultivation of memory which becomes mechanical. Learning is never cumulative; it is a movement of knowing which has no beginning and no end. [68]

"True refinement seeks simplicity."

In conjunction with simplification, one seeks refinement. According to Ted Wong, refinement occurred at a high stage of evolution for Lee and was the essence of the art: "Jeet kune do is simply to simplify, so whatever you do, you want to refine what you have. Refinement and simplification, it comes together." Comprised of only a few kicks and a handful of punches, the aim in jeet kune do is to maximize their use and to understand how they can be used to their fullest extent. Wong referred to advanced JKD as "perfection of the basics." Instead of the conventional thinking that the student learns more complicated techniques as he progresses, the aim in JKD is continually to refine and hone basic skills. Through hard work and understanding of scientific principles, the basics are perfected, both for performance and complete understanding so they can be fully utilized. As Lee wrote: "The mastery of proper fundamentals and their progressive application is the secret of being a great fighter." [69]

Totality: Simplicity Adapting to "What Is"

What did Lee mean when he said, "There is no such thing as an effective segment of a totality?" Did he intend for practitioners to adopt every technique, tactic and training method in an attempt to be ready for every circumstance they may encounter? Martial artists should be well-rounded and resourceful in dealing with the unknown, but to make an endless pursuit of everything under the sun (all things external rather than working inwardly) is to miss his point. Lee was critical of styles because, as he said, "As soon as you have a way, there lies the limitation." If the student has a way, he begins with a conclusion rather than a beginning, thus never developing from personal discoveries. Styles solidify and condition what was once fluid and natural.

However, Lee's view of a totality was not to have more, but rather to have the ability to respond to "what is," which is the ever-changing circumstances in a confrontation, or life in general. The fighter cannot anticipate the outcome of a fight; he must fit in and become one with the opponent (as in yin and yang) moment-to-moment and adapt to the situation in order to come out victorious. Wong stated that adapting to "what is" is the essence of totality:

> *What is the totality of fighting? Totality means fitting in. "Be like water" is a very good example of his philosophy. Any fixed set pattern, you cannot follow that. They always say, "What if?" If my opponent does this, I do this. In real fighting, it is not "What if?" but "What is." "What is" is constantly moving and changing, you cannot be anchored down to a certain way of doing things, okay. Again, able to adapt and make changes to it…. Not the accumulation of many techniques, but rather utilizing your tools to adapt and overcome the opponent.*

---

[68] Ibid. p. 16.

[69] Ibid. p. 53.

In a serious self-defense situation, things develop so quickly the defender cannot respond by thinking. Further, an overly complex system only serves to bog the mind down with multiple-choice reactions and slow the responses. After many hours of training, the student develops the confidence and self-sufficiency to flow with "what is." Without a constant honing of the tools and dealing with "what is" in sparring, the student will not be prepared. Through simplification and returning to his original freedom, he achieves no-mindedness, allowing the unconscious to respond so that "I do not hit. It hits all by itself."

> *The consciousness of self is the greatest hindrance to the proper execution of all physical action.* [70]

> *Art reaches its greatest peak when devoid of self-consciousness.* [71]

> *A good JKD man does not oppose force or give way completely. He is pliable as a spring; he is the complement and not the opposition to his opponent's strength. HE HAS NO TECHNIQUE; HE MAKES HIS OPPONENT'S TECHNIQUE HIS TECHNIQUE. He has no design; he makes opportunity his design.*

> *One should respond to circumstance without artificial and "wooden" prearrangement. Your action should be like the immediacy of a shadow adapting to a moving object. Your task is simply to complete the other half of the "oneness" spontaneously.*

> *When one has reached maturity in this art, one will have the formless form. It is like the dissolving of thawing ice into water that can shape itself to any structure. WHEN ONE HAS NO FORM, ONE CAN BE ALL FORMS, WHEN ONE HAS NO STYLE, HE CAN FIT IN WITH ANY STYLE.*

Jeet Kune Do: It's Only a Name

Despite Lee's radical departure from the formalized styles and forms of martial arts, he realized it was only human nature for students to identify with jeet kune do like a fraternity. He regretted giving his personal art a name, since by doing so he turned his constantly evolving art and philosophy into just another style with formalized techniques, beliefs and traditions. As a result, he decided to close the Los Angeles, Chinatown school on January 29, 1970, and brought the training to his backyard, where the art could be passed to students with careful guidance. He was adamant that he did not create a new style or system, since it would only serve to enslave its followers. In light of the fluid nature of jeet kune do, the student is warned to tread lightly when reading something that purports to be its end-all or final definition. Lee wrote:

> *It is ridiculous to attempt to pin down so-and-so's type of gung fu as "Bruce Lee's Jeet Kune Do." I call it jeet kune do just because I want to emphasize the notion of deciding at the right moment in order to stop the enemy at the gate.*

> *If people say jeet kune do is different from "this" or "that," then let the name of jeet kune do be wiped out, for that is what it is, just a name. Please don't fuss over it.* [72]

---

[70] Ibid. p. 7.

[71] Ibid. p. 8.

[72] Ibid. p. 208.

Note: The following are techniques and principles that members of the Los Angeles Chinatown school and some second-generation students compiled for the First Annual Jun Fan Jeet Kune Do Seminar in 1997. Much appreciation to the following: Bob Bremer, Richard Bustillo, Steve Golden, Larry Hartsell, Herb Jackson, Pete Jacobs, Dan Lee, Jerry Poteet, Ted Wong and second-generation practitioners Chris Kent and Tim Tackett. The Los Angeles school curriculum emphasized conditioning as well as being simple, direct and nonclassical.

Los Angeles Branch Curriculum

Fitness program
- 1) Alternate splits
- 2) Waist twists (three times to each side)
- 3) Run in place
- 4) Shoulder circles
- 5) High kicks
- 6) Side kick raises
- 7) Sit-ups
- 8) Waist twists
- 9) Leg raises
- 10) Forward bends

Punching (hanging paper, glove, glove pad, wall pad, heavy bag)
- 1) Warm-up—the letting out of water (the idea of dropping the hammer loosely)
- 2) Straight punch (left/right)
    - a) Stationary
    - b) With pursuing
- 3) Entering straight right
    - a) High
    - b) Low
- 4) Backfist

Kicking
- 1) Warm-up (left/right)
    - a) Letting out of water
    - b) Whip
- 2) Side kick (left/right) [note: choice of group training method]
    - a) Facing two lines
    - b) In group
    - c) One student comes out

3) Straight kick (left/right)

4) Rear kick

5) Shin/knee/groin kicks

6) Hook kicks (low first) and toe kick

7) Combination kicking—eventually with hand

Basic defense

1) Stop hit

  a) Shin/knee kick

  b) Finger jab (close range)

  c) Any type of kick to fit in

2) Four-corner counter

Power training

1) Isometric (two men)

  a) Upward outward force

  b) Basic power training

  c) Punch

  d) Kick

Classical techniques

1) Pak sao

2) Lop sao

3) Gwa chuie

4) Chop chuie/gwa chuie

5) Pak sao/gwa chuie

6) Double lop sao (a and b)

7) Chop chuie/gwa chuie, lop sao/gwa chuie

8) Jut sao

9) Pak sao/jut sao

10) Chop chuie/gwa chuie/juk tek

11) Inside gate tan da

12) Tan da low/gwa chuie

13) Chop/gwa/lop sao

Combination

1) Right hand feint with groin kick

2) Right kick feint with biu jee

3) Right feint to stomach with right straight to head

4) Right feint to head shift to right to stomach

Lee held that there were three facets to jeet kune do, which he described as follows:

1) Nonclassical

There were and are no classical postures, no unrealistic footwork, no mechanical body movements, no dissection of movement (no "first you do this, then you do this and then you do this") as if it were a corpse. Further, there are no two-man cooperation drills and no rhythmic forms. Instead, the art is "alive" and infused with broken rhythm.

2) Directness

There is no passive defense, blocking is considered the least efficient manner of defense. Everything in the art is stripped to its essential components with absolutely no fancy decoration or ornate movements (i.e., if someone grabs you, punch him). Students are taught to see reality in its suchness and not deliberate about it. Simply experience it as it is, when it is. As if, when someone throws something to you, you catch it—you don't first grunt and go into a horse stance. And similarly, when someone grabs you, you hit him—you don't get involved in elaborate joint manipulations and complex maneuvering.

3) Simplicity

a) A daily minimize instead of a daily increase (being wise doesn't mean to "add" more, being wise means to be able to get off sophistication and be simply simple).

b) The three stages in jeet kune do

      I) Sticking to the nucleus

      II) Liberation from the nucleus

      III) Returning to the original freedom

Or, as Lee described the stages, "Before I learned martial art, a punch was just like a punch, a kick just like a kick. After I learned martial art, a punch was no longer a punch, a kick no longer a kick. Finally, after I understood martial art, a punch is just like a punch, a kick just like a kick."

As Lee taught more and more private lessons, he learned more about his students and, of course, more about himself. This enabled him to refine the components of his art even further, dropping certain technical aspects (such as chi sao and four-corner parries) and emphasizing others (such as footwork and mobility).

Lee's art, like his life, was constantly evolving, but not in the sense of adding more and more techniques to his already considerable arsenal. But rather by reducing technical baggage by "getting off" of sophisticated techniques and martial image actualizing and focusing more and more upon the core tenets of simplicity, directness and efficiency. The result was the student of jeet kune do could ascend to the very zenith of martial discovery—self-actualization. Lee held self-actualization to be the highest form of all art—including martial—and its attainment the true "duty" of a human being.

CHAPTER 6
Comparison of Core Techniques

While in America, Lee transformed his martial arts from the original wing chun gung fu training he received in Hong Kong to Jun Fan gung fu and finally to jeet kune do. A comparison of the techniques of the three eras (Seattle, Oakland and Los Angeles) provides a visual illustration of the development of Lee's art.

The reader may recognize some resemblance to the arts that influenced Lee: wing chun, boxing and fencing. For instance, some punches might look like those from boxing, but they are delivered from the opposite stance, or a technique might not be able to be pinned down to a particular style, but instead appears to be a hybrid of various arts. This resemblance reflects how Lee made the techniques fit him by altering or modifying them, instead of adopting them wholesale. Furthermore, while Lee's original training in wing chun gung fu occurred during the 1950s, the way that art was taught at the time might be very different from the way it is taught today, especially with the proliferation of wing chun around the world. It is not fair to assume an art has remained frozen in time. Each successive generation may take its respective art in different directions, perhaps in many different directions within a single generation. The world is a different place today compared to Lee's time, but nevertheless, he was a huge influence on the way martial artists think.

While certain elements of Lee's art might have been discarded later in his development, they do have a place in the JKD evolutionary path and deserve respect as part of Jun Fan jeet kune do. Whereas Lee got a great jump-start on his martial arts journey by learning wing chun gung fu, "a great style" as he referred to it in writing, he was able to reach for even higher levels with his personal expression known as jeet kune do.

I am completely indebted to Lee's direct students for demonstrating the techniques they learned from their sifu.

Taky Kimura, Seattle

Allen Joe, Oakland

Ted Wong, Los Angeles

Stance

When writing a note to himself describing the root of jeet kune do, Lee placed the on-guard position at the top of the list. Ted Wong referred to the stance and footwork as the foundation of the physical art of jeet kune do. The stance a martial art uses will greatly affect the execution of techniques and overall strategy. While other martial arts may have numerous stances for various purposes, typically one specific stance was used in each respective era of Lee's martial arts development, thereby simplifying the art.

A striking difference between the three stances is their weight distribution. The Seattle by-jong, or "ready," stance has most of the weight on the rear leg with the heel of the front foot up. The emphasis at that time was on keeping the weight off the front leg to avoid being swept while being able to easily deliver a quick front snap kick. Evident of the wing chun gung fu influence, the upper body is positioned squarely, so both hands can be used equally as with straight blast punching. Using the immovable elbow theory, the front elbow is positioned closer to the centerline and extended somewhat forward. The hands are positioned more defensively to protect the centerline, with the higher *tan sao* (palm-up block) protecting the high line and the lower *wu sao* (guarding hand) protecting the lower gate.

The Oakland stance is similar to the Seattle stance. However, as mobility was increasingly emphasized, the weight was more evenly distributed between the legs. The stance was slightly wider or "open" to balance the body over both feet and to employ waist rotation more freely for generating powerful kicks and punches. The shoulders were square with the hands in positions similar to those used in Seattle.

Compared to the Seattle and Oakland eras, the Los Angeles on-guard position is quite different. Based on a fencer's stance, the rear heel is slightly raised, shifting the weight distribution forward, aiding mobility and getting more bodyweight in motion for terrific punches and kicks. The distance between the feet is slightly wider to accommodate for more kicking. With the upper body more bladed off, the hands resemble that of a boxer. The elbows and arms are closer to the body for ease of mobility. The more extended the arm, the more it affects balance and movement. Finally, the stance positions the hands and legs more offensively, ready to attack.

All three stances put the strong side forward. Although wing chun practitioners stress using the lead and rear hands equally, the notion of the strong side forward was emphasized by Lee later. In other combative arts, including boxing, karate and taekwondo, practitioners are generally taught to position their strongest weapons in the rear to maximize momentum and torque by rotating the body. Boxers do so to preserve their energy over many rounds of fighting by jabbing with the weak hand, then delivering powerful punches from the rear. In contrast, Lee believed in putting the strong side forward, since 80 percent of kicking and punching came from the lead foot and hand. Because they are closer to the target, they are structurally faster since they have a shorter distance to travel. To increase power, Lee ensured his body was in proper alignment at the moment of impact, so his body supported the kick or punch, resulting in a more efficient delivery of power. Last, he used footwork not only for a speedy delivery from a distance, but to add momentum to the overall power of a kick or punch.

Kimura demonstrates the earlier Seattle by-jong (ready) stance. The weight is primarily on the rear leg, with the heel of the front foot off the ground. The stance is "square," as the shoulders illustrate, and the hands are positioned defensively, with the front hand in a tan sao and the rear hand in a low wu sao position.

Joe assumes the by-jong stance used in Oakland, which is balanced more evenly between the legs with the feet flat on the ground. The stance is a bit more "open," yet the upper body is still square with the hands in similar positions as those from Seattle.

Wong assumes the on-guard position used during the years in Los Angeles. The weight is shifted slightly forward, as a result of raising the heel of the rear foot and the distance between the front and rear foot is slightly wider than the earlier stances. The upper body is more bladed off in relation to facing an opponent head-on, and the hands are positioned more like those of a boxer, closer to the body.

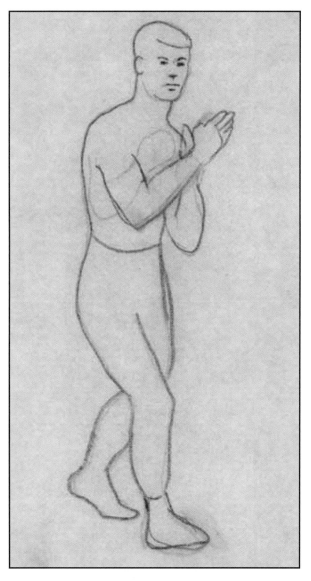 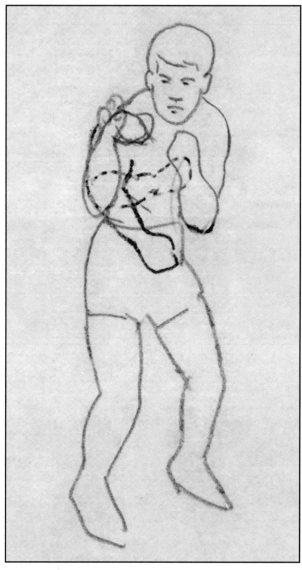

Footwork and Distance

Footwork, mobility and agility were paramount for Bruce Lee during all three eras. Students from Seattle, Oakland and Los Angeles all recall how much emphasis he placed on proper balance and swift footwork. Not only does good footwork make one more mobile, but it assists in learning how to judge distance, maintain it, or "bridge the gap" when attacking the opponent. Lee emphasized footwork even more during the later years after he had studied fencing's techniques for controlling distance. The distance between opponents is lengthened to make it more difficult to launch an attack effectively. The JKD practitioner is trained to cover this slightly increased distance with swift footwork, so he is at an advantage. The later emphasis on kicking also warranted increasing the fighting measure, the proper distance one keeps in relation to the opponent. The on-guard position and proper footwork are used to launch one toward the target like a sprinter exploding off the blocks.

Note the fighting measure or "stand-off" distance between opponents in each of the three eras. In Seattle (Kimura with son Andy), the positioning is closer; in Oakland (Joe and the author), it's slightly extended; and in Los Angeles (Wong and the author), the fighting measure is increased even more to accommodate the additional focus on mobility and footwork.

Kimura and Lee

Wong and Lee

Sidestepping

Lateral footwork opens additional angles of engagement. Early on, Lee had some particular beliefs about how one should move in combat. Referring to his earlier writings, the sidestep technique was performed "unconventionally," with the feet and legs crossing one another when moving laterally. Kimura recalls during this period that protecting the groin and the centerline from being attacked were of chief importance. This resulted in keeping the center covered at all times, so the idea of opening up the stance, even for an instant, was forbidden. Lee described the sequence:

> You should also practice stepping to both sides and their variations while employing your kicking tools and hand tools, all the while covering your centerline and hand and knee positions. For example, when sidestepping to the left, your right or lead leg should cross over in front of your rear leg, in order to protect your groin area. This is immediately followed by a lateral step of equal distance by the rear or left leg so that the by-jong is once more assumed.

Later, as mobility became more important and Lee studied how boxers sidestepped, he adopted the more conventional sequence with the foot closest to the intended direction moving first:

> Remember this simple thought: Move first the foot closest to the direction you wish to go in. In other words, if you wish to sidestep to the left, move the left foot first and vice versa. [73]

By applying circling or curving motions from boxing to lateral motion, flexibility and the ability to adjust to the opponent's movement is enhanced and additional angles of attack are realized:

> Circling right: The right lead leg becomes a movable pivot that wheels the whole body to the right until the correct position is resumed…. Moving to the right may be used to nullify an opponent's right lead hook. It may be used to get into position for the left hand counters and it can be used to keep the opponent off-balance. The important things to remember are never step so as to cross the feet, move deliberately and without excess motion. [74]

---

[73] Ibid. p. 152.

[74] Ibid. p. 149.

Kimura begins the sidestep by first moving the foot farthest from the lateral direction he is going, followed by the other foot moving so that the feet actually cross each other before assuming the same orientation as in the beginning.

When Joe performs the sidestep, he first moves the foot closest to the direction he is heading, followed by the other foot to re-assume the stance.

Wong illustrates curving to the right by stepping out somewhat sideways and forward with the right foot, followed with the rear foot rotating in a circling fashion to position the body at a different orientation to the opponent.

Lead Punch

Although the vertical fist structure was used throughout Lee's evolution in martial arts, his continual refinement of the lead punch is a case study in itself. The vertical fist, or *chung chuie*, complements many wing chun techniques since it helps preserve the centerline. As the punch is being delivered, additional power is generated by cocking the wrist down and snapping the fist upward, striking with the bottom three knuckles.

Lee observed how boxers deliver powerful punches with momentum and leverage by propelling and rotating the body. He started to adopt these methods to generate more power. Lee read boxing books by the likes of Jack Dempsey and Jim Driscoll, which validated some of his earlier wing chun training, such as using the vertical fist, but he also saw ways of using the body for more powerful punches. He continued to use the strong side forward stance to deliver kicks and strikes as quickly as possible, while using body alignment efficiently to generate power.

Fencing was the final element. Lee first increased the starting distance slightly and used footwork to bridge the gap and add additional momentum to the punch. He also adapted some of the key speed components of fencing such as "hand before foot" and non-telegraphic motion. The culmination of all these ingredients was Lee's development of the straight lead punch. Although simple in design, as Wong stated, "The straight lead is more like a fencing move. It is the most difficult technique in jeet kune do. I would say it is the most difficult hand technique in any martial arts. If you read any fencing book, it will tell you that the most difficult technique in fencing is the single straight thrust. Jeet kune do is based on that one technique. So you can see the fencing connection there."

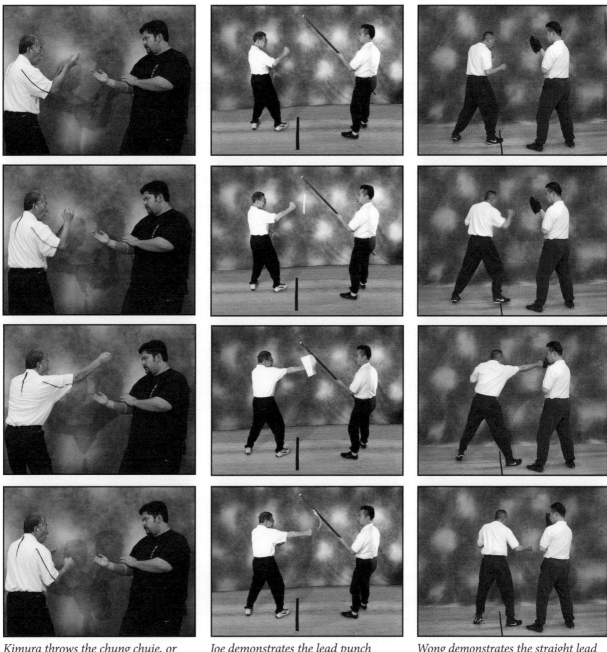

Kimura throws the chung chuie, or vertical fist, lead punch by extending the arm toward his opponent, with a small amount of waist pivot into the target, in order to maintain the square stance and with the weight remaining toward the rear.

Joe demonstrates the lead punch with a hanging piece of paper, hitting something that is insubstantial so the proper distance and amount of penetration can be perfected. As a result, proper mechanics can be refined without the resistance of a heavy or hard target.

Wong demonstrates the straight lead punch on a focus mitt, with the hand moving before the foot, followed by the rear foot explosively pushing off the ground. The waist and shoulders rotate with the arm extending into the target when his body is in proper alignment, with the fist hitting the target at the correct distance, concluding with the natural recovery into the on-guard position.

Kicks

When Bruce Lee first came to America, his kicking arsenal was fairly limited. Southern gung fu styles (more readily available in Hong Kong at the time) tended to emphasize strong, low stances and hand techniques. This was the case with the original wing chun's primary mode of fighting—close the distance on the opponent, engage the opponent's arms and straight blast him with a series of unrelenting punches. Although Lee was integrating some kicks from the northern gung fu styles, they were not designed to inflict much damage unless directed to soft targets such as the groin or the face. In keeping with the philosophy of the southern styles, kicks were kept low, below the waist, so balance was altered as little as possible and recovery time was minimized. Used more as a distraction, kicks were ways to cover distance to get to the heart of the matter with the hands.

One of the most effective kicks Lee employed early on was the stop kick. Using the longest weapon, the leg, to attack the closest target, the knee, made this technique very fast and effective. This effective speed is especially evident when the opponent advances for an attack, since he cannot defend against the countering stop kick to the shin or knee, among the weakest parts of the body.

In Los Angeles, Lee became more familiar with martial arts that emphasized more kicking, such as karate, taekwondo, Thai boxing and even *savate* from France. He started working toward generating more power in his kicks, while delivering them as quickly as possible. Strategically, Lee began to apply and use his legs differently, not just as a distraction or for closing the gap, but truly to integrate kicks into his overall fight plan. As with boxing, where there are just a few types of punches, Lee kept his kicking arsenal to a minimum, maintaining simplicity and maximizing results by perfecting his delivery—but it was the use of kicks and punches in combination that made his kicks effective.

In the by-jong stance, Kimura begins the front kick by raising his knee, followed by snapping his foot toward his opponent's groin, while maintaining the square structure of the stance, so he can close on the opponent and straight blast with both hands.

Joe waits for his opponent's attack and stop-kicks his opponent's knee. Joe remarked, "Bruce liked to call me the shin man since my favorite technique was a kick to the shins. We'd walk to a restaurant and mess around, Bruce trying to punch me."

Wong shuffles his feet to "bridge the gap," then raises his foot and rotates his body as he delivers a high hook kick to his opponent's head.

Hand Strikes

Bruce Lee's most famous punch is his one-inch punch. It was his signature technique throughout his years in America, and he demonstrated the technique at events from Seattle to Oakland to Los Angeles. Coming from wing chun gung fu, Lee was sure to perfect it. When he demonstrated it, Lee proved one does not need to "wind up" by starting his hand way back in left field to gather the momentum to deliver a powerful punch. He positioned his hand on his partner's chest, and with what appeared to be a small

twitch of his body, Lee sent his partner into the seat conveniently positioned behind him or into the air for several feet. This move involved the perfect timing of rotation, weight transfer, alignment, extension of the arm and wrist snap. Lee concentrated all of these elements into the target to maximize impact. It was through the coordination of his entire body that Lee fully expressed his power. As Linda commented, "I remember most that it was tremendously effective. It would just lift people off their feet, literally. And there was so much concentrated power in Lee…. At just the turn of the hip and the expulsion of energy, [he] would just send that person flying with their feet off the ground. They'd land in a chair. That was indicative of Lee's tremendous concentrated focused power."

Lee had amazingly fast hands, and his backfist strike had blinding speed. The backfist did not come from his earlier wing chun gung fu training. Lee adapted the technique from *choy li fut* to add variety to his punches. The backfist is among the fastest of hand techniques due to its relaxed, loose delivery and the natural whipping motion of the hand and arm. The backfist offered additional angles of delivery (side and low) and target areas, complementing straight punches and some of the trapping hands movements from wing chun.

Although the straight lead punch was the signature hand technique developed during the Los Angeles era, Lee was also known for the power in his hook punch, which was demonstrated by the dislocation of a *Black Belt* magazine employee's shoulder, as described earlier. Lee

created tremendous leverage and torque in delivering the hook punch using boxing techniques that emphasized proper body mechanics and timing. Not only did the hook punch provide yet another versatile angle of attack, but also a truly devastating knockout punch, as evidenced by many of the knockouts in boxing history.

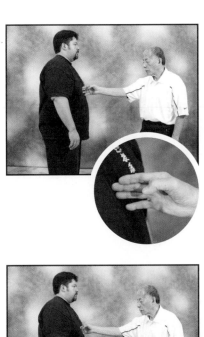

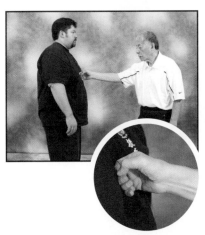

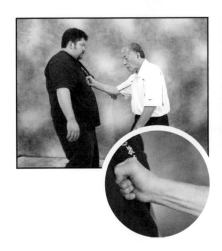

In executing the one-inch punch, Kimura positions his fingertips on his opponent's chest, then rapidly closes his hand into a fist and snaps his wrist in an upward fashion, striking with the bottom three knuckles while his bodyweight is transferred into the opponent.

Joe throws a speedy backfist strike by loosely whipping his hand and arm toward his opponent's temple; then, like the end of a whip, he quickly snaps the hand back after impact. The speed is enhanced not only by delivering the strike quickly, but also by its snapping recovery.

When executing the hook punch, Wong reverses the motion of the straight lead by first rotating his feet, waist and shoulders to the point where there is no free movement in the shoulder joint; then, like a slingshot, he releases the fist in an arc-like path to its target as his bodyweight settles to the rear foot.

Combinations

The evolution of JFJKD is further illustrated with the use of combinations. Straight blast chain punching (*jik chung chuie*) is a very effective combination from wing chun. Lee considered it "the heart of successful close-range attack." Once the distance is closed, the practitioner quickly throws a series of consecutive straight punches typically to the opponent's face. This move is especially effective because the opponent does not expect a follow-up punch to be delivered so quickly. The continuous barrage of punches keeps the opponent off-balance and dazed as each successive punch is delivered with percussive speed. However, straight blasting burns a tremendous amount of energy over a short time, and chasing a backpedaling opponent over an extended period is taxing to the practitioner, as Lee discovered in the challenge match with the gung fu man in Oakland.

As a result, Lee started looking for ways to deliver more damaging punches. Some of Lee's students from Seattle, such as Ed Hart and James DeMile, were experienced boxers, as were James Lee and Leo Fong in Oakland. Through his study of boxing, Bruce Lee integrated waist and shoulder rotation, adding power to his punches. While not as quick as the straight blast in delivering a succession of punches or as many strikes, the mechanics of punching from boxing delivers power more efficiently.

Later, as Lee started to adopt more and more kicks into his arsenal, the use of the foot became integrated into the overall approach. The use of kicks opens three angles of attack: the head, the mid-section and groin, and the knee or shin, increasing the number of targets an opponent must defend. Lee began to use the lead leg as a truly offensive weapon and integrated combinations between the foot and hand as naturally as a one-two combination with the hands.

An important point is that Lee stayed away from set or established combinations, where one simply throws a set series of punches or kicks in a robotic manner, regardless of how the opponent moves or reacts. First, Lee carefully crafted his strategy according to his opponent's strengths and weaknesses, either attacking him or waiting for him to attack. Second, after executing each kick or punch, Lee observed how it affected his opponent, then he selected the proper follow-up technique. Since Lee was performing this process at lightning speed, it appeared that he was executing an established combination.

COMPARISON OF CORE TECHNIQUES

Kimura demonstrates the straight blast chain punching combination, executing a series of straight punches to his opponent's chin. The stance remains square throughout the series so both hands are used equally.

Joe shows the one-two (jab-cross) punching combination influenced by boxing. Notice the use of the waist and shoulders to deliver power in the finishing blow.

Wong illustrates a foot-hand-foot combination. Integrating the foot increases the angles of attack and takes advantage of the more powerful blows possible with kicks.

Principles and Defensive Measures

Wing chun gung fu training emphasizes protecting one's centerline, while attacking an opponent's centerline. Many of the techniques from the Seattle era continue to maintain the wing chun structure. The "four corners" simultaneous attack and defense strategy was an efficient way to defend one's centerline while attacking the opponent's.

One may also simply use his own punch to nullify his opponent's attack and counterstrike with the same technique. When the opponent throws a punch at him, the practitioner controls the centerline by appropriately executing the inner gate punch (*noy moon chuie*) or outer gate punch (*gnoy moon chuie*) simultaneously to deflect and strike his opponent.

By beginning the inner gate punch from the chest, one protects his centerline while maintaining the inside position against an opponent. The punch actually cuts inside the opponent's attacking arm while delivering the counterpunch at the same time. The outer gate punch begins from the shoulder, starting from the outside and ending up at the centerline, an inward motion that deflects the opponent's attack by cutting over the arm while counterstriking at the same time.

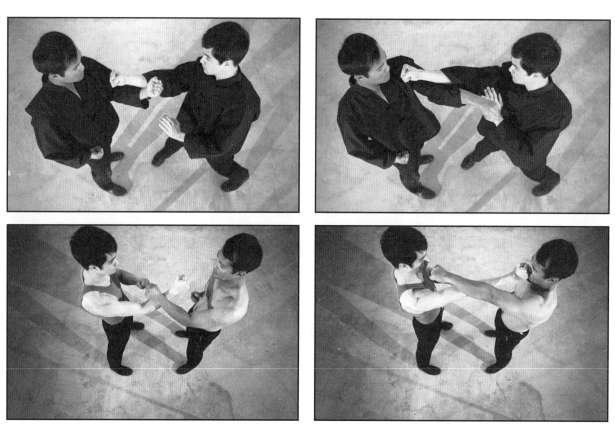

Dan Inosanto with Lee

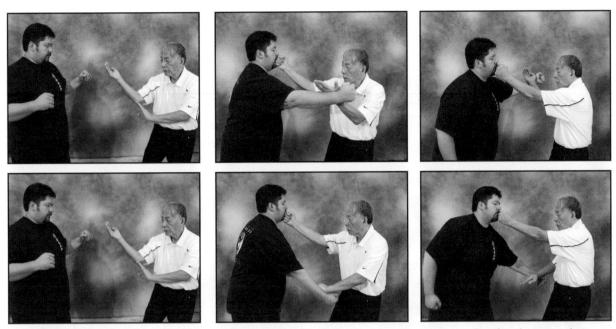

Kimura defends each of the four corners while simultaneously delivering his own counterattack. After the setup, the top row shows the inside high corner followed by the outside high, to both sides. The bottom row shows the inside low concluding with the outside low, to both sides.

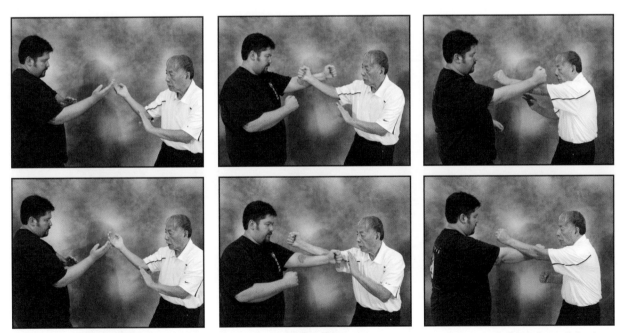

When he is attacked by his opponent's punches, Kimura uses inner and outer gate punching simultaneously to defend and counter his opponent while controlling the centerline.

During the Oakland era, Lee continued to use many of the principles of wing chun gung fu. The fighter protects the centerline by continually "facing" the opponent. When the opponent moves laterally, the fighter must adjust his stance and orientation to the opponent so the centerline is not exposed and open to attack. "Pointing" is a simplified way of preserving the centerline and is used as a guide to continue facing the opponent with the proper positioning. By simply pointing at the opponent's centerline, and ensuring the finger is in front of his own nose, the centerline is automatically covered. With proper body movement synchronized with pointing, the practitioner is automatically facing his opponent so the three fronts or gates (channels of attack) are protected.

Joe protects his centerline by continually facing his opponent by pointing as a guide. By constantly protecting the centerline, Joe does not give his opponent an opening to attack.

Another principle from Lee's earlier training in wing chun, the notion of springing energy, is used to ensure the arms are "alive." When pushed or pulled out of position, the arms must remain resilient, springing back into a protective position and preserving the centerline and vital targets on the body. Cultivating this arm action provides a measure of protection that becomes automatic.

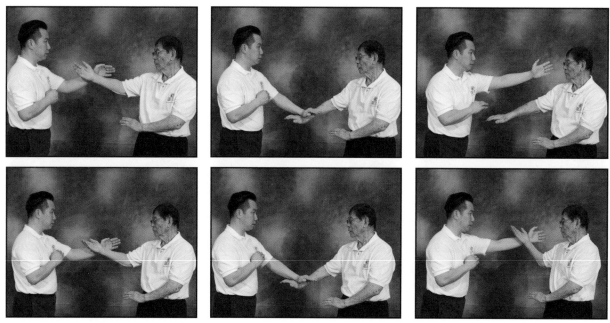

Springing energy: The opponent pulls Joe's arm down in an attempt to create an opening, but when Joe's arm is released, it automatically "springs back" to protect his head. The top row illustrates the attack if the arm does not spring up; the bottom row shows the springing energy.

During the Los Angeles era, Lee was using more of boxing's evasive movements. Slipping an opponent's punch allowed Lee to evade the attack and deliver his own counterpunch at the same time. It was another form of simultaneous attack and defense, except both hands were free to counter the opponent. Curving and circling footwork enabled Lee to move offline and position himself to create new angles of attack. Much of this strategy involved orienting the body so the practitioner is in his strongest position and the opponent is in his weakest. This positioning occurred as the distance between the practitioner and his opponent rapidly closed.

As his opponent attacks with a lead punch, Wong slips the punch, putting himself in an ideal position to counterattack.

Instead of facing his opponent head-on, Wong circles with footwork to create an opening to throw a lead punch to his opponent's nose.

Close-Range Fighting

In Seattle, Lee used a unique method of close-range fighting derived from his wing chun training. The principle of "simultaneous defense and attack" espoused momentarily immobilizing or trapping the opponent's limbs while delivering strikes at the same time. Although these techniques are much better understood today, they were new to America in the early 1960s. Combined with Lee's tremendous hand speed and quick reflexes, his close-range fighting appeared unbeatable—when one could actually see it.

From the trapping hands method of wing chun, Lee predominantly taught the pak sao (slapping hand) and the lop sao (grabbing hand). To subdue an opponent after a trap, he began to implement some of the grappling joint locks and takedowns he learned while experimenting with judo and wrestling. This was a natural progression since, when one is in trapping range, the option of employing grappling techniques is presented. As we see in his movies, Lee showcased his knowledge of grappling by integrating it into his fight scenes.

Later, Lee integrated much more mobility and distance control in his way of fighting. He nullified his opponent's attacks with distance, while mounting his own attacks with devastating speed. He also used positioning, such as moving to the outside, to negate an opponent's weapons and make it awkward for the opponent to counter. As a result, Lee exploited his strengths and neutralized his opponent's advantages. Since he was so physically fast and could read his opponent's movements and intentions quickly, it was efficient for him to keep his distance from the opponent with superior footwork, then bridge the gap to attack or evade the opponent's attack and counter.

Kimura and Lee

As soon as Kimura's arm crosses with his opponent's, he delivers a pak sao (slapping hand) to immobilize the opponent's arm while delivering a lead punch.

When Joe crosses hands with the opponent, he executes a lop sao (grabbing hand) technique with a rear hand punch, followed by an optional armbar joint lock.

Wong maintains his distance from his opponent, and when the opponent executes a lead punch, Wong moves offline to the outside and executes his own counterpunch to the opponent's chin.

Strategies and Tactics

Phon sao (trapping hands) is a unique method from wing chun that Lee continued to use while in Seattle and Oakland. Although most conventional martial arts teach blocking followed by counterattacking, the trapping movements of wing chun employ simultaneously defending and attacking. Its close-range hand movements can be impressive, especially when someone with Lee's hand speed performs the movements. Lee's hands looked like a tornado moving right in front of his adversary's face.

A wing chun practitioner will attempt to connect with the opponent's arms, using a probing hand technique called *mun sao* (asking hand). Once the arms are connected, the opponent's arm(s) is trapped or immobilized, allowing the practitioner to deliver a strike with the free hand. If the opponent blocks the strike, countermovements are employed. All of this is followed with straight blast punching to chase the opponent and overwhelm him. Typical trapping combinations such as the *pak sao-lop sao-gwa chuie* (slapping to grabbing hand with backfist) or the *lop sao-lop sao-gwa chuie* (grabbing to grabbing hand with backfist) were drilled over and over in class so responses became automatic and spontaneous.

Pak Sao-Lop Sao

Double Lop Sao

When Kimura delivers his initial trap, his opponent is able to block his strike, so he executes the proper countermeasure by trapping the opponent's arms again.

The bow and arrow is a form of indirect attack within the trapping range. The initial attack is directed at one angle, causing the opponent to block; the secondary movement attacks the subsequent opening created by the block. During the first half of the movement, one "pulls the bow" by drawing the opponent's response, then "releases the arrow" into the new opening. The "arrow," or follow-up technique, is the finger jab to the throat. This movement from outside to inside lines is cloaked since the strike comes from under the arm used in the initial attack.

The bow-and-arrow technique actually comes from wing chun's third form, *biu jee* (thrusting fingers), as a combination of finger jabs thrown deceptively at the opponent. It employs an indirect attack approach similar to those found in boxing and fencing's close-range techniques. As a result, Lee found some commonality between his previous training and what he later discovered in other forms of combat.

Bow and arrow: When Joe attacks with a lead punch, he draws his opponent's outward block, which he follows with an inside finger jab to the throat.

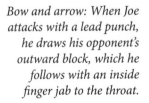

Later on, Lee began to employ broken rhythm and feinting. While not seeking an arm attachment to trap or immobilize, openings are created by faking the opponent into defending an unreal false attack. The true attack is then launched into the newly created opening. The hands and feet are used to add variety, and they actually serve to increase the distance between high and low angles. Lee maintained the distance from the opponent until he either bridged the gap to attack or allowed the opponent to close on him, from which he counterattacked. In close-range fighting, it is more likely an opponent will score, since you are at a distance from which you can hit him, but he can hit you as well. By increasing the distance and controlling it with footwork and mobility, enhanced with lateral movement, the odds are much less that he can score on you. As Bruce told Dan Lee, "Here it is: If you can move with your tools from any angle, then you can adapt to whatever the object is in front of you. And the clumsier, the more limited the object, the easier for you to potshot it."

Broken rhythm: Wong sets up his opponent by first delivering a real attack with a hook kick. He later fakes the same kick so the opponent lowers his guard, allowing Wong to deliver a final blow to the head.

Adapting to "What Is"

In many ways, the Seattle and Oakland eras contain much overlap. Lee was in a state of transition in Oakland: newly married, getting the Oakland Branch of the Jun Fan Gung Fu Institute established, experiencing the birth of his and Linda's son, grieving the death of his father Lee Hoi Chuen (and consequently spending many months in Hong Kong with his family), not to mention Hollywood knocking on his door with a potential television series. In Oakland, his martial arts development progressed as it had during his time in Seattle, absorbing what was useful and rejecting what was useless. Lee continued his refinement as he was exposed to more forms of combat and their strategies and tactics.

During his time in Seattle and Oakland, Lee enhanced and modified his earlier wing chun gung fu with techniques from other styles, such as choy li fut and some kicks from the northern gung fu styles. He also modified the way he performed some of the techniques from wing chun, such as simplifying chi sao and practicing it with a constant forward energy. But the overall approach was still "classical." After the fight with the gung fu man in Oakland, Lee's progression took a giant leap forward. He was forced to re-evaluate his art, taking a critical look at his way of fighting, his level of physical fitness and his ability to adapt. He took time to develop new methodologies in his approach to combat. Much of this influence came from boxing and fencing. Having only a few techniques, boxing is effective because of its practicality and simplicity. It also put much emphasis on generating punching power through the scientific use of the body. Fencing was valuable in terms of attack and counterattack theory, as well as in speed development and distance control.

This is not to say that Lee completely abandoned his earlier training, but as mobility, footwork, distance and kicking became central themes in Los Angeles, many of the techniques Lee relied on from his wing chun training took on less importance. By operating at an increased range and maintaining distance from an opponent with footwork, Lee better controlled the fight, preventing the opponent from effectively attacking. Acknowledging his speed and reactions, Lee had no need to engage his opponent at close range, since he could explosively bridge the gap on him, then be out of range before the opponent could mount a counterattack. Lee's use of broken rhythm and feinting created openings based on the opponent's reactions without having to gain an attachment with the arms.

So, in many ways, the fighting methodology that Bruce Lee later developed did not fit his earlier training. He had transcended his earlier training by discovering new ways that exploited his natural abilities—speed and fast reflexes. As a result, he relied less on his earlier training and it was de-emphasized in Los Angeles. However, he continued to practice chi sao to maintain his close-range reflexes and sensitivity should he be required to use his in-fighting skills.

The need for an approach that was flexible to the situation at hand—"being like water" when adapting to "what is"—came to have primary importance for Lee. Many different techniques would not assist in this process since they would only serve to clog up the mind with a myriad of "what ifs" and multiple choices. To minimize reactions and allow the subconscious to operate, Lee minimized and, therefore, simplified his art. A relatively small number of techniques were honed to be used in response to many different scenarios.

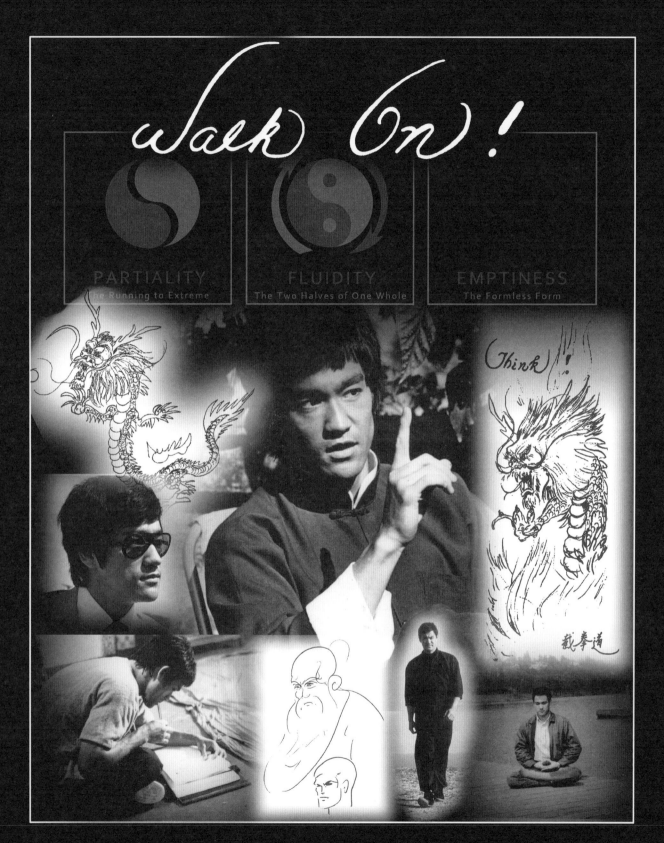

Walk On!

PARTIALITY
The Running to Extreme

FLUIDITY
The Two Halves of One Whole

EMPTINESS
The Formless Form

PHILOSOPHY

CHAPTER 7

The Mind of Bruce Lee: Glimpses into the Soul and Psyche of the Little Dragon

Most people need to overcome the temptation of being completely in awe of Lee's physique and prowess as a martial artist to appreciate fully everything he had to offer, including his intellect. This appreciation for Lee's physicality was especially strong due to his groundbreaking appearances on television and in movies. However, he also developed into a profound thinker, discovering the truth for himself when reading many of the great philosophers of the past and present. It was through this search for the truth that he gained the intellectual self-sufficiency and courage to break away from stifling traditions and evolve his martial arts.

Those who personally knew Lee were able to realize his genius not only as a martial artist, but as a human being. Many personal students mention how good they felt being around him and how he motivated and instilled confidence in them. Stirling Silliphant once said, "In my whole life, no man, no woman, was ever as exciting as Bruce Lee." How is it that a man could have such a positive effect on not only those who knew him, but those who were born after he passed on? Most likely it was how his self-knowledge, his supreme confidence in himself and his positive outlook on life were expressed in his presence on screen and his physical art of expressing the capabilities of the human body that inspire all of us.

Creative Life Force

Even at a young age, Lee felt the creative life force within him and it gave him purpose in life; it drove his being. He knew he would accomplish much since he refused to give in to failure or setbacks. It was this dogged determination that allowed him not only to become, arguably, the greatest martial artist who ever lived, but also the groundbreaking Asian actor who would be universally recognized around the world even today. In a letter to Pearl Tso in September 1962, he expressed this belief openly:

I feel I have this great creative and spiritual force within me that is greater than faith, greater than ambition, greater than confidence, greater than determination, greater than vision. It is all these combined…. Whether it is a godhead or not, I feel this great force, this untapped power, this dynamic something within me. This feeling defies description, and [there is] no experience with which this feeling may be compared. It is something like a strong emotion mixed with faith, but a lot stronger.

When you drop a pebble into a pool of water, the pebble starts a series of ripples that expand until they encompass the whole pool. This is exactly what will happen when I give my ideas a definite plan of action. Right now I can project my thoughts into the future. I can see ahead of me. I dream (remember that practical dreamers never quit)…. I am not easily discouraged, readily visualize myself as overcoming obstacles, winning out over setbacks, achieving "impossible" objectives.

Reflecting on his own self-realization, Lee later wrote in the early '70s about self-discovery and harnessing the powers within one in the screenplay for the *Silent Flute*:

When a man comes to a conscious vital realization of those great spiritual forces within himself and begins to use those forces in science, in business, and in life, his progress in the future will be unparalleled.

Self-Knowledge and Personal Expression

Lee said all types of knowledge ultimately mean self-knowledge. He realized in all learning, whether it is in the martial arts, academia, relationships or anything in life, the experience reveals more of one's being to one's self. In this way, one must be willing to learn from the challenges in life and how to adapt to attain success. Like Krishnamurti, Lee believed learning cannot be accomplished in isolation, but rather through relationships to people, ideas and events. So, although jeet kune do is a martial art, the learning process one cultivates is to be used in everyday life:

> *Self-knowledge is the basis of JKD because it is effective, not only for the individual's martial art, but also for his life as a human being.* [75]

> *To me, at least the way that I teach it, all types of knowledge ultimately means self-knowledge. So, therefore they're coming in [other actors] and asking me to teach them not so much how to defend themselves or how to do somebody in. Rather, they want to learn to express themselves through some movement, be it anger, be it determination or whatever. So, in other words, they're paying me to show them, in combative form, the art of expressing the human body.* [76]

> *To know oneself is to study oneself in action with another person.*

> *Learning is definitely not mere imitation or the ability to accumulate and conform to fixed knowledge. Learning is a constant process of discovery and never a concluding one. In JKD we begin not by accumulation but by discovering the cause of our ignorance, and oftentimes this involves a shedding process.... Truth will not come until we have come to understand personally the whole process of the working of our being. After all, ultimately, knowledge in martial art simply means self-knowledge, and JKD can become intelligible only in the vigorous and constant process of self-inquiry and self-discovery.*

One must be free to express one's self honestly, whether it be in martial arts or acting. The truly great painters and sculptors of the past had a vision in their souls and it was reflected in their works of art. Despite the political pressure they may have experienced, their patrons' intentions or the beliefs of their contemporary artists, the true masters expressed themselves on the canvas or marble. Lee expressed himself in physical form and he realized the need to be devoid of styles or systems in order to have the complete freedom truly to express himself:

---

[75] Ibid. p. 208.

[76] Excerpt from *The Pierre Berton Show*, "Bruce Lee: The 'Lost' Interview." 1971.

I do not believe in styles anymore. I do not believe that there is such a thing as "the Chinese way of fighting" or "the Japanese way of fighting," or any other "way of fighting," because unless a human being has three arms and four legs, there can be no different form of fighting. Basically, we have only two hands and two feet. Styles tend to separate men, because they have their own doctrines, and the doctrine became the gospel truth that you cannot change! But, if you do not have styles, if you just say, "Here I am as a human being, how can I express myself totally and completely?"—that way, you won't have a style, because style is a crystallization. This approach [means] continuing growth.... To me, ultimately, martial art means honestly expressing yourself. [77]

When I look around, I always learn something and that is to be always yourself. And to express yourself. To have faith in yourself. Do not go out and look for a successful personality and duplicate it.... Start from the very root of [your] being, which is "how can I be me?" [78]

As a result, Lee had a personal approach for individual growth:

Research Your Own Experience
Absorb What is Useful
Reject What is Useless
Add What is Specifically Your Own

Contemporary Western Thinking

Whereas Lee's philosophy was a melding of Eastern and Western thought, Ted Wong liked to refer to JKD as contemporary Western thinking. While Lee began his search for truth in martial arts with the Chinese classical philosophies such as Taoism and Zen, he took the extra steps to open up his thinking extensively to many different philosophers. The very fact that Lee was willing to look "outside the box" and not be bound by tradition followed the practical approach of the Western world. For Lee, jeet kune do was nonclassical, not traditional, so its approach was contemporary.

---

[77] Ibid.

[78] Ted Thomas audio interview with Bruce Lee, part 2, 1971.

Lee also realized he possessed unique physical capabilities that many of his students did not. Jeet kune do, as Lee performed it, is not for everyone because the average person simply does not possess the skills and has not invested the amount of training Lee had. Therefore, Lee encouraged his students to find what worked best for them, exploiting and capitalizing on their strengths in their training. This was a nonclassical approach to gung fu, as opposed to the rigid style or system that insisted its followers fit a mold.

Lee and Wong

The Responsibility of a Teacher

Enter the Dragon

"A good teacher protects his pupils from his own influence." [79]

When considering his role as a teacher, Lee taught that he was merely a "pointer of the truth" instead of a giver of truth. As he taught the young man in that early scene from *Enter the Dragon*: "Like a finger pointing a way to the moon. Don't concentrate on the finger or you will miss all that heavenly glory."

Lee realized students often came for training because they were looking for something they were missing. However, the systematic approach to standardized teaching would only serve to make students conform rather than pinpoint the personal need.

Unfortunately, most of the students in martial art are conformers. The student seldom learns to depend upon himself for expression. Instead, he faithfully or blindly follows an instructor, the authority figure, and his instructor's imposed pattern. That way, the student feels he is no longer alone and finds security in mass imitation. However, what is nurtured is the dependent mind rather than independent inquiry, which is so essential to genuine understanding. So through daily conditioning a student will probably be skilled according to a pattern, however, he will not come to understand himself. [80]

---

[79] Lee, Bruce. *Bruce Lee: My Martial Arts Training Guide—Jeet Kune Do*. London: Universal-Tandem Publishing, 1974.

[80] Ibid.

Lee understood that teaching was highly specialized and lessons must be customized to the needs of each unique student: "There is no fixed teaching. All I can provide is an appropriate medicine for a particular ailment." [81]

Lee also realized the teacher must be careful not to instill all of his personal preferences on the student, so that, ultimately, the student must determine what will work for him:

A teacher, a really good teacher, is never a giver of truth; he is a guide, a pointer to truth. Therefore, a good teacher, or, more appropriately, a guide, studies each student individually and helps to awaken the student to explore himself, both internally and externally, and ultimately to integrate himself with his being…. All in all, a teacher acts as a catalyst, and not only must he have a tremendous understanding; he must also possess a sensitive mind with great flexibility and adaptability.

While Bruce was in Hong Kong, extremely busy dubbing one of his films, he expressed the culmination of his thoughts on martial arts in a letter to an individual named John who was interested in learning jeet kune do:

…I'm willing—when time permits—to honestly express or "to open myself" to you, to act as a sort of sign pole for a traveler.

My experience will help, but I insist and maintain that art—true art that is—cannot be handed out. Furthermore, art is never decoration or embellishment. Instead it is a constant process of maturing (in the sense of NOT arrived!).

You see, John, when we have the opportunity of working out, you'll see that your way of thinking is definitely not the same as mine. Art, after all, is a means of acquiring "personal" liberty. Your way is not my way nor mine yours.

So whether or not we can get together, remember well that art "LIVES" where absolute freedom is. With all the training thrown to nowhere, with a mind (if there is such a verbal substance) perfectly unaware of its own working, with the "self" vanishing nowhere the art of JKD attains its perfection.

[81] *Tao of Jeet Kune Do.* p. 9.

Motivation

"Knowing is not enough; we must apply. Willing is not enough, we must do."
—*Johann Wolfgang von Goethe (1749–1832)*

Lee was inspired by this quote from Goethe, a 19th-century German writer, artist and politician, considered among the most important thinkers in Western culture. Not only must we think great thoughts, but we have the duty to take action. Lee encountered many challenges in life, yet he was not beaten down by them; instead, he adapted himself or his circumstances to come out on top. Much of Lee's success can be attributed to his positive outlook on life, turning challenges into stepping stones instead of letting them bog him down.

From the Perry Lee Collection

Captain of My Mind

Lee recognized his thoughts and reactions to challenges in life had a profound effect on what happened to him:

The aphorism "as a man thinketh in his heart, so is he" contains the secret of life. James Allen further added, "A man is literally what he thinks." This might be a shocking statement, but everything is a state of mind.

I've always been buffeted by circumstances because I thought of myself as a human being of outside condition. Now I realize that I am the power that commands the feeling of my mind and from which circumstances grow.

Pessimism blunts the tools you need to succeed. Optimism is a faith that leads to success. [82]

---

[82] *Bruce Lee: My Martial Arts Training Guide—Jeet Kune Do.*

Several 20th-century self-help books and their authors had an influence on Lee, including Napoleon Hill's *Think and Grow Rich*, Napoleon Hill and W. Clement Stone's *Success Through a Positive Mental Attitude*, Norman Vincent Peale's *The Power of Positive Thinking* and Dale Carnegie's *How to Win Friends and Influence People*. Lee used the daily affirmations these authors advocated to reinforce a positive approach to living. Lee wrote the following in his 1967–1972 day-planners:

- *Willpower: Recognizing that the power of will is the supreme court over all other departments of my mind. I will exercise it daily when I need the urge to action for any purpose; and I will form habits designed to bring the powers of my will into action at least once daily.*
- *Emotions: Realizing that my emotions are both positive and negative, I will form daily habits which will encourage the development of the positive emotions and aid me in converting the negative emotions into some form of useful action.*
- *Reason: Recognizing that both my positive and negative emotions may be dangerous if they are not controlled and guided to desirable ends, I will submit all my desires, aims, and purposes to my faculty of reason, and I will be guided by it in giving expression to these.*
- *Imagination: Recognizing the need for sound plans and ideas for the attainment of my desires, I will develop my imagination by calling upon it daily for help in the formation of my plans.*
- *Memory: Recognizing the value of an alert mind and an alert memory, I will encourage mine to become alert by taking care to impress it clearly with all thoughts I wish to recall and by associating those thoughts with related subjects which I may call to mind frequently.*
- *Subconscious Mind: Recognizing the influence of my subconscious mind over my power of will, I shall take care to submit to it a clear and definite picture of my major purpose in life and all minor purposes leading to my major purpose, and I shall keep this picture constantly before my subconscious mind by repeating it daily!*
- *Conscience: Recognizing that my emotions often err in their over-enthusiasm, and my faculty of reason often is without the warmth of feeling that is necessary to enable me to combine justice with mercy in my judgments, I will encourage my conscience to guide me as to what is right and what is wrong, but I will never set aside the verdicts it renders, no matter what may be the cost of carrying them out.*

He Who Thinks He Can

Lee recognized one's state of mind is everything, and it will yield either great success or tremendous failure based on one's outlook, belief in self and determination, along with the action or lack of action that results:

Defeat is a state of mind

Defeat is also a state of mind; no one is ever defeated until defeat has been accepted as reality. To me, defeat in anything is merely temporary, and its punishment is but an urge for me to greater effort to achieve my goal. Defeat simply tells me that something is wrong in my doing; it is a path leading to success and truth.

Negative thoughts are overpowering only if you encourage them and allow yourself to be overpowered by them.

It's not the obstacle—but your reaction to it.

Believe me that in every big thing or achievement there are always obstacles, big or small, and the reaction that one shows to such obstacles is what counts, not the obstacle itself. There is no such thing as defeat until you admit so yourself—but not until then!

I can if I think I can

Thus thoughts are things, in a sense that thought can be translated into its physical equivalent. I begin to appreciate now the old saying "he can because he thinks he can." I believe that anybody can think himself into his goal if he mixes thought with definiteness of purpose, persistence, and a burning desire for its translation into reality.

If you think you are beaten, you are,
If you think you dare not, you don't.
If you like to win, but you think you can't,
It is almost certain you won't.

If you think you will lose, you are lost.
For out of the world we find,
Success begins with a fellow's will---
It's all in the state of mind.

If you think you are outclassed, you are,
You've got to think high to rise,
You've got to be sure of yourself before
You can ever win a prize.

Life's battles don't always go to
The stronger or faster man,
But sooner or later the man
Who wins is the man
Who thinks he can!

This poem, thought to have been published for the first time in 1905 by the Unity Tract Society under the title "Thinking," is widely referred to today as "The Man Who Thinks He Can." It is attributed to late-19th century poet Walter Wintle.

Reflecting on his back injury in 1970, which was a major setback, Lee refused to give in to a defeatist attitude, but rather used the incident to motivate himself. The only true help he needed would ultimately only come from within:

So, action! Action! Never wasting energy on worries and negative thoughts. I mean who has the most insecure job as I have? What do I live on? My faith in my ability that I'll make it. Sure my back screwed me up good for a year but with every adversity comes a blessing because a shock acts as a reminder to oneself that we must not get stale in routine. Look at a rain storm; after its departure everything grows!

Your mental attitude determines what you make of it, as steppingstone or stumbling block.

Having gone through a lot of these ups and downs, I realize that there is no help but self-help. Self-help comes in many forms: daily discoveries through choiceless observation, honesty, as we always wholeheartedly do our best, a sort of indomitable, obsessive dedication and, above all, to realize that there is no end or limit to this, because life is simply an ever-going process.

Notes on Motivation

Most touching are Lee's letters to close friends when they were suffering challenges in their lives. His words were uplifting and raised the spirits of these men. In multiple letters, he gives encouraging words to his good friend Jhoon Rhee and even pens poetry to motivate him:

In conclusion, may I warn you that negativeness very often unknowingly creeps up upon us. It helps occasionally to stop all thoughts (the chattering of worries, anticipations, etc. in your head) and then once more refreshingly march bravely on.

So remember that one who is possessed by worry not only lacks the poise to solve his own problems, but by his nervousness and irritability creates additional problems for those around him. Well, what can I say but damn the torpedo, full speed ahead!

Anyway, I just want to let you know how things are, and also I like you to know that the 1969 Nationals was a steppingstone and not a stumbling block. Your mental attitude determines what you make of it, as stepping or stumbling block. Remember, no man is really defeated unless he is discouraged…. What you HABITUALLY THINK largely determines what you will ultimately become. Remember success is a journey, not a destination.

WHO AM I?

Who am I?
That is the age-old question
Asked by every man
At one time or another.
Though he looks into a mirror
And recognizes the face,
Though he knows his own name
And age and history,
Still he wonders, deep down,
Who am I?

Am I a giant among men,
Master of all I survey,
Or an ineffectual pygmy
Who clumsily blocks his own way?
Am I the self-assured gentleman
With a winning style,
The natural born leader
Who makes friends instantly,
Or the frightened heart
Tiptoeing among strangers,
Who behind a frozen smile, trembles
Like a little boy lost in a dark forest?
Most of us yearn to be one,
But fear we are the other.

Yet we CAN be
What we aspire to be.
Those who cultivate
Their natural instincts,
Who set their sights
On the good, the admirable, the
excellent,
And believe they can achieve it
Will find their confidence rewarded.
And, in the process,
They will discover the true identity
Of him who looks back from the mirror.

WHICH ARE YOU?

The doubters said,
"Man cannot fly,"
The doers said,
"Maybe, but we'll try,"
And finally soared
Into the morning's glow.
While non-believers
Watched from below.

The doubters claimed
The world was flat,
Ships plunged over its edge.
And that was that!
Yet a brand new world
Some doers found,
And returned to prove
This planet round.

The doubters knew
'Twas fact, "Of course,
No noisy gadget
Would e'er replace the horse."
Yet the carriages
Of doers, san equine,
Came to traverse
All our roads in time.

But those who kept saying
"It can't be done,"
Never are the victories
Of the honors won;
But, rather,
By the believing, doing kind,
While the doubters
Watched from far behind.

In a letter to Kimura, Lee consoles his dear student and close friend, who was going through a difficult time in his life:

> *In life there are pluses and the minuses, and it is time for you to concentrate on the pluses. It might be difficult but fortunately for us human beings, we have self-will. Well, it is time to employ it.*
>
> *Life is an ever-flowing process and somewhere on the path some unpleasant things will pop up—it might leave a scar, but then life is flowing on and like running water, when it stops, it grows stale. Go bravely on, my friend, because each experience teaches us a lesson….*

"Walk On"

After *The Green Hornet* was canceled, Lee received only small acting parts in television shows and movies, mostly through connections with friends and students. This time was tough on Lee, but he did his best to support his family. Hollywood was simply not ready for a leading Asian actor. Life seemed even more harrowing when Lee suffered his back injury and the doctors thought he would be lucky if he ever walked normally again. Lee 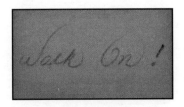 took one of his business cards, wrote "Walk On!" on the back of it, and placed it on a stand that sat on his desk. This card served to remind Lee that despite his circumstances, he would continue to keep a positive outlook, believe in himself and have the determination and courage to continue moving forward.

CHAPTER 8

The JKD Legacy

To understand jeet kune do, and why it is so difficult to understand, we may compare it to Tao or Zen. According to Alan Watts, one of the leading authors on Tao and Zen, the challenge of grasping Tao is "we have been trying to fit the order of the universe to the order of words." Watts continues, "The real basis of Buddhism is not a set of ideas but an experience" and that is "equally true of Taoism, which recognized that experience is altogether something different from words." [83]

Watts explained further in his treatise on Zen: "Books by their very nature are intellectual, and the understanding of Zen is intuitive. What is the difference between intellectual and intuitive understanding? When you talk about these deep matters, people often say, 'I understand what you're saying intellectually, but I don't really feel it.'" [84]

What Watts writes about Tao could be the very reason jeet kune do is so difficult to understand. When approached intellectually, it becomes difficult to reconcile those things that may appear contradictory. Lee expressed his philosophy not only in his words, but also infused it in his actions. His movements have been described as "philosophy in motion." Lee's students may have found it difficult to explain that which is unexplainable. Ted Wong recalled it took him almost 15 years following Lee's death before he felt he truly understood the art and what Lee was communicating. Allen Joe said, "It took me years to understand his philosophy of life." And Taky Kimura commented, "Bruce was able to see all the other parts of the martial arts, see what you were doing and extrapolating the good from the bad—that's how discerning he was."

---

[83] Watts, Alan. *What Is Tao?* Novato, CA: New World Library, 2000. p. 59.

[84] Watts, Alan. *What Is Zen?* Novato, CA: New World Library, 2000. p. 99.

The Perfect Storm

One might conclude that Lee was destined to create jeet kune do—that it was the logical culmination of his life experience combined with his drive and determination; his experiences were like the elements of a perfect storm coming together. Lee had to love martial arts, receive formal training in wing chun gung fu, be exposed to fencing through his brother and Western boxing in high school. He had to move to the United States and become part of the melting pot that is America, which fostered the freedom to look outside the box and not be bound by tradition.

Lee was an experienced performer, having appeared in 20 films before he was an adult. Next, he was given the opportunity to express himself through martial arts, first by demonstrating at fairs in Seattle, then at the 1964 International Karate Championships where he was discovered and led back to acting, first on the small screen in *The Green Hornet*, then back to the big screen in Hong Kong, and finally back to America and a worldwide audience through *Enter the Dragon*. This progression allowed him to prepare himself for an ever-growing audience. Last, Lee had the looks, charisma and determination to see his plan come to fruition, and he single-handedly created the martial arts movie genre in America by importing it from Hong Kong.

 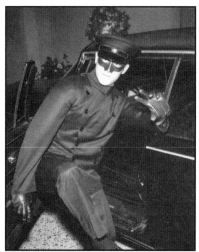 

Lee was constantly expressing and communicating his message, whether it was in a term paper at the University of Washington, lecturing to high school students in a philosophy class, teaching his martial arts students, writing for *Black Belt* magazine, publishing his *Chinese Gung Fu: The Philosophical Art of Self-Defense*, or penning his *Commentaries on the Martial Way* (which was compiled and published as the *Tao of Jeet Kune Do* after his death). Through acting, he could reach out to the masses: explaining jeet kune do on the *Longstreet* television series, then demonstrating adaptability in films during his fights with Kareem Abdul-Jabbar in the *Game of Death* and with Chuck Norris in *The Way of the Dragon* (aka *Return of the Dragon*), then expressing the highest skill in martial arts as "It hits all by itself" in *Enter the Dragon*.

Jeet Kune Do: Occurring Throughout Lee's Life

Although Lee gave his personal expression in martial arts a name in 1967, it had been evolving within him throughout his life. Not to be contained within one system, Lee experimented with different styles of gung fu early in his training. Later, he learned more about martial arts from around the world, such as judo and karate, extracting their strengths and weaknesses. By the time he landed in Los Angeles, his life experiences and research into combative arts, along with his application of science, brought his complete approach to martial arts to fruition. Yet as this approach began to take shape, Lee continued to profess to "be formless, like water" and adapt to "what is."

As Ted Wong said:

> *Jun Fan jeet kune do really is Bruce Lee's lifetime of work and research, and his journey into his own martial art during his lifetime. From the beginning to the end, how he evolved into the*

term he called jeet kune do. But jeet kune do, I think, is just a process of his way of thinking, the research into the martial art, the fighting art…. Jeet kune do [is] from the very beginning, just that his process involved an evolution. Toward the end, he thought that he was so different from the origin, the classical martial art. That's why he decided to give the name jeet kune do. So jeet kune do is really Bruce Lee's lifetime work during his lifetime, his research into his martial arts.

By gaining self-knowledge through martial arts, Lee better understood his strengths and weaknesses. He studied science on his own, thereby gaining another level of self-sufficiency. Ultimately, he gained the confidence and courage to go out on his own, discovering the truth for himself and flowing with "what is." As a result, jeet kune do was not simply a combination or amalgamation of wing chun, boxing and fencing. Lee transcended systems to make it fit him.

According to Wong, the foundation of jeet kune do comprises the combination of its philosophical principles and the physical art, the two halves of one whole. But just like yin and yang, "the philosophical principles are incorporated into the physical art." Using the analogy of building a building, Wong considered the philosophical principles as the "nuts and bolts" of a system, connecting the beams that form the overall structure of the art. The philosophical principles are like a road map, as Wong liked to say, "keeping one in the direction that he would not be lost, telling you where to go." Lee laid out a general map of his personal journey; today, it serves as a guide for others to follow or use as a reference.

Jeet Kune Do: Not Simply a New Style

Lee made it perfectly clear that he did not create a new style, as that would just create another segment of totality, continuing to restrict one to a single way of doing something, and therefore, limiting one's capacity. Defining JKD simply as Bruce Lee's style of fighting is completely to lose its message: "Actually, I never wanted to give a name to the kind of Chinese gung fu that I have invented, but for convenience sake, I still call it jeet kune do. However, I want to emphasize that there is no clear line of distinction between jeet kune do and any other kind of gung fu, for I strongly object to formality and to the idea of distinction of branches."

Lee emphasized in his landmark article in *Black Belt* magazine in 1971, "Liberate Yourself from Classical

Karate," that styles were "merely parts dissected from a unitary whole" and he urged martial artists objectively to seek the truth in combat while on their path to self-discovery. Lee urged readers not to accept prescribed formulas and to be free from the bondage of any style's doctrine, which he referred to as "organized despair." [85]

Eventually, Lee regretted naming his art, fearing his followers would misinterpret his way as the only way to truth in martial arts: "If people say that jeet kune do is different from 'this' or 'that,' then let the name of jeet kune do be wiped out, for that is what it is, just a name."

Unifying Martial Artists

Ultimately, Lee wanted to unify all martial arts (and humans) by not being bound to styles or traditions. Wong commented:

His intention was not just to promote martial arts, but promote martial arts as a peaceful co-existence between different factions of martial arts. He said that martial arts, basically, because of different styles, separate people. You know, different styles say, "I am better than you" or whatever. They are always competing against one another. "My technique is better than your technique." So [there is] always a lot of conflict, a lot of disagreement. I think Bruce Lee's intention was that you should work together peacefully. In fact, he said, "Under the sky, under the sun, there is but one family." He also felt the discrimination throughout his lifetime as a kid, grew up in Hong Kong, invaded by the Japanese. Hong Kong was a colony, controlled by the British. When he came to Hollywood, he also experienced the discrimination. So his intention was, "How can I, through martial arts or his philosophy, bring people together?" I think [we must try] to understand Bruce Lee, not just Bruce Lee as a martial artist, but also as a humanitarian and also a good cause to bring people together.

A large part of this conflict exists in the duality of "for" and "against." Lee looked to the principle of yin and yang to bring about the "oneness" of things, eliminating the duality and conflict. Lee wrote:

Please do not be concerned with soft versus firm, kicking versus striking, grappling versus hitting and

---

[85] Lee, Bruce. "Liberate Yourself from Classical Karate," *Black Belt* magazine, September 1971, p. 27. Reprinted here in Appendix A.

kicking, long-range fighting versus in-fighting. There is no such thing as "this" is better than "that." Should there be one thing we must guard against, let it be partiality that robs us of our pristine wholeness and makes us lose unity in the midst of duality. [86]

The perfect way is only difficult for those who pick and choose. Do not like, do not dislike; all will then be clear. Make a hairbreadth difference and heaven and earth are set apart; if you want the truth to stand clear before you, never be for or against. The struggle between "for" and "against" is the mind's worst disease. [87]

Freedom from knowing is death; then you are living. Die inwardly of "pro" and "con." There is no such thing as doing right or wrong when there is freedom. [88]

"To desire" is an attachment. "To desire not to desire" is also an attachment. To be unattached then, means to be free at once from both statements, positive and negative. This is to be simultaneously both "yes" and "no," which is intellectually absurd. However, not so in Zen. [89]

Bruce Lee with Ed Parker, James Yimm Lee and Ralph Castro

Bruce Lee, Joe Lewis and Ed Parker

Bruce Lee and Kareem Abdul-Jabbar

---

[86] *Tao of Jeet Kune Do.* p. 23.

[87] Ibid. p. 8.

[88] Ibid. p. 16.

[89] Ibid. p. 201.

Applying Jeet Kune Do to Life

During a phone conversation, when Dan Lee commented about Bruce having shown maturity, Bruce clarified: "Not maturity! There is no such word as 'maturity'—maturing. Because when there is a maturity, there is a conclusion and a cessation. That's the end. That's when the coffin is closed. You might be deteriorating physically in the long process of aging, but in your discovery, daily, it's an ever ongoing process."

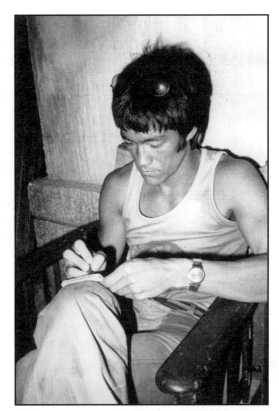

When Alex Block interviewed Bruce and asked the meaning of the martial artist's assertion that man, as a creative individual, is more important than any established style or system, Bruce answered by saying, "Man is always in a learning process, whereas style is a concluded, established, solidified something. You cannot do that, because you learn every day as you go on." [90]

Bruce Lee emphasized, with life as our teacher, we are in a constant process of discovery and learning, a process without an end. And that is why he argued against styles, since they start from a conclusion:

> My purpose in creating jeet kune do was not to compare with other branches of martial arts. Anything that becomes a branch would induce bad feeling. Once there is a formation of a branch, then things seem to stop. Students would labor for regulations and rules. Then the meaning of martial art would be lost. Even today, I dare not say that I have reached any state of achievement. I'm still learning, for learning is boundless.

> If you have mastered a system of gung fu, after you have mastered it, you have to let go of it and head for a higher level. Do not hold to what you have. It is like a ferry boat for people who want to get across waters. Once you have got across, never bear it on your back. You should head forward.

In another phone conversation, Dan Lee pointed out to Bruce that he was approaching these ideals by using the phrases "Using No Way as Way; Having No Limitation as Limitation." Bruce replied, "Yeah, that's the most important thing, man. And because when there is a way, man, therein lies the limitation."

---

[90] Block, Alex Ben. Audio interview with Bruce Lee, 1972.

Linda summarizes Bruce's perspective on not being limited in dealing with "what is" as follows:

The basic thing in this art is learning about yourself. One way you learn about yourself is through relation with another, and fighting is certainly a relation with another: sparring, working out, practicing, or actual fighting, you are always learning about yourself so you can defeat your opponent. Your opponent might be a person or it might be something standing in your path, something blocking you from what you want to do. So you are working in a relationship with this person or this thing, and learning more about yourself as you do, and then you are actualizing what you are learning. And this is what Bruce would always say about JKD, it is a process of self-actualization. He was always in the process of becoming this person or this actualization; it is something you never attain; you are always working toward it. No matter how long you study or how old you are, you are always working toward it and learning more about yourself and then being able to actualize it. So, in just a few words, that's what JKD meant to Bruce…. When you are in a fight, you must respond to what is coming at you, you have to experience the "what is," he would say, what is happening at that time…. You just need to react to what is happening right now. So think about that in terms of living your life; it is the same thing. We all go through situations in our lives where we need to respond, react, or accept what is happening and our lives are always changing, always evolving because there are external forces and things that happen to us that we cannot control. And the "what

is," the "what is happening," and you have to have the philosophical basis, the force within you that allows you to handle situations as they go along.

Last, as Lee gained more self-knowledge, he became self-reliant and self-sufficient. He discovered the power and knowledge that come from within, that can be applied to martial arts, but, most important, to life:

Jeet kune do, ultimately, is not a matter of petty technique but of highly developed personal spirituality and physique. It is not a question of developing what has already been developed but of recovering what has been left behind. These things have been with us, in us, all the time and have never been lost or distorted except by our misguided manipulation of them. JKD is not a matter of technology but of spiritual insight and training. [91]

I wish neither to possess,
Nor to be possessed.
I no longer covet paradise,
More important, I no longer fear hell.

The medicine for my suffering
I had within me from the very beginning,
But I did not take it.
My ailment came from within myself,
But I did not observe it
Until this moment.

Now I see that I will never find the light
Unless, like the candle, I am my own fuel,
Consuming myself. [92]

A Final Thought

Although you have now reached the end of this book, it is the beginning of the journey that is the rest of your life. It is hoped that Lee's life example in the martial arts, which were so dear to him, can be an inspiration for you in your pursuits in life. Lee's life serves as the definitive case study of jeet kune do. Not only did events during his lifetime chronicle its development, but Lee's personality, his thought process, his very essence and spirit are reflected in his art.

Here is where the next chapter of your journey begins: where you, the reader, continue your personal journey of martial arts or life in general. You may have already been heavily influenced by Lee and his writings on JKD, but eventually you will find your own path, one that will take shape as you become better aware of yourself, gaining confidence and becoming self-sufficient in dealing with "what is." You will discover the talents within and use them to guide you on your path of excellence. Remember, you are the captain of your own mind and of your own life, navigating the storms and successes in life. Walk on!

[91] *Tao of Jeet Kune Do.* p. 200.

[92] Lee, Bruce. From original script for *The Silent Flute*, 1969.

截拳道

Chinese characters for jeet kune do
drawn by Professor Dan Lee

Appendix A

Liberate Yourself From Classical Karate

By Bruce Lee

Reprinted from the September 1971 issue of *Black Belt* magazine

WHAT IS *JEET KUNE DO?* I am the first to admit that any attempt to crystalize jeet kune do into a written article is no easy task. Perhaps to avoid making a *thing* out of a *process,* I have not until now personally written an article on JKD. Indeed, it is difficult to explain what jeet kune do is, although it may be easier to explain what it is *not.*

Let me begin with a Zen story. The story might be familiar to some, but I repeat it for its appropriateness. Look upon this story as a means of limbering up one's senses, one's attitude and one's mind to make them pliable and receptive. You need that to understand this article, otherwise you might as well forget reading any farther.

> A learned man once went to a Zen teacher to inquire about Zen. As the Zen teacher explained, the learned man would frequently interrupt him with remarks like, "Oh, yes, we have that too..." and so on.
>
> Finally, the Zen teacher stopped talking and began to serve tea to the learned man. He poured the cup full, then kept pouring until the cup overflowed.
>
> "Enough!" the learned man once more interrupted. "No more can go into the cup!"
>
> "Indeed, I see," answered the Zen teacher. "If you do not first empty your cup, how can you taste my cup of tea?"

I hope my comrades in the martial arts will read the following paragraphs with openmindedness, leaving all the burdens of preconceived opinions and conclusion behind. This act, by the way, has in itself a liberating power. After all, the usefulness of the cup is in its emptiness.

Make this article relate to yourself because, though it is on JKD, it is primarily concerned with the blossoming of a martial artist—not a "Chinese" martial artist or a "Japanese" martial artist. A martial artist is a human being first. Just as nationalities have nothing to do with one's humanity, so they have nothing to do with the martial arts. Leave your protective shell of isolation and relate *directly* to what is being said. Return to your senses by ceasing all the intervening intellectual mumbo jumbo. Remember that life is a constant process of relating. Remember, too, that I seek neither your approval nor to influence you toward my way of thinking. I will be more than satisfied if, as a result of this article, you begin to investigate everything for yourself and cease to uncritically accept prescribed formulas that dictate "this is this" and "that is that."

On Choiceless Observation

Suppose several persons who are trained in different styles of combative arts witness an all-out street fight. I am sure we would hear different versions from each of these stylists. Such variations are quite understandable, for one cannot see a fight (or anything else) "as is" as long as he is blinded by his chosen point of view, i.e. style, and he will view the fight through the lens of his particular conditioning. Fighting, "as is," is simple and total. It is not limited to your perspective or conditioning as a Chinese martial artist, a Korean martial artist, or a "whatever" martial artist. True observation begins when one sheds set patterns, and true freedom of expression occurs when one is beyond systems.

Before we examine jeet kune do, let's consider exactly what a "classical" martial art style really is. To begin with, we must recognize the incontrovertible fact that regardless of their many colorful origins (by a wise, mysterious monk, by a special messenger in a dream, or in a holy revelation, etc.) styles are created by men. A style should never be considered gospel truth, the laws and principles of which can never be violated. Man, the living, creating individual, is always more important than any established style.

It is conceivable that a long time ago a certain martial artist discovered some partial truth. During his lifetime, the man resisted the temptation to organize this partial truth, although this is a common tendency in man's search for security and certainty in life. After his death, his students took "his" hypothesis, "his" postulates, "his" inclination, and "his" method and turned them into law. Impressive creeds were then invented, solemn reinforcing ceremonies prescribed, rigid philosophy and patterns formulated, and so on, until finally an institution was erected. So what originated as one man's intuition of some sort of personal fluidity was transformed into solidified, fixed knowledge, complete with organized, classified responses presented in a logical order. In so doing, the well-meaning, loyal followers not only made this knowledge a holy shrine but also a tomb in which they buried the founder's wisdom.

But the distortion did not necessarily end here. In reaction to "the other's truth," another martial artist, or possibly a dissatisfied disciple, organized an opposite approach—such as the "soft" style versus the "hard" style, the "internal" school versus the "external" school, and all these separative nonsenses. Soon this opposite faction also became a large organization, with its own laws and patterns. A rivalry began, with each style claiming to possess the "truth" to the exclusion of all others.

At best, styles are merely parts dissected from a unitary whole. All styles require adjustment, partiality, denials, condemnation and a lot of self-justification. The solutions they purport to provide are the very cause of the problem because they limit and interfere with our natural growth and obstruct the way to genuine understanding. Divisive by nature, styles keep men *apart* from each other rather than unite them.

Truth Cannot Be Structured or Confined

One cannot express himself fully when imprisoned by a confining style. Combat "as is" is total, and it includes all the "is" as well as the "is not," without favorite lines or angles. Lacking boundaries, combat is always fresh, alive and constantly changing. Your particular style, your personal inclinations and your physical makeup are all *parts* of combat, but they do not constitute the *whole* of combat. Should your responses become dependent upon any single part, you will react in terms of what "should be," rather than to the reality of the ever-changing "what is." Remember that while the whole is evidenced in all its parts, an isolated part, efficient or not, does not constitute the whole.

Prolonged repetitious drillings will certainly yield mechanical precision and security of the kind that comes from any routine. However, it is exactly this kind of "selective" security or "crutch" which limits or blocks the total growth of a martial artist. In fact, quite a few practitioners develop such a liking for and dependence on their "crutch" that they can no longer walk without it. Thus, any one special technique, however cleverly designed, is actually a hindrance.

Let it be understood once and for all that I have *not* invented a new style, composite or modification. I have in no way set jeet kune do within a distinct form governed by laws that distinguish it from "this" style or "that" method. On the contrary, I hope to free my comrades from bondage to styles, patterns and doctrines.

What, then, is jeet kune do? Literally, "jeet" means to intercept or to stop; "kune" is the fist; and "do" is the way, the ultimate reality—the way of the intercepting fist. Do remember, however, that "jeet kune do" is merely a convenient name. I am not interested with the term itself; I am interested in its effect of liberation when JKD is used as a mirror for self-examination.

Unlike a "classical" martial art, there is no series of rules or classification of technique that constitutes a distinct "jeet kune do" method of fighting. JKD is not a form of special conditioning with its own rigid philosophy. It looks at combat not from a single angle, but from all possible angles. While JKD utilizes all ways and means to serve its end (after all, efficiency is anything that scores), it is bound by none and is therefore free. In other words, JKD possesses everything but is in itself possessed by nothing.

Therefore, to attempt to define JKD in terms of a distinct style—be it *gung fu,* karate, street fighting, Bruce Lee's martial art, etc.—is to completely miss its meaning. Its teaching simply cannot be confined within a system. Since JKD is at once "this" and "not this," it neither opposes nor adheres to any style. To understand this fully, one must transcend from the duality of "for" and "against" into one organic unity which is without distinctions. Understanding of JKD is direct intuition of this unity.

There are no prearranged sets or "kata" in the teaching of JKD, nor are they necessary. Consider the subtle difference between "having no form" and having "no-form"; the first is ignorance, the second is transcendence. Through instinctive body feeling, each of us *knows* our own most efficient and dynamic manner of achieving effective leverage, balance in motion, economical use of energy, etc. Patterns, techniques or forms touch only the fringe of genuine understanding. The core of understanding lies in the individual mind, and until that is touched everything is uncertain and superficial. Truth cannot be perceived until we come to fully understand ourselves and our potentials. After all, *knowledge in the martial arts ultimately means self-knowledge.*

At this point you may ask, "How do I gain this knowledge?" That you will have to find out all by yourself. You must accept the fact that there is no help but self-help. For the same reason I cannot tell you how to "gain" freedom, since freedom exists within you, I cannot tell you how to "gain" self-knowledge. While I can tell you what *not* to do, I cannot tell you what you *should* do, since that would be confining you to a particular approach. Formulas can only inhibit freedom; externally dictated prescriptions only squelch creativity and assure mediocrity. Bear in mind that the freedom that accrues from self-knowledge cannot be acquired through strict adherence to a formula; we do not suddenly "become" free, we simply "are" free.

Learning is definitely not mere imitation, nor is it the ability to accumulate and regurgitate fixed knowledge. Learning is a constant process of discovery, a process without end. In JKD we begin not by accumulation but by discovering the cause of our ignorance, a discovery that involves a shedding process.

Unfortunately, most students in the martial arts are conformists. Instead of learning to depend on themselves for expression, they blindly follow their instructors, no longer feeling alone, and finding security in mass imitation. The product of this imitation is a dependent mind. Independent inquiry, which is essential to genuine understanding, is sacrificed. Look around the martial arts and witness the assortment of routine performers, trick artists, desensitized robots, glorifiers of the past and so on—all followers or exponents of organized despair.

How often are we told by different "sensei" or "masters" that the martial arts are life itself? But how many of them truly understand what they are saying? Life is a constant movement—rhythmic as well as random; life is constant change and not stagnation. Instead of choicelessly flowing with this process of change, many of these "masters," past and present, have built an illusion of fixed forms, rigidly subscribing to traditional concepts and techniques of the art, solidifying the ever-flowing, dissecting the totality.

The most pitiful sight is to see sincere students earnestly repeating those imitative drills, listening to their own screams and spiritual yells. In most cases, the means these "sensei" offer their students are so elaborate that the students must give tremendous attention to them, until gradually they lose sight of the end. They end up performing their methodical routines as a mere conditioned response, rather than *responding to* "what is." They no longer "listen" to circumstances; they "recite" their circumstances. These poor souls have unwittingly become trapped in the miasma of classical martial arts training.

A teacher, a really good sensei, is never a *giver* of "truth"; he is a guide, a *pointer* to the truth that the student must discover for himself. A good teacher, therefore, studies each student individually and encourages the student to explore himself, both internally and externally, until, ultimately, the student is integrated with his being. For example, a skillful teacher might spur his student's growth by confronting him with certain frustrations. A good teacher is a catalyst. Besides possessing deep understanding, he must also have a responsive mind with great flexibility and sensitivity.

A Finger Pointing to the Moon

There is no standard in total combat, and expression must be free. This liberating truth is a reality only in so far as it is *experienced and lived* by the individual himself; it is a truth that transcends styles or disciplines. Remember, too, that jeet kune do is merely a term, a label to be used as a boat to get one across; once across, it is to be discarded and not carried on one's back.

These few paragraphs are, at best, a "finger pointing to the moon." Please do not take the finger to be the moon or fix your gaze so intently on the finger as to miss all the beautiful sights of heaven. After all, the usefulness of the finger is in pointing away from itself to the light which illumines finger and all.

Appendix B

The Bruce Lee Library

Linda recalls Bruce started his collection of books while in Seattle. As time passed, the library continued to grow. In fact, it is estimated to contain approximately 2,500 books on a variety of subjects.

Bruce was a tremendous reader, Linda says, and he researched all types of combative arts, as well as physical training and science. For example, although there was a limited amount of information about nutrition at the time, he read what was available and applied it to his routine, adding protein shakes to his diet. According to Ted Wong, Bruce Lee was really a self-made man in that much of what he accomplished in his life was a result of his hard work and determination to achieve his goals. A large part of that success came from continuously researching diverse fields of study and discovering ways he could better himself. This appendix describes the types of books Lee had in his library.

Chinese Martial Arts

Lee believed many of the classical *gung fu* styles and prominent masters had developed valuable techniques and training methods, and he wanted to explore what these arts offered. There were just a few English-language books available about Chinese gung fu, such as those by James Lee, but there was a bounty of books available in Chinese. Bruce Lee periodically traveled to Vancouver, Canada (where there has always been a large Chinese community), and bought Chinese-language books about various gung fu styles. Many were about *tai chi*. He wanted to read about internal styles, which he knew less about than the external styles.

Boxing

According to Ted Wong, Lee looked into boxing, "because it is the most scientific out there." Amassing an impressive collection of approximately 300 books on boxing, including many rare books from the 1800s, Lee gained tremendous knowledge about boxing's history and methodology.

Lee also had a collection of many boxing matches on film so he could study their movements and tactics. Linda recalls, "He would watch boxing films in slow motion with a projector where he would turn the film frame by frame. He was very impressed by early boxers. He followed Muhammad Ali's career, studied his movements. He learned a lot about combative arts from studying boxing, although it was backward, because boxing is left lead and Bruce was right lead. He would put the film in his projector backward, so they would look like a right lead." By observing boxing in films in real-time, he was able to gather the timing of a perfect knockout, the slip and the counterattack.

Fencing

Although books on fencing were not as readily available in the United States when compared to boxing, Lee had 68 books on Western fencing and its methods. He used much of his knowledge gained from studying fencing to work on speed and tactics. Fencing is a refined art with a long, rich history. In fact, fencers played a role in the development of modern-day boxing in the 1800s. It can be said that boxing actually came largely from fencing. Lee looked very deeply into the strategies and tactics of fencing, helping him formulate his five ways of attack.

Wrestling and Grappling

Lee was one to research any and all martial arts. He had 63 books about wrestling alone, and he also had books about judo, *chin na* and *jujitsu*. Although he did not formalize it into his teaching, he expanded his research in the grappling arts and he experimented with it. Approaching unarmed combat openly and objectively, Lee communicated a total approach to fighting by showing in his films the fluid transition from kicking and punching to grappling by fitting in with his opponent and situation.

Philosophy

Lee read Western and Eastern philosophy. From the Western, he read Plato, David Hume, René Descartes, Thomas Aquinas. From the Eastern, he read much Chinese and Japanese philosophy, including such ancient classics as the *I Ching,* Lao Tzu's *Tao Te Ching,* the writings of Chuang Tzu, Sun Tzu's *The Art of War,* Miyamoto Musashi's *The Book of Five Rings,* and more contemporary books such as Eugen Herrigel's *Zen in the Art of Archery*, and many works by Alan Watts and Jiddu Krishnamurti, who brought the Taoist and Zen approaches to the masses in America.

From *The Art of War,* Lee learned the ancient art of war strategy, and he discovered some valuable lessons for personal combat. For instance, from Sun Tzu's saying "To subdue the enemy without fighting is the acme of skill," Lee promotes the art of fighting without fighting in an early scene in *Enter the Dragon.* He learns that a battle plan requires constant assessment and re-assessment to adjust so that victory is ensured and "to change with change is the changeless state." Sun Tzu wrote, "In the art of war there are no fixed rules. These can only be worked out according to circumstances." Lee inscribed next to this saying: "Art of no art."

One of Lee's favorite passages from Krishnamurti's *Think on These Things* dealt with the meaning of learning. Real learning, said Krishnamurti, means constantly learning, with no one special instructor teaching you. You let even the simplest things of life teach you. You don't need a guide or a guru. Essentially, life is your teacher. Lee's collection of books (22 of them by or about Krishnamurti) is a testament to Krishnamurti's writing.

Psychology

Lee read books by psychologist Carl Jung, who sought to help people work toward "wholeness" by establishing a healthy balance between the conscious and unconscious parts their personality. The premise that the unconscious mind plays a critical role in the development of the individual had an effect on Lee.

He was also inspired by Carl Rogers, one of the founders of the humanistic approach to psychology, which emphasized the inherent drive toward self-actualization and the ongoing process of personal development and learning. Rogers wrote that, "Life, at its best, is a flowing changing process in which nothing is fixed. … It is always in process of becoming." [93] Lee also read the works of Frederick "Fritz" Perls, one of the founders of Gestalt therapy, with its core being enhanced awareness of sensation, perception, bodily feelings, emotion and behavior in the present moment. Gestalt emphasized relationship, along with contact between the self, its environment and the other.

How-To Books (Self-Help and Positive Thinking)

Lee referenced James Allen, author of *As a Man Thinketh*, when writing that "everything is a state of mind." Allen (1864–1912) is considered by many as a pioneer of the self-help movement. Lee was also highly influenced by the writings of Dale Carnegie (*How to Win Friends and Influence People*), Napoleon Hill (*Think and Grow Rich*, *The Master-Key to Riches* and *Success Through a Positive Mental Attitude* with W. Clement Stone), Norman Vincent Peale (*The Power of Positive Thinking*), Maxwell Maltz (*Psycho-Cybernetics*) and Gyula Denes (*Change Your Life with Positive Action*). Lee used these books as positive motivation when navigating the various challenges he encountered in life. In light of his huge successes, one can easily conclude these books helped him to maintain his drive and his perseverance in achieving his goals, no matter how daunting attaining them appeared to be.

---

[93] Rogers, Carl. *On Becoming a Person*. New York, NY: Houghton Mifflin, 1961.

Science and Training

Lee liked to refer to his approach to martial arts as "scientific street fighting." He had a collection of approximately 140 books on physical fitness, kinesiology, physiology and weight training/bodybuilding. He sought out the various sciences to help him determine the optimum way to train his neural system or develop his body. By studying kinesiology and human movement, he delved into what is known today as biomechanics so he could find the most effective way to execute techniques. By applying physics, notably Newton's three laws (inertia, acceleration, reaction), Lee adjusted his stance and body positioning to acquire more speed and power in his techniques. As a result, he developed tremendous yet efficient force in his punches and kicks using proper body alignment.

Lee studied various athletic training manuals to find out how the body gains coordination and mastery of athletic pursuits as a result of different training methods. From books about physiology and workout methodology, he learned how practice trains the nervous system. Synapse theory purports that training stimulus and impulses create connections in the central nervous system that cultivate movement. In this way, agonist and antagonist muscles work together to execute a technique efficiently.

Lee also had many books about strength training and bodybuilding, including both weight training and isometrics. He also read the fitness magazines of the day, including *Strength & Health*, *Ironman*, *Muscle Builder*, *Mr. America*, *Muscular Development* and *Muscle Training Illustrated*. When he found an article that was particularly useful, he clipped it and saved it for future reference. Seeking knowledge from the past and present, as always, Lee bought a used copy of *Strength & How to Obtain It* by Eugen Sandow, published in 1897, from a second-hand bookstore.

Acting and Filmmaking

Recognizing his potential for a successful career in the movie industry, Lee continued to hone his craft by reading books about acting and filmmaking, amounting to around 200 books on the subject. Gathering books on these subjects continued even into 1973, after he was hugely successful in Hong Kong. For Lee, simply being successful was not enough; he wanted to get better and better at his craft, and he wanted his future projects to be of high quality.

If Lee had never moved to America, things might have been very different. It was his dependence on himself, instead of his *wing chun sifu* and seniors, and his intense thirst for knowledge and understanding that led to his radical growth and evolution in martial arts. As Ted Wong said, "Now, had Bruce Lee never come to America, stayed in Hong Kong, probably he would have been a wing chun man. So when I have said that jeet kune do is not an Oriental martial art, but a Western-influenced martial art, you better believe it." The knowledge that Lee gained from his 2,500 books had a huge influence on making him the person he was.

Appendix C

Biomechanics and the Evolution from Jun Fan to Jeet Kune Do

By M. Shorten, E. Pisciotta, J. Pisciotta

"The true science of martial arts means practicing them in such a way that they will be useful at any time, and to teach them in such a way that they will be useful in all things."
—Miyamoto Musashi

The name Bruce Lee has become synonymous with the martial arts. Many who hear his name think of him as a philosopher, while others may think of him as an actor. In this chapter, we hope to demonstrate that Lee was also a scientist—someone who applied the scientific method and biomechanical principles to the development of *Jun Fan jeet kune do.*

Lee once said, "Knowing is not enough, one must apply. Willing is not enough, one must do." The acquisition and application of knowledge are both evident in the history of jeet kune do—in Lee's continuing effort to learn what he could from the mechanical principles of boxing, fencing and other sports, and in the resulting evolution of his techniques over the years. We can emulate him by using the study of biomechanics to gain insights into his thought processes. We can also observe how he used the scientific method to ask questions about the effectiveness of different styles and techniques and use the answers he gleaned to discover what was useful, to reject that which was not and to add elements that were uniquely his own.

It is clear that Lee's martial arts style changed between the early years in Seattle and the later period in Los Angeles. Change can occur for many reasons but we can reasonably describe this progression as "development" or "evolution." "Evolution" is especially appropriate because it describes a process of change that is driven by competition, with the most effective or most adaptable competitors surviving.

Evolution

Most people recognize evolution as a fundamental concept in biology. In the mid-19th century, scientists familiar with the fossil record and the results of breeding domestic animals and plants understood that species change over time—they evolve—but the mechanism driving the process of change was unclear. In 1859, Charles Darwin, in his book *On the Origin of Species,* described the process of "natural selection" and explained how the small variations in the members of a population and competition among them were all that were required to explain the evolution of new species. [94] Natural selection is a simple process. Individual organisms inherit characteristics from their parents and they differ slightly from one another. Sometimes, those small differences give an advantage to individuals with certain characteristics, making them more likely to survive, reproduce and pass on those characteristics to their offspring. The advantage may be very small. A herbivore with a slightly longer neck than his neighbors' can reach edible leaves higher in the trees. The difference may not be meaningful most of the time, but if a drought reduces the availability of food in general, the long-necked vegetarian has a slightly better chance of finding enough food. That individual is more likely to survive the drought and pass on his genes for the long-neck trait to his offspring, making long necks more common in the next generation. If occasional droughts persisted over time, millions of years, the descendants of our herbivore could look something like a giraffe.

While "evolution through natural selection" is commonly used in the context of biology, it is a fundamental process that describes many other kinds of change over time. Ideas, societies, technologies and martial arts styles, among other things, evolve in the same way.

Evolution of Martial Arts

For an evolutionary view of martial arts, we need only to consider various disciplines as "species," small differences in style among practitioners as "genetic variation," and the teacher-student relationship as the means by which those variations are passed from generation to generation. The measure of success or failure is persistence over time ("survival") just as in the biological model. While martial arts styles do not compete for food, they do compete for practitioners, and survival depends on their techniques being

---

[94] In popular jargon, natural selection is often referred to as Darwin's theory of evolution. Darwin actually described a process that explained the observable fact that species evolve. His contemporary, Alfred Wallace, developed a very similar concept of natural selection at about the same time.

taught to—and adopted by—successive generations of students. This may sound like a popularity contest, but we prefer to think that survival depends on how well the system achieves a certain goal. Effectiveness is one obvious criterion of success. Martial art forms are quintessentially fighting tools so effectiveness in combat is an obvious selection criterion. If we look at it crudely, warriors are more likely to re-use techniques and strategies that help them win, while losing strategies fall into disuse. Students, too, are more likely to seek out winners, rather than losers, as their teachers.

In the modern context, most combat is simulated. Winning and losing remain important but less so, and survival of a style depends on other criteria, too. We can summarize those criteria with a question: "How well does a form, technique or style fulfill the goals of the martial artist?" Those goals are common to most martial arts systems and based on the same four core principles of skill and knowledge that practitioners seek to acquire:

    a. Self-defense
    b. Self-discipline
    c. Self-expression
    d. Self-discovery

Martial arts systems or styles that give practitioners a higher probability of meeting these goals are more likely to be passed down or "inherited" over generations of students. The goals themselves may vary slightly based on geographical and cultural factors, access to weapons, crime rates, terrain, climate or even political influences. Responding to these different local "environments" has caused martial artists in different places and at different times in history to "adapt" their styles in different directions. The result is the great diversity of schools and styles we see today, most of which have their origin in a specific locale and time that caused survival of the art to depend on successfully adapting to local conditions.

Punctuated Equilibrium

Biological evolution is not a continuous process. Species and their habitats may remain stable for thousands or even millions of years. (Crocodiles, for example, have changed little since they shared the earth with dinosaurs.) Throughout the earth's history, long periods of ecological stasis have been occasionally interrupted by periods of rapid change during which many species went extinct and many new ones emerged. The periods of rapid change in the fossil record were often associated with cataclysmic events—asteroid impacts, continents merging or dividing, climate change, or shifts in the earth's axis. The most well known example of an "interruption" is the cataclysmic event that ended the age of the dinosaurs.

Biologists use the term "punctuated equilibrium" to describe these bursts of change in biological diversity in an otherwise stable world. Transforming events of this type can also be seen within the martial arts. In the evolution of martial arts, individual styles often adhered to traditions, and remained little changed in structure for long periods of time.

The history of judo includes two major "punctuations," for example. The art of *jujitsu* (柔術) was born in the early 16th century when Hisamori Takenouchi combined elements of older Japanese styles to create one that was effective in close combat. Jujitsu represented a significant departure from other forms of the time, foregoing weapons in favor of throwing, joint locking and choking techniques. In close combat against armored opponents, weapons were useless, but jujitsu could effectively disable an opponent. Thus a collection of miscellaneous techniques rooted in different styles was transformed into a coherent and effective martial art form.

In the 1880s, jujitsu was practiced much as Takenouchi-san taught it. Around that time, Jigoro Kano began to adapt the style by applying concepts of maximum efficiency and minimum effort. He also understood that those concepts were part of a larger philosophical approach that incorporated mutual welfare, self-improvement and social change. In a second burst of rapid change, Kano's combination of ideas transformed jujitsu from a martial art (*bujutsu*) to a martial way (*budo*) and jujitsu became the ancestor of an Olympic sport—judo.

The history of judo illustrates two more important aspects of the evolution of martial arts. First, "natural selection" is not necessarily "natural" in this context. Cultural change may be guided or goal-driven, making the process more similar to the evolution of domesticated animals than to that of their wild counterparts. Second, it is clear that the development of martial arts has been occasionally "punctuated" by the work of visionary individuals like Takenouchi and Kano, whose ideas led to rapid and indelible transformations in traditional forms.

Bruce Lee's Innovation

In the 1960s, another innovator emerged, a man who taught us to be like water. The "style of having no style" would have viral effects on martial philosophy and systems. Bruce Lee's philosophy and application of knowledge "punctuated the equilibrium" and modern martial arts have been forever changed due to his teachings.

While Lee's influence is unique, the *processes* that led to his innovative style were not. In several ways, his path to innovation followed trails left by founders of great traditions in the past.

First, he was not bound by tradition and was not afraid to analyze and adapt the best, most useful techniques from other styles. He studied other martial arts forms and martial art mechanics. He also investigated activities ranging from fencing to track and field, deducing fundamental mechanical principles that could be applied to his own art. Second, like Kano, Lee was driven in part by a quest for greater efficiency and effectiveness. In the natural world, during periods of equilibrium, random mutations can produce changes that have no particular value. Creatures can evolve or retain characteristics that are essentially useless. Our own bodies carry many examples—vestigial claws (nails) on our fingers and toes, an appendix in our intestines left over from an earlier herbivorous

BIOMECHANICS AND THE EVOLUTION FROM JUN FAN TO JEET KUNE DO

lifestyle, and the remnants of a bony tail at the base of our spine. As long as they have no effect on survival or reproductive success, these superfluous characteristics are not a problem, although they may become important if major environmental changes increase the pressure to adapt. Do martial arts styles accumulate inefficiencies in the same way? Perhaps they do. Perhaps, over time, a tradition may accumulate elements that are more stylistic rather than functional. Certainly, Bruce Lee is not the only innovator to have seen the need to refocus on efficiency and effectiveness.

The accumulation of non-adaptive features in nature and of inefficient or unnecessary stylistic elements in martial arts forms can only occur if there is no pressure to adapt—when survival is not a big issue. In martial arts, the disappearance of real, potentially injurious combat from competition allows inefficient and ineffective elements to survive. Lee's focus on "effectiveness" and "efficiency" and the elimination of unnecessary movement reflects his belief that the style should be "real"—rooted in the street fight and martial combat. Those roots are what caused the mixed martial arts community to respect Lee as a founding influence. The commercially successful Ultimate Fighting Championship league clearly reflects Lee's emphasis on *applied* JKD and the "reality of combat."

Bruce Lee's path to innovation did differ from others in at least one way. He believed that an understanding of mechanical and biomechanical principles could potentially inform his decisions about what was effective and efficient and what was not. He exploited this potential to choose the best of existing style elements and even to devise new elements of his own.

Biomechanics

One of the authors of this appendix once asked Lee, "How can you punch so hard, Sifu?" Lee responded, "F = ma [force equals mass times acceleration], Jeff. It's all about the biomechanics."

"Biomechanics" is the study of *bio*logical systems using *mechanical* principles. As an academic discipline, biomechanics has a wide range of applications—from analyzing the way trees bend in the wind to figuring out the hydrodynamics behind the ability of whales to engorge thousands of shrimp in one gulp. More commonly, biomechanics is used in orthopedics, sports medicine, robotics sports equipment design and other areas where human bodies need to be fixed, protected, duplicated or enhanced. Although the term "biomechanics" was not employed until the 1970s, the idea of using physics and mechanics to help understand how living bodies work is not new. Leonardo da Vinci is said to have modeled the flight of birds to establish mechanical principles that could be adapted to achieve human flight.

> The primary goal of Biomechanics is to understand how biological systems move and how they respond to loads (forces). In this context the "system" of interest is the human body. Understanding requires knowledge of the forces acting on the body, the motions they produce, and the ways in which force and motion are produced and controlled. Biomechanics utilizes the laws of physics (Newton's laws) that govern all physical objects and applies them to the musculo-skeletal system.

As a student of biomechanics, Bruce Lee was ahead of his time. Many of his original notes and thoughts regarding proper martial technique and economy of motion emerged when biomechanics was still in its infancy and incorporated biomechanical principles. In the *Tao of Jeet Kune Do*, specifically the "Qualities" chapter, there are numerous references to biomechanical principles such as power, body alignment, center of mass, projection of force and conservation of energy. Lee appeared to realize that "correct" techniques (i.e., more efficient and more effective ones) used natural mechanisms to maximize force and velocity.

The Scientific Method

The core philosophy and techniques of Jun Fan jeet kune do were "distilled" using a process that closely replicates the scientific method. This consists of four steps:

1. Careful observation
2. Deduction of natural laws (principles)
3. Formation of hypotheses
4. Experimental observational testing of the validity of the predictions (hypotheses) thus made

Each experiment produces a new set of observations, so the cycle starts again at Step 1. Consequently, over time, the principles and hypotheses are gradually refined until their predictions closely match the observations.

Lee studied the science of biomechanics, collected an extensive library of different martial arts books (from traditional karate and gung fu to Western boxing), and even analyzed films of the great boxers of the era such as Muhammad Ali. From these observations, he deduced fundamental principles of efficient and effective techniques, and then "tested" his hypotheses in his own training and sparring. Based on the outcomes, he applied the principles that worked in realistic combat to JKD.

Biomechanical Principles

Although this section is not meant to serve as a biomechanics textbook, a few basic concepts should facilitate the reader's understanding of the discussion that follows.

Biomechanics is fundamentally about force and motion. The relationships between force and motion are well known and embodied in physical principles. For most practical purposes, those principles are embodied in Newton's laws of motion. [95] When forces act over a distance, they are doing work, which changes the *energy* of the object. The rate at which work is done (also the rate at which energy changes) is called *power*.

---

[95] Newton's laws explain the observations we make at "intermediate" scales, those between the size of an atom and the size of a galaxy. At the atomic level (smaller scale), Newton's laws break down and quantum mechanics is a better model. Similarly, Einstein's relativity theory provides a better description of our observations at intergalactic scales.

Newton's Laws of Motion

Newton's three laws of motion form the basis for classical mechanics. The laws were first compiled by Sir Isaac Newton in his work *Philosophiæ Naturalis Principia Mathematica,* originally published in 1687. Newton used them to explain and investigate the motion of many physical objects and systems. They describe the relationship between the forces acting on an object and the resulting motion. The laws have been expressed in many different ways over the past three centuries, most of them as incomprehensible as Newton's original (17th-century English style, but written in Latin).

- **First law**

  We call this one the "couch-potato rule." If there is no force acting on an object, its motion does not change. It simply continues to move (or not) in the same direction and at the same speed. If it is not moving, the object remains motionless until an external force makes him get up and go to the grocery store.

- **Second law**

  External forces cause objects to accelerate; that is to change the speed and/or direction of their motion. The change occurs in the same direction as that in which the force is applied. Larger forces produce more acceleration but heavier objects are harder to accelerate. Consequently, the acceleration depends on both the size of the force and on the *inertia* (mass) of the object. The equation for this law (Force = mass x acceleration or F = ma) may be familiar from high school physics class.

- **Third law**

  This is the "push-back rule": When one object exerts a force on another, the action is counterbalanced by a reaction force of equal size in the opposite direction. Press your fingertip against this book. The page may yield slightly in response to the force you apply (the action), but the pressure you feel on your fingertip is the book pushing back (the reaction).

Vectors are quantities that have direction as well as size. A speed of 30 mph is a *scalar*, but adding a direction makes it a vector—"30 mph north," for example. Again, the distinction can be very important. The two vectors "30 mph north" and "30 mph south" have the same scalar magnitude and the same units but clearly have very different effects on where your travel takes you.

In biomechanics, because force and motion have important directional components, most of the numbers we use are vectors.

Example: If you are a JKD practitioner, you already know that the direction of a punch, not just its speed, is important. Lee emphasized the importance of correct body alignment and the techniques he developed have strong directionality. The most effective punch or kick is one that strikes the target directly (e.g., a frontal blow to the head). A punch that strikes at a small angle, even if it has the same speed and strikes the same target, is slightly less effective because a small component of the velocity vector is not directed at the target. Similarly, the striking techniques are more effective when legs, hips, shoulders and arms all move in the same direction.

Motion and Time

Displacement: A change in position caused by motion from one place to another. Displacement is a vector equivalent of "distance." As a vector, displacement has both units (e.g., meters or feet) and direction. Typically, we handle the direction component of displacement (and other vectors), reducing it to three scalar values, each aligned with one axis of three-dimensional space.

Velocity: The rate of motion, calculated as the displacement per unit time. Velocity is the vector equivalent of "speed."

Acceleration: The rate of change of velocity. Acceleration = change in velocity/change in time.

Example: The JKD one-inch punch continues to accelerate into and through (penetrates) the target. The subtle wrist "snap" toward the end of the technique also accelerates the hand to maximize impact velocity.

Force, Mass and Inertia

Force: Something that causes a change in the motion state of an object. Forces acting on an object change the object's state (velocity, acceleration, direction of movement). The amount of change depends on the object's inertia (mass). Force = mass x acceleration.

Example: The "impact" produced by a punch or kick upon contact with an object is a result of the force generated.

Mass: The amount of matter within an object. Weight and mass are often confused. Weight is a force, the product of mass and the acceleration of gravity. An astronaut on the moon has the same mass as on earth but weighs less because the moon's gravitational acceleration is only one-sixth that of the earth.

Example: Larger objects may produce more force. A kick produces more force due to the increased mass of the leg compared with the punch.

Inertia: The tendency of an object to resist changes in motion—the basis of the "couch-potato rule."

Example: The JKD ready stance was optimized to initiate movement from a "static"/stable but mobile position.

Momentum and Impulse

Momentum: The product of an object's mass and velocity. Momentum = mass x velocity. *Conservation of momentum* is an important principle that governs impact situations (referred to as "collisions" in biomechanics and physics).

Example: The "impact" produced by a punch or kick upon contact with an object is a result of the force generated. The final impact force is determined by the momentum of the strike combined with the momentum of the target/opponent (a "collision" similar to two automobiles crashing into each other).

Impulse: A force exerted over time causes an equivalent in change momentum. Impulse = force x time.

Example: In his writings on JKD, Lee discussed the importance of a technique going in toward the target fast but returning even faster. The net effect is to produce a shorter contact time coupled with a large force and do more "damage" to the opponent. The JKD finger jab, for example, is one of the fastest (speed) techniques to execute, and therefore, was emphasized heavily by Lee.

Biomechanical Analysis

In 2009, we embarked on a study of the motion patterns of JKD practitioners. There were two motivations for this study. First, we sought to preserve in some way the techniques employed by Bruce Lee's original students. Second, since the sifus we studied represented different eras in the development of jeet kune do (Seattle, Oakland and Los Angeles), we hoped to find evidence of the changes ("Evolution") in Lee's technique over the course of his career.

During two sessions of data collection in Los Angeles and Portland, Oregon, we recorded five sifus performing twenty-six different JKD skills; about two hundred examples in all. In order to track motion in three dimensions, our subjects wore a "motion capture" body suit with reflective markers attached at specific locations on the head, body and limbs. Ten digital cameras were arranged around the lab and used to track the motion of the markers, with each camera capturing one hundred frames per second (Figure 1).

A computer recorded the camera outputs and did the math required to reconstruct the position of the body segments from the marker coordinates. This part of the process was performed in real time (much to the amusement of sifu Allen Joe, who appeared to enjoy seeing his movements copied by a manikin on a computer screen). Later, we analyzed the recorded motion data to calculate joint angles, velocities, momentum changes and biomechanical parameters. Much of this work is beyond the scope of this appendix. Here, we focus on some basic techniques from different eras of jeet kune do.

Figure 1. Motion analysis setup (with Allen Joe as subject)

Evidence for Evolution

We had planned to compare the execution of techniques from Seattle, Oakland and Los Angeles to see whether and how those techniques changed across the three eras. In fact, each era was represented by a different skill set, with few techniques in common. It appears that Bruce Lee's progression in JKD was marked as much by the selection of new, more effective techniques as by making existing methods more effective.

Comparisons of three fundamental techniques that were common to all three eras did reveal evidence of the "biomechanical evolution" of JKD: the ready stance, the straight lead and the side kick.

Ready Stance

The ready stance is the platform from which all other movements, both offensive and defensive, are launched. The importance of a "strong" (stable) stance is recognized by all martial arts systems, traditional and modern.

Our observations of JKD sifus showed that the ready stance changed significantly from its wing chun roots and "adapted" … probably the result of Lee's insights from the biomechanics of boxing and, later, fencing.

During the Seattle era, the ready stance had most of the body's weight on the rear foot (75 percent) and 25 percent on the lead foot. This posture is characteristic of classical wing chun. It is very "static" in nature, i.e., it does not facilitate body movement very well. The stance emphasized stability and defensive techniques, especially the use of the front leg for kicking.

In the Oakland era, the ready stance was more aggressive and appeared to be strongly influenced by Lee's study of Western boxing. In this stance, the weight is distributed evenly (50/50) between both legs. The center of mass is positioned equidistant within from either foot and centered in the base of support. Although stability is retained, this body alignment is more balanced, and it allows greater mobility compared with the Seattle stance.

During Lee's Los Angeles era, the ready stance continued to evolve (Figure 2). It retained the 50/50 weight distribution between both legs. The incorporation of a raised rear heel slightly elevated and shifted the center of mass forward. A slightly higher center of mass emphasizes mobility and, coupled with a forward shift, the net effect is an emphasis on forward mobility and offensive techniques. Further, the raised heel slightly increased muscle tonus (tension) in the calf muscles (gastrocnemius and soleus muscles), the primary movers of the rear leg during the "push-off" step. This simple adjustment has the effect of "taking up the slack in the system (muscle)," allowing the muscle to initiate motion more quickly and to propel the body (step) more quickly than a "flat-foot" stance. This subtle but highly effective change was attributed to Lee's insights from fencing. It was also consistent with Lee's philosophy of interception. One must be able to move forward quickly (explosive movement) toward the opponent either to intercept his attack or to launch an attack.

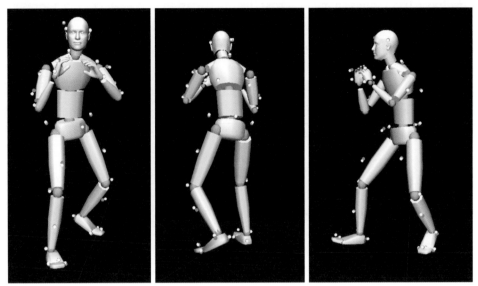

Figure 2. JKD ready stance (Los Angeles)

Straight Lead

Our recordings of the straight lead (or straight punch) also illustrated specific biomechanical changes as part of its evolution. The main biomechanical goal of the punch is to produce force and "project" the force to an external object (the opponent). The momentum of the fist, through the momentum-impulse transfer, translates into impact force at the point of impact.

Although most body movement is continuous, it is often convenient to identify "phases" or distinct time periods in a movement for the purpose of biomechanical analysis. Describing a motion as a sequence of movement phases frequently provides a "structure" that gives biomechanists some insight into the characteristics, the underlying process of the organization, and biomechanical goals of the movement. Bruce Lee broke techniques into phases and used the term "phase" in his own writings.

In the JKD straight lead (Los Angeles era, Figure 3), we can identify four distinct phases in the movement sequence.

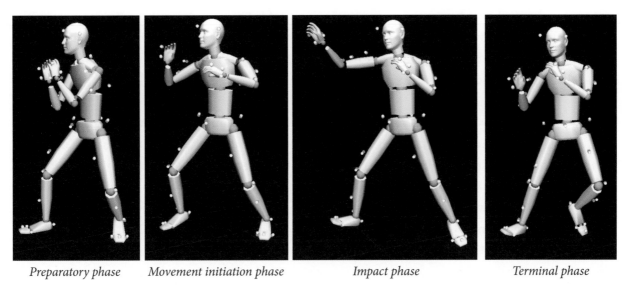

Preparatory phase	*Movement initiation phase*	*Impact phase*	*Terminal phase*

Figure 3. Phase analysis of JKD straight lead

The straight lead that Lee taught in Seattle was the traditional wing chun straight punch. The straight punch relied heavily on linear motion of the elbow and fist. Any footwork that accompanied the punch was of the "step-slide" type employed in classical wing chun. Overall, this technique is generally linear and restricted to a single plane (sagittal). Although the straight punch is very effective, only a few of the body's smaller segments contribute to the momentum of the technique, and they limit the resultant final impact force that can be produced.

During the Oakland era, Lee continued his scientific analysis of martial arts, and incorporation of his insights from the "sweet science" (boxing) appeared in the Oakland evolution of JKD. Specifically, Lee utilized rotational (angular) motion in conjunction with linear velocity. Upper body motion in the Oakland straight punch was similar to that seen in Seattle, but the addition of body pivot and hip rotation (angular movement) added more powerful body segments (in particular the back leg and shoulder) to contribute multi-planar motion, and momentum to the final impact. The JKD principle of producing force "from the ground up" began to emerge. The pivoting of the feet and hips used both ground reaction force (Newton's third law) and angular velocity. Mechanically, the effect of these additional movements is like adding a large first-stage rocket to a smaller rocket. When the smaller second-stage rocket fires, it is already moving at high speed and inherits momentum created by the first stage. In the Oakland punch, the elbow and fist are initially propelled by the large muscles of the legs, butt and shoulder. The smaller muscles of the arm that extend the elbow and fist add to the momentum already created, rather than starting from scratch.

Lee explored and tested a few other technical concepts during the Oakland era. The alignment of body segments and the "line of force" in relation to the point of force application (all biomechanical principles) was considered, tested and validated by Lee. Boxing techniques that successfully used these same principles, such as the cross and hook punches, were added. Complementary footwork was also introduced, again borrowing from boxing technique. The primary step coupled with the straight lead evolved to a "push" from the rear foot rather than the "pull" from the front foot found in the traditional step-slide from wing chun.

Lee's scientific analyses of martial arts and his development of jeet kune do culminated in Los Angeles, the final stage in the evolution of JKD. His understanding of the importance of momentum was enhanced by his study and analysis of fencing and the Los Angeles straight lead added insights from the fencing "lunge" to the Oakland method. The straight lead was further refined and optimized. The adjustments to the Los Angeles ready stance mentioned earlier (raised heel, etc.) facilitated efficient transfer of momentum from the lower-body segments to the striking fist. Both linear and angular components of velocity and acceleration were present. The rear foot became a "piston" that "drove" the whole body forward into the strike. Alignment of the body segments optimized the "line of force" to ensure the momentum was transferred to the point of force application (the fist). In effect, the entire body and the fist used projectile motion.

If the Seattle rocket had a single stage and the Oakland rocket two stages, then the Los Angeles version had three stages and a few additional boosters on the side. In reality, the whole body had become a projectile. Instead of the fist striking like a hammer, the fist was now striking like an arrow (but with great mass) shot from a bow. One of the best descriptions of the execution of the JKD straight lead was given by sifu Ted Wong, who described it as "the fencing lunge without a sword" and as a "three-point landing (fist/front foot/rear foot)." The timing of the three points "landing" facilitated transfer of momentum, ground reaction force and maximum impact force in the punch.

Only a very few scientific studies have measured the velocity of various martial art striking techniques (punching and kicking). The research published shows that highly skilled martial artists have produced punch velocities of 9–12 meters/second and total movement times of 0.1–0.2 seconds. Our JKD sifus were within these ranges for both velocity and the total movement time.

Using data from JKD sifus skilled in styles used in Seattle and Los Angeles, we can estimate the effects of technique evolution between the two eras. Impact velocity of the fist was 13–16 percent greater in the Los Angeles style. Since kinetic energy is proportional to velocity squared, the energy of the punch was 28–34 percent greater. The "rocket" effect of the legs added about 25 percent to the velocity of the whole body center of mass, and at least a portion of the additional momentum is likely to be transferred to the target.

In the straight blast (a series of punches in quick succession), it is not possible to take advantage of the whole body rotation and leg propulsion on every punch. In our measurements, punches in a sequence had about 16 percent less lower velocities than a single punch. However, with our sifus delivering 8–10 such punches in the space of a single second, there is no questioning the technique's effectiveness.

Side Kick

Differences among side kicks from different eras show a pattern of evolution similar, but less dramatic, to that seen in the straight lead.

The process closely paralleled the changes for the straight lead but with only minor refinements. The side kick began in Seattle more or less "linear," and then evolved to "linear" + "angular" with increased hip contribution. However, ensuring proper body alignment and the correct direction of the line for force limited the extent to which the side kick could be adapted compared to the straight lead revisions. Instead, Lee incorporated the "pendulum step" as the ideal footwork to facilitate transfer of momentum. Lee also appears to have recognized the value of the hook kick as a tool in his arsenal of JKD "weapons." The hook kick allowed for more angular velocity with minimal disturbance to the equilibrium of the stance. Appropriate alignment and sequencing (timing) of the body segments and the addition of angular components to the kick helped generate higher terminal velocities and hence larger impact forces. With the JKD sifus, kicks in the Seattle style delivered that foot to the target at an average velocity of 10 meters per second (33 feet per second). Side kicks in the Los Angeles style averaged 24 percent higher impact velocities and hook kicks were 7 percent faster still. The hook kick may have been Lee's ultimate "expression" of speed, balance and force generation in a kicking motion.

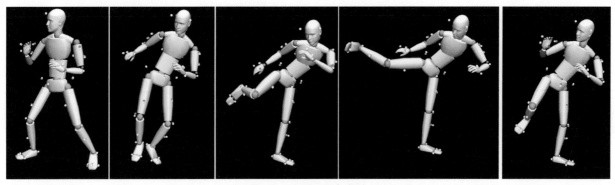

Figure 4. JKD side kick

Attack By Combination (ABC)

It is worth noting that Lee, through his analysis of the fighting arts, was able to demonstrate there were a limited number of ways to attack an opponent regardless of style or system. Through his deductions, the "five ways of attack" were born, once again highlighting Lee's analytical approach.

Lee used biomechanical principles in devising attack combinations. His written notes on which combinations appeared to work better together are reproduced in the *Tao of Jeet Kune Do*. Lee "experimented" with different combinations and looked for those that would facilitate optimal (minimal) movement patterns in the transition between techniques. In other words, he sought techniques that "flowed" into each other, with minimal disturbance to balance and equilibrium while maximizing force. His design of JKD offensive combinations also considered fighting strategy and creating openings in the opponent's defense.

Countermovement

The JKD motion analysis also revealed an interesting phenomenon. Most movement involves a subtle countermovement to take up the "slack" in the musculoskeletal system. The JKD practitioners in this study did not appear to display any countermovement. They immediately initiated the techniques in the direction of the line of force at their target.

Conclusions

Jeet kune do went through an evolutionary process over the course of a few years, driven by Bruce Lee's research into the different martial arts and their techniques, his insights from the field of biomechanics, and his use of an experimental ("scientific method") approach to testing his ideas and optimizing his techniques.

The ready stance evolved from a "static" posture that emphasized a foundation of stability and balance to a quasi "dynamic" one that facilitated equilibrium, mobility and the ability to initiate explosive forward movement. Subtle changes in body alignment, weight distribution and the raised heel aided in overcoming inertia and the initiation phase of movement. The JKD ready stance of the Los Angeles era had applied principles from sprinting biomechanics, boxing and fencing. The JKD man was standing on a "hair trigger," ready to explode into movement and maximize acceleration, transfer of momentum and striking force.

The straight lead progressed from a simple linear biomechanical "model" to a more complex model that optimized the transfer of momentum and ability to project force along a direct (efficient) line and focus at the point of application. It became the ultimate expression of a strike. Instead of just a fist striking the opponent, the whole body became the fist in a manner of speaking.

The side kick evolved along similar lines to the straight lead, adding angular velocity and whole-body momentum.

During the Los Angeles era, JKD techniques emphasized correct alignment of the body and body segments to maximize acceleration and momentum. Lee stressed "snap" in each technique, meaning great acceleration and quick recoil (impulse) both to improve the delivery of impact force to the target and to defend against counterattacks. All the JKD techniques utilized Newton's laws to improve their "biomechanical goal" of producing force.

The biomechanical analyses in the present study demonstrated the practicality of the biomechanical principles incorporated within the evolution of jeet kune do.

Discussion

Bruce Lee's writing and teaching suggest that he relied heavily on his understanding of Newton's laws and biomechanical principles to develop and advance the JKD style. He understood the principles of force, mass and conservation of momentum and the mechanics of motion, while intuitively realizing they implied there is a "balance" in the way we move and execute techniques. Nothing is free. His own research, as reflected in his writings, consistently focused on force, time, speed (velocity and acceleration) and the mechanics of motion.

He subjected all the techniques and styles he encountered in his research of the martial arts to the litmus test of analysis and testing based on the principles of scientific investigation. Thus, the evolution of jeet kune do is intimately tied to the evolution of Bruce Lee as a martial artist, his evolution as a scientific thinker, the refinement of his techniques/tools and the development of a core philosophy that evolved into his art of JKD.

Lee's personal epiphany and the evolution of JKD appeared to be his journey from asking the "What?" to the "How?" to attempting to ask/understand the "Why?" As a martial artist, he went from simply learning techniques ("what") to understanding the basic "attributes" of combat ("how") and eventually deducing the principles of biomechanics that governed effective fighting methods and the underlying skills ("why"). In that sense, the evolution of Jun Fan jeet kune do was perhaps best summed up in his own words as "Learn the principle. Abide by the principle. Dissolve the principle." His evolution as a martial artist correlated with his scientific approach to the martial arts, the refinement of his techniques/tools and the core philosophy that evolved into his art of JKD.

Final Thoughts

The evolution of martial arts forms in response to changing need is inevitable and obvious to any student of history. The art of combat evolves continuously and even drives its own evolution. New, more effective attacks lead to the "natural selection" and development of more effective defenses and vice versa. Although forms have remained stable for long periods, this equilibrium has been punctuated by rapid changes in the fighting environment. More than 2,000 years ago, the invention of steel and the development of sharp-edged swords and spears caused the "extinction" of blunt instruments, virtually overnight. More recently, the invention of gunpowder and bullets wiped out swords and steel armor. Cavalry charges were made obsolete by tanks and trench warfare. Defensive strategies have evolved through eras of dirt fortifications to stone walls to tank armor made from depleted uranium. The deployment of atomic weapons has made just about any other form of large-scale attack irrelevant, while driving the creation of "mutually assured destruction" and "détente" as defensive political strategies.

Although martial arts forms evolve, methods that are outdated and extinct as effective fighting forms remain in abundance. Sword fighting, for example, is no longer effective in modern combat, but the art has been preserved by tradition. Its meaning and importance now come from the context of sport rather than warfare.

Tradition effectively allows extinct techniques to survive extinction. Bruce Lee's transforming idea was that his style should not be bound by tradition but should continue to evolve. He was also an innovator in using science, in particular biomechanics, as a tool for driving that evolution. Nor was he afraid to step across discipline boundaries in order to learn effective techniques from other styles. "Evolution" was a fundamental characteristic of Lee's progress as a martial artist.

It is no surprise then that, since Lee's death, there has been discussion about whether the techniques of Jun Fan jeet kune do should be preserved as he left them or whether they should continue to change over time—to evolve.

The choice between conserving the art or preserving the principles underlying the art is one that we cannot resolve. If anything, our investigation suggests the two were so intimately connected as to be inseparable.

MARTYN SHORTEN

Before starting his research and development consulting business in 1992, Martyn Shorten was employed as director of the Nike Sport Research Laboratory and as director of research design and product development for Puma AG. He is an R&D consultant to leading athletic shoe and sports surface manufacturers. Shorten has been an active member of the International Society of Biomechanics since 1983 and served on the society's executive council from 2001 to 2003. In 1993, he established the ISB's Technical Section on Footwear Biomechanics. Shorten is chairman of the ASTM Committee F08 on Sports Equipment and Facilities, chairman of the Athletic Footwear subcommittee, and a member of the Committee on Standards.

Although Shorten's basic and applied research has won international recognition, he is a self-styled "recovering academic," preferring to use science and technology as tools for developing applications and products. He is a frequent author and invited speaker on topics related to the biomechanics of human performance and injury, and their links to athletic footwear and sports surface and protective equipment design.

ERIC PISCIOTTA

Eric Pisciotta is an avid jeet kune do practitioner. He received his Bachelor of Science degree in human physiology from the University of Oregon in 2011. Driven by his study of JKD, he volunteered as a research assistant in the motion analysis lab on the U of O campus where he began his studies of human motion. Upon graduation he was employed at BioMechanica, in Portland, Oregon, where he assisted in biomechanical testing and learned about sport and footwear biomechanics. He is currently attending graduate school to pursue his studies in biomechanics. He seeks to advance his understanding of JKD through biomechanics; or perhaps it is better stated as advancing his understanding of biomechanics through JKD.

JEFF PISCIOTTA

Jeff Pisciotta is a biomechanist and martial artist. He has studied wing chun gung fu under a few different masters, most notably William Cheung. A fateful encounter with Bruce Lee gave him a "crash course" in JKD and a "lecture" on the science of biomechanics that forever changed his approach to his study of the martial arts. Lee's influence also led Pisciotta to pursue graduate studies in biomechanics and to his eventual career. He continued his JKD training under various instructors, but credits sifu Ted Wong as his ultimate JKD instructor and for facilitating his understanding of the science of jeet kune do.

Pisciotta began his biomechanics research at Children's Hospital Medical Center in Boston in 1983 and has worked in clinical gait analysis, orthopedic biomechanics and sport biomechanics. He worked in the Nike Sport Research Lab for 17 years, eventually becoming its director. His research led to many applied footwear innovations and patented new technologies. More recently, he founded Applied Innovation Research, a biomechanics consulting company in Oregon. He is also acting CEO at JKD Biomechanics LLC, where he seeks to perpetuate the science of JKD.

Appendix D

654 Jackson Street

By Tommy Gong

When my grandmother was having health problems in the mid-70s, my mother and aunts decided to rent and share an apartment in San Francisco's Chinatown near my grandparents' residence. Instead of staying in a hotel each time during their weekly visits, they had a place to serve as a second home, and it was cheap since they split the monthly rent.

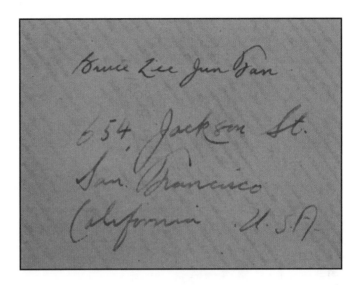

During the '80s and '90s, my eldest sister, Rosemary, lived there when she began her advertising career in San Francisco, and I visited her from time to time when I was attending UC Berkeley. On one occasion, the landlord was there. Somehow we got into a conversation about my JKD training. He claimed to have known Bruce Lee; that, in fact, Bruce stayed in these same apartments during the summer of 1959 when he arrived in San Francisco from Hong Kong and stayed there for several months before leaving for Seattle.

I didn't know whether to believe him, but when many of Lee's personal belongings were auctioned off in Beverly Hills during the 1990s, I saw his earliest driver's license in California: 654 Jackson Street! I had not spoken to the landlord for many years, but in preparation for Bruce's 70th birthday celebration in San Francisco, I decided to contact him to find out more about Bruce's short stay in that city.

Bruce stayed with Kwan Ging Hong, the apartment's tenant, who was in his 50s at the time and quite a

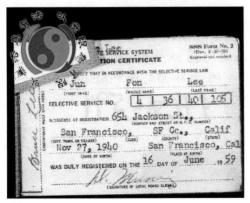

1959 selective service card

bit older than Lee. Kwan, a single man, actually taught the landlord to read and write Chinese when he was a teenager. Kwan Ging Hong was also involved with the Chinese Opera; it was through those connections to Bruce Lee's father that Bruce had a place to land when arriving in San Francisco.

The landlord's initial introduction to Bruce Lee occurred when, while trying to study for his college finals, he heard a constant "clicking and clanging noise coming from across the hall." When he couldn't ignore the sound any longer, he went across the hall to see who was making the noise, and a young man about his age opened the door; it was Bruce Lee. They became fast friends during that brief period of Lee's life.

The landlord recounted stories Lee told him about his appearances in Hong Kong movies as a child actor and that he had to leave Hong Kong because he was getting in trouble fighting, taking on sailors on leave and Hong Kong police. He was particularly indignant at the treatment that white Hong Kong policemen showed toward him and other Chinese kids. The landlord also recalled telling Lee that he only knew how to "slow dance," so Bruce showed him how to do the cha-cha in the apartment. At the end of the summer, Lee told him he was off to Washington State to go to college.

For many years, prominent JKD instructors such as Ted Wong and Dan Lee stayed at the apartment on separate occasions when teaching my students in San Francisco during the 1990s. When the Jun Fan Jeet Kune Do Nucleus formed in the late 1990s, I made sure to show Linda Lee the apartment that Bruce first stayed at when he arrived in America. I have also taken a few die-hard Bruce Lee fans up to the second floor to see it. After more than 30 years of occupancy, my parents decided to forgo the apartment, which had offered many good memories and a small connection to Bruce Lee.

Appendix E

Glossary of Chinese Terminology

By Sherry Mei Gong

Biu jee	標指	Thrusting fingers
Bong sao	膀手	Elbow up-in-air block
But doan jiang	不動肘	Immovable elbow
By-jong (also **bai jong**)	擺樁	Ready position
Chi sao	黐手	Sticky hands or sticking hands
Chop chuie	插捶	Low horizontal fist
Chum kiu	尋橋	Searching for the bridge (second form in wing chun)
Chung chuie	冲捶	Vertical fist punch
Fook sao	伏手	Bent-arm elbow-in block
Gaun sao (also **gong sao**)	摑手	Low outer wrist block
Gnoy moon chuie	外門捶	Outer gate punch
Gung fu (also **kung fu**)	功夫	Skill, martial skill
Gwa chuie	掛捶	Backfist
Ho Oi Yee (also **Grace Ho**)	何愛瑜	Bruce Lee's mother
Jeet kune do (JKD)	截拳道	The way of the intercepting fist
Jian jie de dong zuo	簡捷的動作	Economy of movement
Jik chung chuie	直冲捶	Straight blast chain punching
Jiue ying	追形	Theory of facing
Joan sien	中線	Centerline theory
Jun Fan gung fu	振藩功夫	Bruce Lee's martial art
Jun Fan jeet kune do (JFJKD)	振藩截拳道	Term coined by Shannon Lee to express Bruce Lee's complete body of work from Seattle to Oakland to Los Angeles
Jut sao	窒手	Jerking hand
Lee Hoi Chuen	李海泉	Bruce Lee's father
Lee Jun Fan	李振藩	Bruce Lee's Chinese name
Lee Siu Loong	李小龍	Bruce Lee's stage name
Lin sil die dar	連消帶打	Simultaneous defense and attack
Lop sao	擸手	Grabbing hand
Mo si tung	無時停	Never sit still

Mo sum; Mandarin, **wu hsin** (also **mushin**)	無心	No-mindedness
Mo wei; Mandarin, **wu wei**	無為	Non-action
Mook jong	木樁	Wooden dummy
Mun sao	問手	Asking hand
Noy moon chuie	內門捶	Inner gate punch
Pak sao	拍手	Slapping hand
Phon sao	封手	Trapping hands
Saam moon	三門	Three fronts/gates
Saam seen kune	三線拳	Three line fist
Sai fong	細鳳	Little phoenix
Sai gok	四角	Four corners
Sil lum kung fu	少林功夫	Shaolin kung fu
Sil lum tao (also **siu nim do**)	小念頭	A little idea (first form in wing chun)
Sim; Mandarin, **Ch'an** (also **Zen**)	禪	"Absorption" or meditative state
Sun yee hop yut	身意合一	Unification of mind and body
Tai gik; Mandarin, **taiji**	太極	Tai chi
Tan sao	攤手	Palm-up block
Tao (also **Dao**)	道	The way or the truth
William Cheung	張卓慶	Bruce Lee's wing chun senior brother
Wing chun gung fu	詠春功夫	Bruce Lee's first formal training in martial arts
Wong Shung Leung	黃淳樑	Bruce Lee's wing chun senior brother
Wu sao	護手	Guarding hand
Yee mo faat wai yao faat; yee mo haan wai yao haan	以無法為有法；以無限為有限	Using no way as way; having no limitation as limitation
Yip Man	葉問	Bruce Lee's wing chun teacher
Yum/yeung; Mandarin, **yin/yang**	陰 陽	Dark and light

Note: *Special thanks to Professor Dan Lee for his Chinese terminology suggestions for this edition.*

Appendix F

Preserving Bruce Lee's Legacy for Future Generations
Conserving "Commentaries on the Martial Way"

By Tommy Gong

While serving as a member of the board of directors for the Bruce Lee Foundation, I have been fortunate to peruse some of Bruce's personally handwritten notes on topics ranging from martial arts to motivational notes. I was especially moved when I viewed his *Commentaries on the Martial Way*, which he penned when recovering from his back injury in 1970. The commentaries are comprised of seven black binders, each containing 300 to 400 pages. These were essentially Bruce's last writings on the martial arts, and they served as the source material from which the *Tao of Jeet Kune Do* was derived.

Ted Wong and the author review Bruce Lee's commentaries

When reading his notes in their original form—in his handwriting—I witnessed Bruce's personal thoughts on the martial arts and it had a tremendous impact on me. How fortunate the world was when he sustained that back injury. Otherwise, we might never have seen the genius that is Bruce Lee.

Ted Wong and I read through the commentaries in 2009 for research in preparing this book, and we noticed the pages were beginning to deteriorate. After making inquiries to Brown's River Marotti (BRM, currently known as Kofile Preservation), a document conservation company, we found out the pages should be de-acidified and encapsulated to slow their aging process and provide protection. De-acidification removes the acids that leave paper dry and brittle over time. In addition, the pages could be digitally scanned so they could be viewed electronically. By conserving the seven volumes, we would increase their longevity from about 50 years to 300 to 400 years. All of this was a natural fit with the goals of the Bruce Lee Foundation to preserve his legacy.

The cost of de-acidification and restoration is not cheap. Fortunately, BRM donated its services to complete the first volume. Estimates were made to restore the remaining volumes, and I asked several individuals for matching donations, and we had funding! As a gesture of appreciation, Shannon Lee agreed to have the donors' names placed on a dedication plate that was attached to the inside cover of each volume. The donors are Linda and Bruce Cadwell, Shannon Lee, Ted Wong, Allen Joe, Gregory B. Smith Sr., Jeff Pisciotta, Louis Awerbuck and myself.

The seven volumes were completed during 2009 and 2010. A huge debt of gratitude is given to BRM and the donors for preserving this part of Bruce Lee's legacy for many more generations.

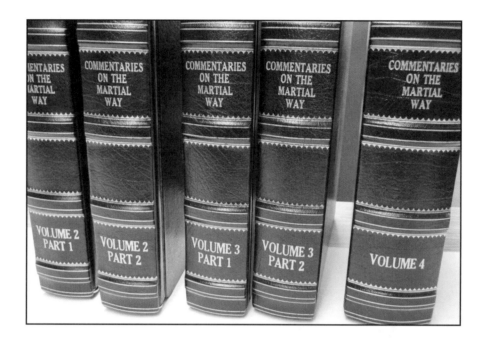

BLAM

By Shannon Lee

The Bruce Lee Action Museum (BLAM) is a project of the Bruce Lee Foundation (BLF), a 501(c)(3) public charity whose mission is to preserve and perpetuate the legacy of Bruce Lee for generations to come. The BLF seeks to carry out its mission primarily through educational means with the Bruce Lee Action Museum being the ultimate expression of this mission.

More Than Memorabilia

The vision for the Bruce Lee Action Museum is one of community, education, inspiration and innovation. The BLAM will not only be a place to view Bruce Lee memorabilia, but it will be an interactive place of learning that will explore the idea of action in all its forms as exemplified by the legacy of Bruce Lee. It will take a close look at Martial Action, Film Action, Social InterAction, Self Actualization and Action for Change through the lens of Bruce Lee's life and accomplishments. More important, however, the space will engage visitors to turn the very same lens onto themselves as a means of sparking a discussion and an exploration into how people might utilize action within their own lives to accomplish their own goals and create positive change.

A Legacy Comes Home

Seattle was a place very dear to the heart of Bruce Lee. He attended the University of Washington, he met and married his wife, he opened his first martial arts school and he is laid to rest all in Seattle. Every year people travel to Seattle to visit the gravesites of Bruce and Brandon Lee, and with the realization of BLAM, those visitors and many more will have a home for all things Bruce Lee to visit as well. No other museum in the world will explore the rich East/West legacy of Bruce Lee as well as the notion of action in such a complete and meaningful way as the Bruce Lee Action Museum!

The Bruce Lee Action Museum Where Actions Speak!

Galleries
Museum Store
Theater
Training Center
Research Library
Meditation Area

To find out how you can help make BLAM a reality, go to bruceleeactionmuseum.org.

255

OTHER BRUCE LEE BOOKS AND DVDs

Bruce Lee's Fighting Method: The Complete Edition

by Bruce Lee and M. Uyehara

This restored and enhanced edition of *Fighting Method* breathes new life into hallowed pages with digitally remastered photography and a painstakingly refurbished interior design for improved instructional clarity.
492 pgs. (ISBN-13: 978-0-89750-170-5)

Book Code 494—Retail $34.95

Chinese Gung Fu: The Philosophical Art of Self-Defense
(Revised and Updated)

by Bruce Lee

This new edition gives martial arts enthusiasts and collectors exactly what they want: more Bruce Lee, including digitally enhanced photography, previously unpublished pictures with Lee's original handwritten notes, and introductions by his widow and daughter.
112 pgs. (ISBN-13: 978-0-89750-112-5)

Book Code 451—Retail $12.95

To order, call toll-free: (800) 581-5222 or visit blackbeltmag.com/bruce_lee

OTHER BRUCE LEE BOOKS AND DVDs

Bruce Lee's Fighting Method: Basic Training and Self-Defense Techniques

by Ted Wong and Richard Bustillo

This video covers the first two volumes of the book series *Bruce Lee's Fighting Method,* with topics including warm-ups, basic exercises, on-guard position, footwork, power/speed training and self-defense. (Approx. 55 min.)

DVD Code 1029—Retail $29.95

Bruce Lee: Wisdom for the Way

by Bruce Lee

Bruce Lee: Wisdom for the Way pulls from many of Bruce Lee's sources—quotes, pictures, sketches—to create a visually comprehensive reference of the master. 144 pgs. (ISBN-13: 978-0-89750-185-9)

Book Code 491—Retail $15.95

Bruce Lee Foundation Mission Statement

The Bruce Lee Foundation, a California 501(c)(3) public benefit corporation, seeks to preserve, perpetuate, and disseminate Bruce Lee's life example, philosophies, and art of Jun Fan Jeet Kune Do® through inspirational events, educational programs, martial arts instruction and the Bruce Lee Action Museum. We believe that the Bruce Lee Foundation can enrich lives, open minds and break down barriers through the active proliferation of Bruce Lee's legacy of undaunted optimism in the face of adversity, unwavering humanism, mental and physical perseverance, and inspirational presence of mind toward the betterment of our global community.

For More Info

For further authentic information on Bruce Lee or the
art and philosophy of Jun Fan Jeet Kune Do®, please contact:

BRUCE LEE FOUNDATION
11693 San Vicente Blvd., Suite #918
Los Angeles, CA 90049

bruceleefoundation.org